THE HISTORIAN
AS DIPLOMAT

Charles Kingsley Webster
and the United Nations
1939–1946

THE HISTORIAN AS DIPLOMAT

*Charles Kingsley Webster
and the United Nations
1939–1946*

P. A. Reynolds and E. J. Hughes

Martin Robertson

First published in 1976 by Martin Robertson and Company Ltd., 17 Quick Street, London N1 8HL

ISBN 0 85520 131 2

Typeset by Santype (Coldtype Division) Ltd., Salisbury.
Reproduced, printed by photolithography and bound in Britain at The Pitman Press, Bath.

Contents

Acknowledgements

We wish to acknowledge the assistance given by the Keeper of the Public Record Office and his staff. Transcripts of Crown-copyright records in the Public Record Office appear by permission of the Controller of H.M. Stationery Office. Originals of these transcripts, printed in Appendices A, B, C and E, are held by the Public Record Office under references CAB 66/33, CAB 66/38, CAB 66/52 and PRO FO371 U8785/180/70 File 40725 respectively.

Assistance in the form either of supply of information or of comment on parts of the text has also been generously given by the Archivist of *The Times*, by Mr. W. W. Lockwood of the Woodrow Wilson School of Public and International Affairs, Princeton University, by Dr. W. Diebold, Jnr, of the Council on Foreign Relations, New York, by Mr. Brian Urquhart of the United Nations, and by Mr. D. T. Travers of the University of Lancaster.

The manuscript, repeatedly revised after correspondence between geographically separated collaborators, was typed with skill, speed and inexhaustible patience by Hazel Walker.

To the memory of

Charles and Nora

INTRODUCTION

Sir Charles Kingsley Webster, 1886–1961

Before the middle of this century it was rare, in comparison with the United States, for teaching members of British universities to be allowed or encouraged to play much part in the formation of government policy. This was perhaps particularly so in the field of foreign affairs, and indeed may still be more so in this field than in many others. The Foreign Office has for long prided itself on its excellence; but whether the failures of British foreign policy in this century suggest incompetence by officials or their political masters, or reflect changes in Britain's external environment to which no effective response was possible, may be matters for debate to which this book may offer some small contribution. Charles Webster was one of the small number of dons who have succeeded in being accepted into the official hierarchy.

Throughout his life Webster kept a personal record of those of his activities that seemed to him to be of more than private importance. On his death in 1961 he bequeathed part of these diaries to P. A. Reynolds (whom he had appointed to his staff at the London School of Economics in 1946), and part to Noble Frankland, co-author with him of the volume on Bomber Command in the official history of the second world war, and now Director of the Imperial War Museum. The material left to P. A. Reynolds forms the core of this book, in chapters 2–6: these chapters have been written by E. J. Hughes, who also conducted the research on which they are based. This Introduction, chapter 1 and the Conclusion have been written by P. A. Reynolds. Naturally both authors have made contributions to the work of the other, and they share responsibility for the work as a whole. The diaries are written in a barely legible longhand, and frequently contain grammatical and spelling abbreviations. We have not attempted to alter this style, though where necessary words or parts of words have been added on the first occasion of their appearance to make the meaning clear. The Webster papers are deposited in the Library of the London School of Economics and Political Science.[1]

Webster's first brief incursion into official life was in 1918 when as a young professor of 32 he was seconded for a few weeks to the Foreign Office from the War Office (where he was a Major in M.I.6) in order to write a monograph on the

Congress of Vienna, a task that led on to his appointment as Secretary to the Military Section of the British Delegation to the Paris Peace Conference. The purpose of the monograph lay in the hope that knowledge of 1814—15 would save the peacemakers of 1918—19 from misjudgments or errors made by the conquerors of Napoleon, but as Webster ruefully admitted in the 1934 reissue of his essay the monograph had had no observable effect whatsoever.[2] Webster had enjoyed the sensation of being close to the heart of things, however, and he believed that life-long study by persons of intelligence and integrity fitted them to make some contribution to the solution of the great problems of the day. Not incorrectly he judged himself to have experience and qualities of this kind. He had, moreover, a strong desire to leave the world a better place than he found it, and he longed therefore for the chance to give what he thought he had it in him to offer. The scholar in him came first, but he wished also to use for practical good the insight and understanding that scholarship had nurtured in him. When therefore he was asked immediately after the outbreak of the second world war to become head of the American Section of the Foreign Research and Press Service, he was glad to do so.

The request was a not unnatural sequel to the reputation he had established in the previous two decades. For ten years after the first world war he had occupied the Wilson Chair of International Politics at Aberystwyth, a chair whose holder was at that time required to be present in Aberystwyth only for one term in the year, and which enjoined upon the Professor the practice of foreign travel so that he should have direct experience of the world about which he taught. Webster used these opportunities to the full, so that he became well-known in many countries of the world, but particularly in the United States where for some years he occupied a chair at Harvard simultaneously with his Aberystwyth incumbency. Moreover he was a leading member of the League of Nations Union, and he was an indefatigable speaker on behalf of that organization, perhaps, until 1936, the most successful interest group operating between the wars in the United Kingdom. In these years he produced what many think to have been his finest work of scholarship, the two volumes of *The Foreign Policy of Castlereagh*, and in 1932, shortly after the publication of the second volume, he moved from Aberystwyth to the London School of Economics and Political Science, thus fulfilling an intention he had formed many years earlier to spend the latter part of his working life in London. The move was from this point of view perhaps a little early, since he began his tenure of this, his third chair, still at the age only of 46.

At London he began work on the next phase of his life's ambition to write the definitive history of British foreign policy from 1815 to 1878. His Castlereagh, following *The Congress of Vienna*, had established him as the master of a new craft of diplomatic history. Unable, however, to go forward to Castlereagh's successor as Foreign Secretary, George Canning, since (to his great regret) H. W. V. Temperley had forestalled him, he moved on to the next great figure in the line, Lord Palmerston. Research among the mass of papers at

Broadlands, the home of Lord Mount Temple, and as in the case of Castlereagh in the archives of the capitals of Europe, occupied him until the outbreak of war; and it was not until 1951 that the first two volumes were published of a study which, had it ever been completed, would have run to three volumes, if not four. He was diverted from its completion, however, by an invitation to write the Bomber Command volume in the official history of the second world war, and this task in collaboration with Noble Frankland was to occupy him until immediately before his death in 1961.[3]

During his years before the war at the London School of Economics, he continued strongly to support the League of Nations. His ardour was gradually quenched however as, in common with one of the men he most greatly admired, Lord Cecil of Chelwood, he recognized that the governments of Britain and France were unwilling, or thought themselves unable, to use the League's machinery to check the rising dictators in Italy and Germany. His judgment and his realism caused him powerfully to oppose the Munich agreement, and, to his great resentment, he was one of those (how many were there?) whose letters to *The Times* condemning the settlement were not published.

His scholarship, his judgment, his energy, his international reputation, and his wide range of contacts in Britain, made it almost inevitable that on the outbreak of war he should be summoned to public service. The initial opportunity was a narrow one, but he enlarged it with characteristic vigour and opportunism. His manner of doing this, and the use he made of his opportunities, are described in later chapters of this book.

CHAPTER 1

Principles and Problems of World Organization

The replacement of political structures made inappropriate by technological advance or by changes in economic and social forms has rarely been achieved without violence. The political structures known as sovereign states which emerged in western Europe in the sixteenth and seventeenth centuries, and which spread all over the globe in the twentieth, were the dominant structures in the global arena in 1945. The western European prototypes had developed from the disintegration of feudalism, from the establishment of money economies, from the concentration of authority in a sovereign monarch, and from the disruption in the Reformation of a universal Christian church, finally accepted in the *cuius regio eius religio* principle of the Treaty of Westphalia at the end of the Thirty Years' War in 1648.

In the succeeding three centuries these structures grew ever stronger. Spain and Portugal, France and England spread their influence overseas, while Romanov, Habsburg and later Hohenzollern concentrated on extending their sway on the mainland of Europe. The strongest of them, France, first under Louis XIV and later under Napoleon, was checked partly by the organization of coalitions against her, but mainly because of the dispersal of her strength between her imperial interests and her mainland ambitions. But the decline of Spain and Portugal left the other five in positions of such predominance that only their mutual rivalries enabled smaller states to survive: the fate of Poland, three times partitioned, and finally to extinction in 1795, showed what could happen when three of the major powers were sufficiently agreed.

The system known as the balance of power expressed their interaction. Behavioural relationships were limited in more ways than one: first, in that no friendship was so close and no enmity so bitter that alignment of any with any other was excluded; secondly, in that none was prepared to push a quarrel to the point of destruction of another, recognizing that the security of each was best served by the preservation of all; and, thirdly, in that the range of contacts hardly extended beyond dynastic relationships, governmental exchanges (whether officially through the diplomatic system or quasi-officially through espionage and intrigue), and clashes of largely mercenary armies. The peoples were barely engaged.

This system was transformed by the French Revolution. The destruction of one monarchy united the others against its destroyers. Mass involvement in the Revolution, not merely in the overthrow of the Parisian aristocracy but in the peasant acquisition of land ownership, was mobilized for its defence in Carnot's *levée en masse* in 1793; and patriotic fervour joined with revolutionary enthusiasm under the superb leadership of Napoleon and his marshals to threaten every state in Europe. His final defeat required the mobilization of similar popular involvement, particularly in Prussia, Russia and Britain. The passage of the revolutionary armies however, beaten back though they eventually were, left behind ideas of nationhood that were swiftly to grow in Italy, Germany and Greece, and thereafter among Poles, Bulgars, South Slavs and Czechs. At the same time the slow but massive processes of economic and social change evolving with the industrial revolution as it moved forward rapidly in Britain and more slowly on the mainland of Europe, brought into question internal political structures, and began slowly to extend the range of contacts between peoples in different states.

These were the circumstances from which emerged the first attempt in modern Europe at international organization. Like its global successors, this first attempt reflected in its formation and its working the different interests of the states that composed it, as those interests were perceived by political leaders in relation to new and unmeasurable sources of instability in their domestic and external environments. In very broad terms the new organization, the Concert of Europe, was seen by a succession of British foreign secretaries, Castlereagh, Canning and Palmerston, as a means by which the great powers meeting together could reach among themselves agreed settlements of international problems in ways that prevented the powers from getting into war with each other. Human affairs cannot be static. Change is bound to occur. What is important is that inevitable changes do not inevitably lead to war.

The seemingly self-evident sanity of this approach was fortified by the British interest in maintaining peace (since trade flourishes in peace, and Britain's long-standing trading activity was on the brink of huge expansion in consequence of her industrial lead), and by the slowly-growing popular participation in Britain's internal affairs leading to sympathy for attempts similarly to increase participation elsewhere (particularly if such participation weakened Britain's great power adversary-partners). But these partners in the Concert, and especially the persisting east European autocracies of Prussia, Russia and Austria, saw the Concert mainly as a means by which the great powers could defend their interests and their position by agreeing on measures to suppress 'popular' movements, liberal or national or both, wherever they might arise. At any conjuncture in international affairs there will be states more interested in preserving things as they are and states more interested in stimulating or going along with change; and there will be states that for strategic or technological or economic or ideological reasons see unyielding opposition to change as the best means of preserving their interests, and there will be others that seek their salvation by accommodating to and perhaps moderating change by peaceful means. Neither is right in all circumstances. Most historians would agree that the attempt of Metternich through the Concert of Europe to suppress liberal-nationalism was bound to fail — but liberal-nationalism if successful was bound to destroy the Austro-Hungarian empire anyway. Most historians would also agree that the Anglo-French failure at an early stage to resist Hitler's attempts at international change led to far more serious consequences for them in the end than if they had acted otherwise. One major problem for international organization, then, is the conflict between change and the *status quo*, and the different attachments of state-members of the organization at different times and on different issues to one or the other.

The last major meeting of the Concert of Europe was in the Congress of Berlin in 1878, which settled for the time being the problems and conflicts arising out of growing Balkan nationalist feeling against both the Turks and the Austro-Hungarians. A pale reflection of the Concert, in the form of a Conference of Ambassadors, met in London at the time of the first Balkan war in 1912, but it succeeded in producing only a temporary halt to the fighting; and the Concert did not operate in relation to the crisis sparked off by the assassination of the Austrian Archduke at Sarajevo in 1914 which led to the first world war. It is difficult to suppose that it could have done so. Though the powers of 1815 had different conceptions of what they needed to do to preserve and advance their interests, there remained sufficient flexibility in their relations to render possible the operation of a modified balance of power system in which the Concert served as an additional mechanism. By 1914, however, the alliance system had ranged the powers in two opposed blocks, France and Russia, with Britain less firmly committed, on one side, Germany and Austria-Hungary, with Italy wavering, on the other. The rulers of Austria-Hungary felt themselves increasingly unable to control the nationalist sentiments of Pole, Czech, Slovak, Croat and Slovene, especially now that Bulgar, Greek, Roumanian and Serb had largely freed themselves from Turkish rule. But Russian ties with the Balkan Slavs meant that an Austrian punitive move against the Serbs could not go unchallenged, and the alliance system with its administrative and strategic imperatives did the rest.

On a wider scale, however, there were broader conflicts arising out of the globalization of the industrial economies of Europe. By 1914 most of Africa, and much of Asia, had been brought under the suzerainty or indirect or direct colonial control of Britain, France, Germany, Italy, Belgium, Holland, Portugal or Spain (the latter mainly relics of earlier imperial expansion), and J. A. Hobson and Lenin found ineluctable causes for world conflict in the exhaustion of new markets and new regions for exploitation and the investment of surplus capital. However much these considerations contributed to the outbreak of war, it is certain that economic activity had become in substantial degree world-wide.

The war gave confirmation of this. The prolonged military stalemate, not accompanied by pauses in the slaughter, gave increased emphasis to economic means of defeating the enemy, so Britain intensified the economic blockade of Germany (thus antagonizing the neutrals, particularly the United States), and Germany in a desperate attempt to starve out Britain launched unrestricted submarine warfare in 1917 (thus bringing in the United States against her). The war thereby demonstrated that the globalization of economic activity likewise globalized strategy, and that major conflict in any one part of the world must henceforth always carry the potential of spreading to all other parts of the world. But at the very time when the pointless horror of the first world war and its ultimate world-wide nature revealed a common interest shared by all men round the globe, the sacrifices demanded by the war intensified the passionate attachment of peoples to their own states or nations, and their hatred of their enemies. The magnitude of the efforts required to fight the war meant that peoples had to be mobilized in terms of commitment and participation on a scale previously unknown, and their mass involvement in politics gave a new dimension to the environment of statesmen.

1919 thus saw revealed a second major problem of international organization. The world was in significant degree unified in economic and strategic terms, and if conflict now widely seen as being unendurable was not to recur, some institutional expression of this internationalism would have to be devised. But peoples were now participants in politics, and were more profoundly committed than ever before to the states that enshrined their customs, habits, ways of life, and beliefs (this was as true for the Russians as for the rest, though not at first for their Bolshevik leaders). Moreover Woodrow Wilson, finding one cause of the war in nationalist aspirations, encouraged the emergence of new political entities, which likewise found the attribute of sovereignty precious. The framers of the League Covenant thus had to reconcile the need for structures reflecting the ways in which man's activity was international, with the powerful allegiances of peoples to the states of which they had long been members, or had recently become so. Moreover it was felt that, in order fully to satisfy the aspirations of those peoples who had only recently won statehood, they should be regarded as equal in status to the rest.

Inevitably, since politicians are leaders of states and not leaders of mankind, the League of Nations Covenant leaned heavily towards sovereignty and away from internationalism. The League was an association of sovereign states pledged to co-operate for specified purposes. The disaster of 1914 being seen to have resulted at least in part from the absence of consultative machinery and from the inexorable way in which step followed step, once the crisis broke, the Covenant was primarily devised to create machinery to impose delay. Members of the League accordingly bound themselves to submit any dispute likely to lead to a rupture to settlement by the Permanent Court of International Justice, or to arbitration, or to enquiry by the League Council; and they undertook not to resort to war until three months after the judicial decision, the arbitrators' award, or the report of the Council respectively. Resort to war in violation of these obligations would lead to the imposition of economic sanctions and to recommendations by the Council on members' contributions of armed forces to protect the covenants of the League. All members were members of the Assembly, and recommendations had to be unanimous, apart from parties to a dispute. The Council, composed partly of permanent and partly of elected members, came to act very much as an executive committee of the Assembly (there being little differentiation of function between the two), and in the Council too recommendations had to be unanimous apart from parties to a dispute. But the essence of the League lay in undertakings of members in certain circumstances to act in certain ways, and the organs of the League could do no more than recommend that they should do so. This was a realistic recognition of the relative weight of attachment to sovereignty as against internationalism, but even so Wilson had gone too far for the United States Senate, which repudiated his signature.

From this blow the League never recovered, but even had it not fallen, effective action within the framework of the Covenant might well never have been possible given inevitable divergent and diverging interests among its members. One of the earliest and most serious of these was the desire of the French and a few supporters to see and use the League to strengthen the *status quo*, as against the British view that its main value should be as an agent for peaceful change and conciliation of disputes. In addition to its primary political function, the Council supervised a number of economic and social committees the purposes of which were to seek agreements among states on matters where international regulation would be beneficial (such as drug traffic), or on questions that might indirectly threaten peace and security (such as economic exploitation or instability).

Evidently there was nothing in the Covenant that provided for, or envisaged, a deliberate and fixed determination on the part of the leaders of a state to go to war, whatever the reason for such determination might be. This could be done perfectly legitimately within the Covenant three months after a Council report. Still more, any state prepared to rely upon differences of view or of interest among members of the League, which would permit illegal resort to war to pass without effective response, would be in no way inhibited by the Covenant. Such a state would be deterred only by the certainty or high probability of a counter by forces seriously rivalling its own. In these circumstances the only recourse for a state with smaller resources than a potential predator was alliance. But the most effective alliances are those in which the *casus foederis* is strictly limited and defined, because few states can contemplate the assumption of widely-dispersed commitments and obligations. Alliances thus tend to be regional and specific, and they accordingly weaken commitments to universalism.

The experience of the League thus exposed a third problem of international organization. Peace is indivisible, and therefore machinery is needed with global reach and range. The commitments of states when a dispute arises must, however, vary with their resources, with the nature of their interests, and with their geographical location. Once this variation is recognized the emergence of a proximate and powerful threat must cause states to seek alliances, but these in turn tend to reduce still further the effectiveness of the principle of universalism. Moreover, in addition to their undermining of universalism, regional alliances may positively increase the difficulties of maintaining international peace and security by aligning hostile blocks against each other.

These were the three great problems — preservation of the *status quo* versus peaceful change, sovereign equality of states versus world unity, and limited or regional alliances versus universalism — with which any blueprint for a new international organization after the second world war would have to deal. As in 1919, the choices among these alternatives to which political leaders would be likely to lean were only too clear. Stalin had consolidated his hold on the Soviet Union through the doctrine of socialism in one country, through the identification of the cause of world communism with the existence and strength of the U.S.S.R., and through reiteration of the threat of capitalist encirclement and the inevitable enmity of capitalist-controlled states. The notion of the inviolability of state sovereignty fitted easily into these precepts, and a regime putatively the expression of an internationalist philosophy ironically became the most ardent exponent of a rigid and exclusive form of state sovereignty.

Roosevelt was leader of a nation that throughout its history had had to pay relatively little heed to the views and aspirations of others, so long as the British fleet validated the Monroe doctrine, and British capital furnished the means for satisfaction of economic aspirations by internal growth within the American continent. The conditions making possible this degree of isolation from the world changed with the decline of British pre-eminence and growing United States involvement in the world economy, but one hundred and fifty years of tradition do not die overnight; and however much Roosevelt and his colleagues might recognize that the United States was now inescapably mixed up in the world, they could not but recall the Senate's rejection in 1919 and 1920 of such a recognition by Woodrow Wilson. So at Yalta in February 1945 Roosevelt observed that he would not be able to keep United States troops in Europe for more than two years after the end of the war. As part of this tradition was Washington's injunction to his successors to make no permanent commitments, and Jefferson's to shun entangling alliances. Roosevelt could therefore contemplate 'the establishment of a wider and more permanent system of general security' (in the words of the Atlantic Charter revised from Sir Alexander Cadogan's 'effective international organization'), but this system would have to be one that on the one hand could not be represented as an entangling alliance, and on the other reserved fully to the United States her ability herself to decide in all circumstances what action to take.

Churchill's views were in principle not dissimilar. He represented a country whose traditions and interests were very different from those of the other two.

Britain was a world-wide maritime power whose diplomatic influence derived largely from the imperial system of which she was the centre, and whose economy depended critically on a high level of world trade and on the free flow of food and raw materials to the United Kingdom. Moreover, as Sir Eyre Crowe had pointed out in his classic memorandum of 1907, a great naval power is the neighbour of any state with a seaboard, and in order not to create perceptions of menace that could lead to combinations against her, it was desirable to follow a policy that would harmonize with the interests of as many other states as possible. So Britain had developed the policy of protecting the interests and independence of small powers, such as Greece or Portugal. Churchill's experience in and before the war, however, of inability to act simultaneously in the Far East, the Middle East and on the European mainland, reinforced his earlier view that the League should have been seen and used as a European agency to deal with menaces in Europe, and that it had been fatally weakened by its indiscriminate and equal commitment to deal with any problem anywhere in the world. He therefore attached himself powerfully to the notion of regional councils with responsibilities for peace-keeping in their areas, and he saw little virtue in any global organization beyond a continued association of Britain, the U.S.A., the U.S.S.R. and, regretfully, China (since the U.S.A. insisted) to form the core of a World Council to which the regional councils should be in some sense subordinate. But within the World Council itself he hankered after a maintenance of the intimate war-time collaboration between Britain and the United States, involving certainly the continuance of the Combined Chiefs of Staff, and possibly moving forward towards common citizenship between the Commonwealth and the U.S.A.[1]

This was the political context within which Webster had to work when in January 1944 he was seconded to Gladwyn Jebb to work on proposals for a new world organization. His daily irritations, frustrations, hopes and fears are frankly recorded in his diary. He fully accepted that international peace and security depended on the willingness and ability of the four great powers to maintain it (five, if France was included), but he profoundly believed that the association of the four powers must be embedded within a universal organization. Strategically, as the Chiefs of Staff likewise argued, it was not possible to draw boundaries separating one region from another, particularly for a power with major maritime interests and forces. Economically the development of institutions and practices aimed at reducing economic causes of conflict could not realistically be imagined except on a global basis. But it was the political arguments to which Webster gave primary attention. Small power jealousy of the great powers had been a cause of international instability at least since the Concert of Europe and it was essential that they should have a role in the new structure which would enable them to swallow great power hegemony. Britain particularly had to take account of this because of the extent to which her influence derived from association with middle and smaller powers in the Commonwealth (and among these Webster saw Canada as being the most important, although it was Australia in the person of Herbert Evatt who at San Francisco proved the most unaccommodating). Traditional attitudes of the United States towards Europe might make her participation in a European Council improbable, and the formation of such a Council without her might dangerously encourage isolationism. Finally, Churchill's emotional desire to reunite the English-speaking peoples was reciprocated by few in the United States, and even fewer in Canada, and advocacy of such an exclusive partnership would be likely not merely to be self-defeating but might destroy the chance of any effective participation of the United States in international post-war co-operation.

These were the great issues to which the diary entries in chapters 3–6 of this book refer. Together with the Appendices they go some way towards closing the gap noticed in Herbert Nicholas's observation, 'About the evolution of British official thinking [about plans for a world organization] curiously little has been disclosed'.[2] These four chapters are preceded by a shorter chapter showing how Webster became involved in the affairs to which he subsequently made a major contribution. The concluding chapter of the book offers some reflections based upon the diary on the interplay of politician, official and outside expert in the processes of decision-taking and negotiation.

CHAPTER 2

F.R.P.S. to Foreign Office

The Foreign Research and Press Service (F.R.P.S.), to which Webster was seconded from the London School of Economics on 11 September 1939, was located at Balliol College, Oxford. Formally it was part of the Royal Institute of International Affairs, but in practice it worked for various government departments, especially the Foreign Office. Its functions were to prepare a weekly digest of the foreign press, produce detailed background memoranda on foreign countries, and undertake long-term planning including preparatory work for the peace conference.[1] Even before joining this organization Webster had considered a draft statement of war aims which affirmed, 'The aims of the British people were stated by their leaders at the beginning of the last war to be the creation of a world organisation which should make another great war impossible. That was our aim throughout the war and it was our aim in the peace which followed the war. It is still our aim.'[2] At the F.R.P.S. this interest in the formulation of war aims was continued with Webster participating in the background work for the Cabinet War Aims Committee and the Reconstruction Committee.[3] But Webster's colleagues at the F.R.P.S., no less than he, were by no means content with their role and wished to work directly under the Foreign Office,[4] whilst for his part R. A. Butler* freely acknowledged '. . . that the good brains of Chatham House such as Professor Webster, Clark, McCartney and others are dragging only small carts when they might be dragging big ones and that we should use them more than we do.'[5]

Consequently, when Webster was asked by the Minister of Information, Duff Cooper, to travel to the United States he accepted with alacrity. The object of the visit was '. . . to get in touch with the Universities, the Foundations and other intellectual organisations and in particular to ascertain what was being done as regards researches into the problems of reconstruction, to inform them, so far as was desirable, of similar efforts in Britain and to discuss the possibilities of further contacts in the future. A secondary object was to obtain information about the United States for the FRPS . . .'[6] Between 31 March and 15 May 1941 Webster travelled throughout the United States. In Washington he talked to a

---

* Brief biographical notes on persons referred to in the text are contained in the List of Persons on pp. 189—92.

number of senior State Department officials.   '7 April Monday   Visited Horn-beck at State Depart[ment]. He is very white haired but otherwise exactly the same, trenchant and dogmatic. Reviewed the course of events in [the] Far East & said he had protested every time since 1931 at the Japs not being stopped. Was very down on British policy & said he had compiled a list of 20 instances where they had been wrong since 1900, beginning [with the] 1905 renewal of [the] Japanese Alliance to [the] closing [of the] Burma Road. I intimated U.S.A. had not been very helpful on this & he agreed but said [there was] no reason why Britain should acquiesce in Jap aggression claiming U.S.A., in spite of great faults of omission, had never assented to Jap wrongdoing. He believed Japs would be stopped by firm stand. He also said he was constantly preaching the two wars were one. He shewed me a memorandum on the importance of Singapore to American interests strategic, economic. Very good & shewed its importance to whole war effort. Then went to Pasvolski [sic] on floor below. Discussed approach to peace aims. He said there was a rather informal departmental committee.[7] Little done but to gather materials. He had himself always insisted peace aims being worked out in action and no clean slate at end of war. Was quite sound on transitional period and its importance in constructing permanent machine, also on necessity of publicity and discussion.'

Two days later, Webster lunched with Adolf Berle.   '9th April . . . He [Berle] was at first a little buttoned up. He always speaks very softly and slowly. He tested me with a few thrusts at England re rubber monopoly etc to which I assented & talked of Smoot Hawley tariff.[8] This got us on mutual ground and he gradually became very communicative and even intimate. He said that he could not survive a German victory except in a concentration camp any more than I could. Obviously thoroughly believed in Anglo-American cooper[ation] after war. Was absolutely sound on Security as our joint job. It is clear that State Dept are now thinking along lines of joint Anglo-American force control in future. But he [Berle] is also much preoccupied [with] economics where his previous lines have been altered I think. He is more disposed to admit planned economy into world scene. He described the two kinds of Washingtonians (1) those liberals who believed in controlling and hampering capitalist enterprise & (2) those who want state action as substitute . . . He clearly belonged to the latter & while he did not go so far in [the] international sphere he was prepared to go a good way. On the deeper issues of the war he was splendid & I think at [the] end we both felt that we were completely in tune on this point, the more so since we both condemned in the same way the errors which led up to it. He thought [the] war would be long.'

From Washington Webster travelled to New York where he talked to W. H. Mallory, who told him in confidence of the '. . . special work the Council are doing for the State Department which is rather like that of FRPS for British Government. They have written 170 Memoranda. They have 4 special committees, Military, Political, Economic and Financial & Territorial. Isaiah Bowman is head of latter and the Greenland information produced by his committee was what the Pres[ident] relied on in his recent move. All this is very secret and they cannot therefore justify themselves to those who criticise them for doing nothing.' (14 April.) Contacts in Washington and New York caused Webster to conclude (10 April) 'All these people that I have met have same scale of values as us. They are neither American nor Anglo-American but want to use the combination for something wider and deeper. This is the most comforting thing I have found in U.S.A. On the immediate issues they are wild and jittery. Their imaginations are so big that they see impending disaster or victory so close that their judgment not good. But this very fact makes them realise the longer and deeper issues better than many Britishers.'

The visit certainly reinforced Webster's perceptions of the importance of the United States to British foreign policy. On 16 June 1941 he wrote to Lord Halifax bemoaning the fact that many officials in the Treasury and elsewhere wanted to keep the United States at arm's length — 'They do not seem to realise that the future of the democracies depends on the co-operation of the United States and the Commonwealth or that the attitude of the United States towards our security problems may be affected by our attitude on economic problems.'[9] On 27 July 1941 Webster wrote a detailed paper expressing his personal opinions on the 'Future Relations between the United States and the United Kingdom'. Based on the premise that the United States would enter the war, Webster analysed the reasons for closer co-operation — the danger perceived by both peoples and the similarity of defence interests. But the limitations of co-operation were set out: 'The history and traditions of both countries militate against a close fusion. Such a connection as federal union implies is not supported by any responsible politician in either country. In both countries there is a tendency to eschew clear-cut solutions and to rely on time and opportunity to remedy obvious defects in an imperfect scheme of things. In both countries statesmen are apt to wish to keep a way of retreat in case there has been a miscalculation of forces. We may expect, therefore, that proposals for collaboration will tend to be tentative and limited to the emergency of the moment rather than far-reaching and irrevocable. There will need to be a habit of collaboration formed before public opinion in either country will welcome complete fusion of defence forces or permanent economic organisations. It may be that if the organs set up for this purpose are described as temporary they will work better than if tradition is too strongly challenged at the outset.'

In addition, Webster realized that there were many obstacles to co-operation, particularly in the economic field where there might well be conflict over access to raw materials and in the size of the respective merchant navies. Nevertheless, he was guardedly optimistic — 'In the immediate post-war period the two countries in accordance with promises already made, will have the task of producing and directing reconstruction in many devastated and suffering areas. It may be hoped that this common task will lead to economic and financial co-operation, which could hardly be obtained for any other end. If during this period the advantages of such co-operation become manifest to the public opinion in both countries there will be a great demand that it be prolonged until it may well become permanent. At the same time it would be unwise to underestimate the opposition to such a policy which is certain to come from vested interests both of capital and labour which feel themselves threatened by it.

'It is suggested that while the problems of creating an Anglo-American partnership are many and difficult, they are not more so than those that remain if no partnership exists. This is true for both countries. It would appear also that the difficulties become less rather than greater if the area of security is made as wide as possible and the interests of other countries are fully taken into account in economic reconstruction. The partnership may also then be truthfully described as in the interests of the world as a whole.'[10]

Within months of returning to Britain, however, Webster agreed to leave the F.R.P.S. and become Director of the British Library of Information in New York.[11] On September 21 he wrote to Frank Walters reporting on a North Atlantic Relations Conference which the American Committee on International Studies had organized in Maine, 4–9 September 1941.[12] 'From the first I tried to strike the note that no power which did not take a full share of the war was likely to be much listened to at the peace. Powers which would not act against such aggression as is now taking place in the world would hardly be listened to if they said they would act against aggression in the future, and so on . . . The tone of the conference was exceedingly good; its basis was a complete Nazi defeat, and if it was rather amateur in some of its approaches, it was ready to accept a great deal.

'After some manoeuvring I got both George Fielding Elliott and Corbett to accept the thesis that an Anglo-American security scheme should be temporary and later fused into a general association. Elliott, who was very intransigent at first, also accepted the idea that if we had special obligations in Europe that would not necessarily prevent joint obligations for world security being undertaken by an Anglo-American force.'[13]

From August 1941 to May 1942 Webster energetically pursued his job as Director travelling in both Canada and the United States, emphasizing the shared interests of Britain and the North American continent in the prosecution of the war and the establishment of a better post-war world. But in the spring of 1942 the Ministry of Information and the Foreign Office agreed that the British Press Service in New York and the Library should be amalgamated, and Webster was deprived of his position after acrimonious correspondence with Brendan Bracken, who had succeeded Duff Cooper as Minister of Information in July 1941.[14] Webster now considered the alternatives of returning to the London School of Economics or of taking up a new appointment at the F.R.P.S. It was not until September 5 that he decided to return to Balliol, having been urged to do so by Sir Orme Sargent and having received intimations that the F.R.P.S. might be moved to London and given a more important planning role.[15] Before leaving for Oxford, however, Webster talked to Amery and Cripps, and the interviews reveal two of the themes that later caused Webster so much anguish when they reappeared in the ideas of Churchill himself:

Monday 31 Aug [1942]
... In the afternoon I saw Amery at the India Office. We discussed U.S. reactions and I described U.S. opinion including Pearl Buck etc. ... I ventured to hint that we should not still merely stand on our old offer but be ready to discuss [proposals] so as not to leave impression in America we were merely negative. But he said that he must take into consideration feelings of Indians on Viceroys council which was a sound enough reason. When he pressed, however, idea that present situation meant Indians really governing India I had to point out that Americans knew Viceroys real powers and it was no use pretending about them. Later we discussed future of world and he shewed that he still had all his old ideas. He said that Europe and other Continents must be united. I said that if I thought that Brit Empire did not matter I might accept continental areas, a remark which did not please him. I also said oceans unite as much as they divide. We parted rather cooly [sic] .

Wed 2nd Sept
... Went to Gwydyr House ... I thought it was to be for a few minutes but it turned out to be a long interview. He said he w [oul] d like to go to U.S. but was prevented by circ [umstance] s ... we discussed U.S. attitude towards India and Colonial questions generally. This led him to expound his views on all reconstruction esp [ecially] European which he had obtained during his Russian visit and discussed with diplomatists there, Jugoslavs & others. He wants regional federation, Scandinavia, Balkan etc. I said security was global & they should be made to see their security linked up with all the rest. He said they could only be led to this through seeking the security of their region. He asked me to read some of his reports on this subject. He said also that he had got Eden to set up the planning dept in [the] F [oreign] O [ffice] and told me I should join it. He knew all about Jebb. I told him I was going to FRPS but hoped we might be transferred at a later stage.[16]

This question of the F.R.P.S. transferring to London was very much in the minds of the senior members at Balliol. In Toynbee's absence[17] Zimmern and Webster presented their case to Jebb. They argued that the F.R.P.S. should become an entirely official body severing all connection with Chatham House and becoming more integrated into the formulation of policy.[18] Jebb was favourably disposed towards the idea and after tortuous negotiations both within the Foreign Office and with the Council of the Royal Institute of International Affairs it was agreed that the F.R.P.S. should become the Foreign Office Research Department from 1 April 1943.[19] The possibility was thus created for Webster to play a major role in policy planning within the Foreign Office. The formal incorporation of the F.R.P.S. into the Foreign Office in no way guaranteed such a role, but with typical determination Webster seized the opportunities offered by this change in status, as the following chapters show.

CHAPTER 3

Planning for a New World Organization

By the beginning of 1943 some progress had been made in the establishment of bureaucratic machinery to consider post-war British policy. In October 1942 Anthony Eden had decided to establish an informal interdepartmental committee under Richard Law which would consider the problems of the armistice period.[1] There had also been an important change in departmental responsibilities within the Foreign Office. On 26 June 1942 an Economic and Reconstruction Department (E & R) had been established. Though originally conceived as a co-ordinating department for such practical matters as wheat supplies and relief work, it soon became a 'planning' organization under Gladwyn Jebb's energetic leadership.[2] In May 1943 Nigel Ronald, the superintending Assistant Under-Secretary for E & R, noted that one of the new Research Department's functions would be to provide memoranda for E & R.[3] Indeed, within a month of the formal establishment of the Research Department, Arnold Toynbee was able to write 'Relations between R.D. and E & R Department have had a most satisfactory beginning in the consultations that have already taken place between Mr. Jebb and Professor Webster.'[4]

Characteristically, Webster had not waited for the formal date of incorporation of the F.R.P.S. before establishing a closer working relationship with the Foreign Office. In February 1943 he and his assistant W. M. Jordan were given access to Foreign Office archives so that they could write detailed historical memoranda on the experience of the first world war. Between January and August 1943 five papers were produced – 'The Political and Procedural Problems of the Armistices of 1918'; 'A Note on the Working of the Supreme War Council 1917–18'; 'The Problem of a Preliminary Settlement 1918–19'; 'The Maintenance of Order in Europe 1918–19'; and 'The Administration of the German Armistice and the Politico-Economic Direction of the Rhineland Occupation 1918–19'.[5] In addition Webster became engaged in work which was much more policy-oriented. By March 1943 he had completed a paper that analysed the various ways in which the war could be brought to an end – 'Some Considerations on the Time Table and Instruments of Peacemaking'. In this he outlined the advantages of obtaining political objectives quickly, and argued that

18

whichever mode of practice was followed work should be begun on drawing up alternative documents beforehand.[6] 7 June 1943 saw a further paper dealing with the problem of post-war European reconstruction. Although entitled 'Plebiscites arising from the Last Peace Settlement', the analysis considered the adequacy of this special device in a way that differed significantly from the five strictly historical memoranda. Webster accepted that there were advantages to plebiscites − they appealed to the world's sense of justice and might be '. . . the only method to resolve a deadlock between those States which have the power of decision'. But there were myriad difficulties: the vote might be influenced by temporary factors such as whether one state employed conscription; the possession of an economic monopoly might have a crucial bearing on the outcome and 'Post-war votes are inevitably held in abnormal conditions. If one of the competitors is a defeated combatant, voters may hesitate to link their fortunes to her fallen star.' The memorandum was clear that the disadvantages of plebiscites outweighed the advantages.[7]

Webster was now being consulted not only on the future shape of a European settlement but also on the larger question of the relationship of the great powers and the establishment of a replacement for the League of Nations. Two Cabinet memoranda had already been submitted on this topic: 'The Four Power Plan' of 8 November 1942 and 'The United Nations Plan' of 16 January 1943. Both were outline proposals only, positing leadership by the four great powers − U.S.A., U.S.S.R., U.K. and China − in a World Council (to which France might later be added) below which would be a number of subordinate regional councils. They showed how similar Foreign Office thinking at this time was to the ideas that Churchill was later to express.[8] On March 26 Gladwyn Jebb drafted a more detailed paper, which after much revision ultimately emerged on July 7 as a Cabinet memorandum − 'The United Nations Plan for Organising Peace'.[9] Webster played an important role in this revision and this began the close collaboration between him and Jebb on planning for a United Nations Organisation which lasted until San Francisco and after. Though both men were 'great power' advocates, Webster had a deeper understanding of the problems of international organization and a greater sensitivity to the feelings of smaller powers about any system that might appear to be too dominated by the great powers. In a note 'Some Considerations on a United Nations Organisation' he suggested a number of amendments to Jebb's draft:

> It is essential to discover the appropriate language in which to present the plan of leadership to the smaller powers. In its present shape it might only obtain their acquiescence for the immediate post-war period, and that with much protest. The same consideration applies to the Dominions. Since the 'Executive Committee' [the four powers] will necessarily have to summon representatives of the smaller powers to their meetings in order to adjust their disputes, etc., might it not be well to promise to do so when matters closely affecting any of the small powers are under discussion, thus recognising a principle which goes back to the Conference of Aix la Chapelle of 1818? . . . The Great Power meetings are apparently to be spasmodic, without

regularity of place and time, and without a central secretariat. It is not stated whether all are to be obliged to meet at the summons of one. This is a return to the 'Concert' system which, in fact, often means 'crisis' meetings and the reluctance or even refusal to be present on the part of one of the powers. Sir Austen Chamberlain regarded the regularity of the meetings of the principal statesmen as one of the greatest contributions of the League to international affairs. Judging by the experience of the nineteenth century, 'spasmodic' meetings would nearly all take place in the United States as the strongest power . . .
A general assembly of nations acts as an advertisement for world solidarity as well as a vent for suppressed emotions, especially those of vanity. It is probably a British interest that it should exist because of our special interest in world unity.
There is no mention of any system of machinery for the settlement of disputes. There is no mention of the World Court. But the integration of some kind of such machinery with the Great Power organisation is essential unless the principal statesmen are prepared to spend the whole of their time in settling disputes. No small power will accept a distasteful regional decision if it has the right of appeal to the Great Power Committee. The more decisions can be made by technical bodies the better for all concerned.[10]

These observations contributed to changes in the paper presented to the Cabinet. It proposed that small powers should be given adequate representation on the Council: 'In addition, smaller Powers should always be summoned to sit on the Council when their special interests are under discussion.' Reference was also made to the necessity of 'Judicial and Arbitral Machinery', and it was further suggested that the Council should meet at regular intervals with an 'Assembly of all the United Nations' meeting every two years.[11] However, the July 7 Cabinet paper could not ignore the known views of the Prime Minister. On January 30 and May 22 Churchill had outlined his plans respectively to the Turks and to a representative group of Americans.[12] His stress on the importance of regional councils was reflected in the Cabinet paper which paid lip service to the idea of such councils. The Foreign Office emphasis, however, was on smaller, specific-purpose regions. Not only were the ideas of No. 10 in conflict with those of the Foreign Office planners, but Churchill's exposition of his ideas, even though avowedly on a personal basis, caused concern and irritation. In his diary Webster recorded his reactions on being told by Jebb of the Prime Minister's statements in Washington.

Tues 15 June
. . . They are incredible. The S[ecretary] of S[tate] has agreed in principle — though he was never consulted. They are a mixture of Cripps and Lord Davies. They would have been up before Cab[ine]t tomorrow if J[ebb] had not got his master to stop them. He has been allowed to draft comments for E[den] to send to W[inston] and we went through these and I made one or two emendations. This shews the danger which I have foreseen all along that these preparations & studies will be made and then precipitate and unconsidered action by the PM will take matters entirely out of the hands of the experts. He

would never even organise a small commando raid without taking some expert advice even if he did not follow it. But here he is trying to shape the whole of the future without saying a word to his Cabt, For Sec or their officials. The scheme is crude in the extreme and is more like that of a too donnish thinker than of a man of action. It is often so when men of action deal with something on which they have little experience. Winston has never really taken much part in foreign policy. It is an appalling thought that he should take such decisions so recklessly and that there should be no one to stand up to him. The Americans lapped up the stuff as they had no experience to correct it. There are of course good points in it but these are vitiated by impossible suggestions which will very likely wreck the whole scheme. Meanwhile it will prevent any other scheme being set on foot. I do not yet see how we can save anything out of this wreck though of course the demarche is not official. But who is to disavow a Prime Minister? No one indeed in this Cabinet is likely to run his head into danger by pointing out the obvious dangers and impossibilities of the scheme. It looks as if Winston might do exactly what he said he never would do "preside over the dissolution of the British Empire"[13] . . .

'Wed 16 June

. . . I saw J at 6. There had been a satisfactory meeting with the S of S who had agreed to read P.M. J's minute of yesterday which I saw and amended a little. He also agreed to the suggestion (which I had made to J) that a Cabt C[ommi]ttee should be made for peace aims like the Defence Cttee. J thought Law & Cadogan might sit on it and an official secretariat be attached. I doubt if they will let Law but at any rate a Cttee of any kind would be a barrier to such exploits as the PM's recent one. The paper on necessity of taking up Armistice terms with major allies is before Cabt today but PM's idea of taking his own US demarche, which has been circulated to War Cabt is stopped. There is some chance, therefore, of pulling something out of the mess.[14] But much depends on todays Cabinet . . . I told J there was no precedent which I knew for a PM acting on his own initiative without consultation with Cabt or indeed anyone so far as is known . . . [Jebb also said] that the latest idea was that Regions should elect not ministers of the states composing them in Central Council but independent persons! Fantastic! These are the ideas of the more futile kind of international wallahs of the last 20 years. . . . I shall hear tomorrow morning the result of this days fatal discussions — or perhaps more likely there will be compromise and confusion and no real result . . .

'Thurs 17 June

Result of Cabt was not so bad. The P.M. fumed and was in bad temper but Attlee was good and in contradistinction to P.M. said we were not prepared last time. P.M. actually insisted we were! The result which I suspect due to Bridges drafting as much as to anything else was to allow the armistice paper to go forward & US & USSR to be approached through Ambassadors. We also decided to make new draft of United Nations plan in the light of all this and I spent a couple of hours with J going through it. The last paras in which regional stuff comes in he left to me ... it took some time to draft as one must accommodate the language all the time to the phantasies of the Washington meeting. However, I think I have got our essentials in without being too challenging ...'

Some success had been achieved in advancing planning on an international organization, but with Italy in the throes of defeat Webster was forced to direct his attention to the urgent problems of European reconstruction in addition to his work on world organization. Throughout the war Webster had been conscious of the crucial importance of the U.S.A., but on August 7 he voiced his concern about American tactics on the Italian armistice:

'Sat 7 Aug
... The telegrams re the armistice are pouring in. The Americans are accepting our terms. But they have not let in the Russians or the smaller allies. ... I told him [Jebb] all the long term plans would be useless if we antagonised the Russians and the French to say nothing of the smaller allies by trying to run everything as an Anglo-American shew. If we gave them their rights we would still have substantial control in the southern area because we were there. J entirely agrees but the Americans seem to be either entirely stupid or are even more stupid in trying to be Machiavellian. Hull still refuses to recognise the French Cttee and de Gaulle's complete ascendancy in it makes the rift very dangerous ... As regards our plan [on world organization] this is now before a special planning Cttee of the Cabinet. It is made on party lines. Attlee, Cripps, Sinclair, Cranborne, Assheton, Mabane, & another liberal I forget. Bridges & J are the Secs. He [Jebb] shewed me minutes of 1st meeting.[15] So far they have accepted it pretty well. Have refused special position of 4 powers on Council on grounds that if they are united it does not matter & if not nothing can be done. They were foolish on Court & judicial machinery. It was referred to Malkin who is back and says [he] has written a good minute. They now insist they must review the future of Germany before they can go further so the F.O. paper on Germany will be taken next on Wed ...

'Monday 9 August
Lambert telephoned me and on seeing him I found that the Cttee on the plan wanted an F.O. Memo on the relations of the Technical organizations to the World Council. It is one of the many lacunae in that document. He asked me to write it ... I saw Malkin who is much better. He had few ideas on the subject but agreed with mine so far as I was able to state them. Later I discussed the whole question with Frank [Walters] without telling him the exact purpose. We decided the Bruce report[16] applied and with much difficulty I got a copy in fact two one from the F.O. and one from Chatham House. I tried to see J but he was out so I told Lambert to tell him of my ideas before he left as rather big issues are at stake ... The time for the memo is extended a week as it will be impossible to get one printed and circulated before [the] next meeting of the Cttee on Wed ...

'Tues 10 Aug

Bridges sat next to me at lunch. He told me that the recent Cabt meeting at 1.30 was about the Italian armistice and the first thing asked was the precedents. He had sent for my armistice paper and it could not be found![17] He said he had told them to sew one on to the tail of his pyjamas. I told him things were bound to get into a mess with no real machine on the highest levels and he seemed to agree. He was rather impatient and nervy though exceedingly nice to me . . .

'Thur 12 Aug

Discussed my draft [on technical organizations] with Lambert & Coulson. The latter made some objections but saw the light. I also talked with Hood and discovered [that] Macmillan [was] here. Lambert said Cabt Cttee had discussed German dismemberment and were divided. He was not very communicative . . .'

In his diary entry for August 14 Webster noted that Eden would 'soon be abroad', a reference to the Anglo-American meeting at Quebec which began on August 17. During this conference Cordell Hull gave Eden a copy of the American draft of a Four Power Declaration which called for the establishment of an international organization.[18] Gladwyn Jebb had also crossed the Atlantic in August, having discussions in Washington with State Department officials.[19] On Jebb's return both he and Webster were concerned about the lack of real progress in the Attlee committee considering world organization. They were also involved in preparations for a three power foreign ministers' meeting at Moscow. For some time there had been considerable correspondence between Roosevelt, Stalin and Churchill about a possible Big Three meeting, but on August 25 Stalin had finally agreed to a meeting of 'representatives in charge of foreign affairs'.[20] Since the Americans had already taken the initiative on international organization with their Four Power Declaration, the Foreign Office concentrated on the more immediate problems of a liberated Europe.

'Mon 30 Aug

. . . J rang up and asked me to dine which we did at the Travellers and then went to the office where he shewed me the Quebec dope . . . 4 power declaration proposed, general but on right lines. Then a Protocol with Senate consent. Proposed 3 power meeting by Stalin. In Sicily. All to the good.

'Later we discussed the latest brickbrats [*sic*] of the Plan Committee . . . J. will write an impatient critique for the S. of S. saying we must avoid going into details. I told J I knew nothing while he was away. He said Ronald should not have stayed away so much and admitted Lambert [was] rather overwhelmed . . .

'Tues 31 Aug

. . . J's paper did not come but at 5 I went across and found he had a draft of one for the Attlee Cttee, which I altered a good deal before it was finally agreed, on the United Nations Commission for Europe.[21] They also wanted one on an Int[ernational] Police Force which Hood drew up & I vetted.[22] All this is very ridiculous and J. has got the S. of S. to sign a very good paper he had drawn up telling the Cttee they must not begin to investigate details but get the principles passed so that consultation with the Allies could begin . . .[23]

'Sat 4 Sept

. . . Attlee Cttee on the plan has not met A[ttlee] being too occupied with [the] armistice. So everything on the permanent side is held up . . .

'Tues Sept 14

. . . I find that Attlee had summoned his Cttee on the plan for Wed to discuss Eden's notes telling them to get on with it and now Eden won't go but wants to remain in the country. This is too bad as it is the only chance to get general approval immediately to the principles of the plan. After lunch I walked up with Bridges and told him of this. He was very indignant and said a telegram had come from the great man at Washington [Churchill] urging them to get on with it.[24] He said he would get on to Gladwyn and try to make Eden go, but I have little hope he will succeed. He said we needed two Sir John Andersons and two Richard Laws. I said first not possible but that they could easily get a second Under Sec of S[tate] for F[oreign] A[ffairs] if they would not play politics . . .

'Fri 24 Sept

I saw J. at 11 o'clock. He shewed me a great many things and I began to realise the exact state of the transactions with Moscow. The question of Confederations was to be discussed there and J. said there was a meeting at 5 in Strangs room. He rang up Christopher Warner and got me invited . . .

. . . At 5 I found Warner, Roberts, Howard, Coulson, Geoffrey Harrison, Geoffrey Wilson, J and I at Strangs. I was first there and he said he had read all my papers. He also was convinced of necessity of setting up machinery to deal with the problems and spoke bitterly of the present arrangements which left everything in the hands of the Combined Chiefs of Staff in Washington . . . The meeting turned out to be one for the consideration of the Agenda [for the Moscow Conference]. A real brick has been made about the British Agenda for it was originally intended as a list of subjects for our people to consider and by mistake turned into a list to be submitted to the Russians! The result is that all the thorny questions are on it including Confederations and the future of all the S. East States, besides [the] future of Germany, Poland and the establishment of machinery — and all in 10 days. Of course most of this will never be touched except perhaps to refer the problems to other bodies. Still we went all through the Agenda to see how each question stood. The young FO men merely considered (a) what had been said in it (b) what expediency of the moment might make us do. I once or twice ventured to point out that there was also the consideration of what was in the best interests of all the states in a permanent settlement. Strang backed me up on this and so the young men became a little less hard boiled. But they are immersed in this nauseous atmosphere and look on every negotiation as an intrigue. When at last we came to "Confederations" I waited for the appropriate moment and then broached my principles. J backed me up. Strang was bitten and the young men climbed on the bandwagon. J and I were instructed to draw them up.[25]

'Sun 26 Sept — Sat Oct 2

... As regards the Conference my principles[26] have been approved right up to the S of S with small alteration ... I have seen all the Agenda and also the Cabinet Paper on Germany which they will take on Monday.

'Tue 26 Oct

Saw J in the afternoon and all the corres[pondence] put in to Moscow Conference. It has gone very well and we should get a European Commission in London.[27] I told J he could then combine his own job with the Sec[retary]ship of the Commission. He was bucked up at the impetus it would give our work here. So far my own special document has not been tackled. It will I think be referred to the Commission. This may of course be sabotaged by the USA and ultimately be of no avail but at any rate it is a move in the right direction.

'Sat 30 Oct

... I went to FO ... I read the rest of the Moscow corres. The result is splendid, far better than we had hoped. My own declaration is dropped, I am sorry to record, as Molotoff did not like it and Eden dropped it.[28] But it can be revived later I dare say at the London Commission. I discussed this with J who has already written Cadogan a memo about it ...

'Mon Nov 15

... Dined with Geoffrey Wilson and David Owen ... Geoffrey told me a great deal about Moscow Conference. He had been present at all Plenary meetings and kept a record ... Russians suspected my draft. Asked why they should deny spheres of influence which only journalists had talked of. They had sent in a paper on Federations wh[ich] they refused to call Confederations. Eden was not interested and just let the matter fall ...

'Sat 20 Nov

In evening I went to see J. He is off with the big three on Tuesday. He agreed that European Advisory Commission had slumped. I warned him agst giving up his present job for it. He now agrees. Strang who is to be British rep[resentative] under Eden is very upset about [the] difficulty of getting adequate Russian and United States representation — only Amb[assa]dors. The truth is that there has been a reaction in Washington agst it and Hull cannot go so far now he is back home. The World Plan will be done at Washington and J agreed that I would be useful there but I do not expect results ...'

Following the establishment in July of the sub-committee on Post-War Settlement, which had proved a failure, there had been no further consideration of international organization in the Cabinet during 1943. Instead attention had been focused on the meetings at Moscow and Teheran. However, on November 19 Howard Bucknell of the United States Embassy in London wrote to Anthony Eden informing him that the United States government, with the concurrence of the other signatories of the Moscow Declaration, wished to make an announcement welcoming adherence of the United Nations to the Moscow Declaration and specifically to the clause that envisaged a new international organization. The Foreign Office view was that it had been agreed at Moscow that there should in the first place be tripartite discussions before any adherence to this declaration. Richard Law so informed Bucknell[29] and on November 29 Lord Halifax reported that the State Department now proposed four power discussions in Washington on the subject of a new League.[30] This was welcomed in the Foreign Office,[31] and an enquiry from Law about ideas in the Office on world organization, beyond those sketched in the U.N. Plan, was followed by a minute from Jebb stressing that such a meeting as was now being considered would require detailed preparation.[32] An informal interdepartmental committee came into being to supervise the preparation of briefs, and on 14 February 1944 Jebb suggested to Eden that this informal committee should be formalized and placed under a new sub-committee of the Cabinet. This was agreed by Churchill at the end of February, and thus the interdepartmental committee under Law, called the Committee on Future World Organization, came to be established.[33]

In the meantime the necessity of preparing briefs had caused an outburst of hectic activity in the Foreign Office, and the sudden involvement of Webster.

'Wed 5 Jan
... Jebb rang and asked me to see him urgently. I find that [the] S of S had allowed taking up the great plan departmentally and J had the job. He asked me to be seconded to him. I was a bit staggered at this but said I would consider it with Arnold [Toynbee] ... Nora [Webster] thought I ought to do it but it is a heavy job and may very likely lead to nothing at all.
'Thur 6 Jan
... I at last saw Arnold about J's proposal. He was a little bit perturbed ... but behaved very well and agreed it would be good for FOR[esearch] D[epartment]. He insists on seeing Ronald. I said I would say it could be done but would insist on reasonable conditions.'

By the middle of February considerable progress had been made in drafting detailed memoranda on a new international organization, and in preparing agenda for the Washington discussions. The date for these discussions remained undetermined, however, because the Americans found, like the British, that they needed time to prepare their proposals.

'Tues Feb 15
Went to J who had done wonders overnight — got out new draft & got S of S approval through Law [of the Summary of Topics — consisting essentially of chapter headings of the detailed papers to be submitted as agenda for the talks in Washington] ... I left to see Lord Cecil at 5.30. He was in good form though he has been ill. We agreed on nearly everything. He said the essential failure was in not making the people realise that they must put force behind the League — a remarkable and characteristically objective statement. He agreed that the main

thing was to get US in but said unless you put some definite good world before the people they might despair with incalculable results. I agree but it is hard to find the right mean of not promising more than can be done with reasonable fortune and promising enough to stir up their faith. If it is exploited again it may disappear for good i.e. look to entirely new social forms and probably wrong ones — for where no cure for ills is seen men turn to nostrums and quacks . . .
'Thurs Feb 17
. . . Jack Ward lunched with me and was very frank about FO personalities. He said J's manner had nearly caused his fall. The S of S had not wanted him to go to Cairo.[34] He was in better odour now but he might be in the bad books again at any time. I said I had long realised this. It was only partly due to his bad manner and was even more caused by what was much to his credit his courage and energy. He said Strang did not stand up to Eden — hence the lamentable decision re the E[uropean] A[dvisory] C[ommission]. If Eden had put himself in we might have had good US and Soviet representation. As it was neither Winant nor Gousev cut any ice at home and the whole thing was a flop and would soon be ridiculous. It was wasting the time of the best Ass[istan]t Under Sec. At Washington the War Dept were all powerful in such matters. Like ours, in peace time the soldiers had a bad time and they made up for it in war. . . . I got an SOS from J and found Chiefs of Staff had refused to accept the Security paper. They said they had no time to consider such things while fighting a world war. Nor had they any belief in an int[ernational] org[anisation]. They wanted an Alliance. J stuck up to them as far as he could but though they admitted he had done quite right to put something up they would give no lead. So we face [the] Washington discussions without any policy on the most important part of them. However they may not come off at all. The PM and the Cabinet must be brought in. I helped J draft a minute for Eden to send to [the] PM. He had not been tactful but I hope I got the thing in better shape. But who can say what the result will be? The PM may blow up, in which case J may well be the sacrifice.'

It was this minute, Churchill's initialling of which being taken to signify approval, that led to the establishment of the Cabinet sub-committee under Attlee, which was called the Armistice and Post-War Committee.[35] This sub-committee did not however hold its first meeting until April 22. The delay was caused by a decision that since the planners' papers would require the agreement of the Dominions, they should first be considered by a Ministerial Committee which was preparing papers for the May meeting of the Dominion Prime Ministers.[36] However, it was ultimately recognized that the planning papers were outside the real competence of the Dominions Committee.[37] Accordingly, the previous decision in principle to establish a new committee was implemented. The first meeting of the Armistice and Post-War Committee (A.P.W.) considered five detailed memoranda drawn up by the planners. These were: A. Scope and Nature of an International Organisation; B. Guarantees and the Pacific Settlement of Disputes; C. Security; D. Co-ordination of Economic and Political Machinery; E. Method and Procedure for establishing a World Organisation.[38] Webster describes his part:

'Sunday 16 April

For a fortnight I have been too pressed to keep this diary because the papers of the World Organisation scheme had to be finished by this Sunday. ... substantially the Covering Brief, Memos A, B and E are my work. I did a lot in P.H.P. [Post-Hostilities Planning Sub-Committee] on C and I discussed and helped Fleming with E [*sic*]. So I have a grave responsibility for the final result. ... This morning J and I went over them [the papers] again and tidied up a few ends. Then Cadogan had a go. I waited till 6 ... but the only news was that he had no observations on the first 3 so I left for home . . .'[39]

'Dick Law [w] as too busy to attend ... the meetings but I had half an hour with him on Friday [April 14] to coach him on what we had done. He has been with Stettinius, Bowman and the others at Chequers this weekend. I told him what to say to PM about regionalisation and I told Bowman to say the same thing so I hope some impression will be made but the old man may still blow the whole thing up. The Cttee of Ministers will probably have Attlee in the Chair so I have told Evan (after consulting J) about the whole thing and prepared him to advise his master. But it is a bad time to consider these key parts of the whole Post War plan. The [Dominion] PM's arrive in a fortnight and they will see the papers if they are passed by the Ministers. It will take something pretty drastic to stop the whole thing now but who can say what the PM will do?

'I was pretty tired in the middle of the week. I had written two of the key papers in 4 days. But I stood the dust up at the Committees all right and got nearly all my stuff through. Of course the papers have got a bit woolly by change of some sentences and continuing elisions and insertions.

'Falla has been a great help. He is a brilliant philologist with a sense of language and a good drafter. I have got on well with Gladwyn. I have given way a good deal on details but I think I have kept the essentials. Now it is to be seen whether the Cabinet will stand for my plan. For my plan it is.'

As this extract shows, the United States Under-Secretary of State Edward Stettinius was in London from 7 to 29 April and it was with this visit in mind that Webster had written to Jebb on March 9:

In view of the visit of Mr. Stettinius and the fact that he may wish to discuss the 'headlines' of a permanent organisation it might perhaps be worth while looking again at the 'principles' which I drew up some time ago.

Principles for the Washington Discussions

1.   Subject to the necessity of preserving harmonious relations with the Dominions and maintaining Imperial rule, the entrance of the United States and the U.S.S.R. into a permanent organisation is more important than the exact form of the organisation itself.

2.   While it is essential to establish the power and responsibility of the Great Powers in the maintenance of world peace, it is possible to obtain this end without such explicit definition as would offend the susceptibilities of the Dominions and the lesser Allies.

3.   A World Council with final responsibility for the preservation of peace in every part of the world is of greater importance than any regional organisation such as the 'Councils of Europe and Asia'. Moreover, the former can become at once a reality while the latter must for a considerable period be merely an aspiration.

4.   On the other hand, some recognition of regionalism such as a Western Europe security organisation or a North and South Atlantic system would be of advantage to British interests in the event of failure of the permanent organisation.

5.   It is a British interest to prepare in every possible way for the recognition of a revived France as a Great Power.

6.   It is a British interest to obtain as specific security arrangements as possible in the machinery of world organisation.

7.   Some recognition of the final control at the political centre of the economic organisations is essential if the Secretary of State for Foreign Affairs is to maintain final control of Foreign Policy.

21 January 1944

Both Jebb and Ronald liked these 'principles' which Ronald thought might be a useful introduction to a brief for Ministers on the subject.[40]

The months of April and May were crucial for Webster as he waited, sometimes with foreboding, for Ministerial approval of the papers on world organization.

'Tues 18 April
Bowman came to see Jebb and me this morning and at 12 we went to Cadogan's room where Law joined us for some time. He told us all about his interview with the PM at Chequers with which he was well satisfied. . . . The PM was in a mellow mood and only once complained that he was made to go into the question of a World Organisation when he was running a war. B[owman] talked a good deal about Colonial Trusteeship but on our questions his thoughts ran very much along our lines as on previous occasions. To me the most satisfactory thing was Cadogan's interest. He now intends to attend the meeting of Ministers [A.P.W. Committee] and is taking up the whole thing seriously . . .
'Thur 20 April
. . . Eady has sent me a very nice letter asking to discuss the fundamentals of the WO at a lunch. I welcome this as it may have good effects later on. By a curious coincidence I met him in the station going home. . . . We had a few words about his letter. I said I had not allowed the proportions of the papers to be disturbed and not given way on essentials. We agreed it had been a good Committee [the Law interdepartmental committee] and everyone had tried to help and not sparkle. . . . He said the Ministers ought to pass it. I said they would certainly if I had a Minister to fight for it — but Eden is sulking in the country and even Dick Law suggested he might go away for the weekend when he heard Cadogan would

attend. J told him he must at least go to present his papers and he reluctantly consented. The irresponsibility of Ministers is almost beyond belief but I have had so much opportunity of seeing it in my official life that I have now come to expect it. No wonder that the Civil Service which, whatever else it is, is conscientious often comes to despise them.

'Friday 21 April

Rather an anxious and difficult day in which I have done a good deal to get the way prepared for the consideration of my papers tomorrow. The Cabt Cttee will be Pres of Council (Attlee) Sec of S. Doms (Cranborne), Sec of S. India (Amery), Minister of Labour (Bevin) Sec of Air (Sinclair) with Law and Cadogan. Eden is still in the country. I do not know if Alexander (Navy) will be there. Sir James Grigg (Army) is sulking because he is not on the permanent Cttee and refuses to go. At first he said no W[ar] O[ffice] rep. was to be present but I believe General Nye is to go. He will know little or nothing about it. I got Evan to come in to shew me the note he had written for Attlee. This was shockingly puerile. He had not read all the papers and did not understand them. I had only a ¼hr with him at F.O. and he promised to put in all I told him but he cannot understand it I am afraid.

'After lunch Gladwyn & I saw Sir V. [*sic*] Laithwaite who is War Cabt Sec. He also had written a lot of rot for Attlee. He accepted all our corrections easily enough but he again does not understand the issues involved . . .

'At 5 Gladwyn & I saw Cadogan who really does understand it [the papers on world organization] and asked some excellent questions. I rely on him to see the thing through as Law will not be quick enough. He said he hoped the Cttee would accept on grounds that everything was to be discussed with Dominions and then whole thing could be reviewed in the light of their comments . . .

'Saturday 22 April

I saw Bowman with Malkin this morning about the World Court. He said there was now no criticism among their Congress confidants though there had been much at the beginning. They might accept the Hague, though not Geneva as a centre. At 1 o'clock Falla came in to say that my covering brief and papers & Jebb's on Security had all been passed with small alterations of no consequence. This is a great relief for us, this Cabinet Committee was a strong one. They should now pass the Cabinet and go to the Dominions. With any luck they should be the foundation of our discussions with the USA. Flemings paper on the other hand on coordination of economic and political organisation has foundered. They would not have him make a re-draft and as Lionel Robbins was away I had to make one from a directive. This was peculiarly foolish in parts. However I saw Laithwaite and Cadogan and after consultation with them drafted a new D which I hope will at any rate do no harm. This is an extraordinary way to get out so important a paper and Cadogan who was present at the Cabt Cttee said they did not know what they were doing. However I think I have left the way open for the future to do what is necessary . . .

'On the whole I am pretty satisfied with this weeks work. I must wire

Gladwyn on Monday.[41] I dare say there will be shocks next week.'

This presentiment of difficulties ahead was more than justified.

'Monday April 24
. . . I hear that the P.M. is a bit uncertain about our papers and Chiefs of Staff
are going back on C so we are not out of the wood yet . . .
'Wed April 26
I went to Dominions Office and with Sir John Stephenson and Shannon worked
out the necessary changes in my covering brief for the use of the Dominion P.M.'s
later on. Beaverbrook's office had rung up Donald Hall with [an] absurd
suggestion to solve the question of Dominions & World Council i.e. that [the]
British Commonwealth should be on it and one sit for the whole after
consultation. We all laughed at this. I was not impressed by Stephenson but he
was useful to keep Shannon in order and we easily agreed. When I was off to
Stettinius cocktail party at Claridges I ran into Dick Law. He was pleased re
papers and I congratulated him on producing the right atmosphere. We regretted
D which I said was out of proportion. He blamed himself for it but he said he
had not had time. Nevertheless he is partly to blame. He, Hood, Donald Hall and
I went in his car to the party. I saw Bridges there and he said we must go softly
with PM re papers. He had a plot for Sec of State to handle him. They should
ask for comments and later S of S [should] get PM to agree. I said we would be
in a terrible position if the papers [were] now turned down and he agreed but
seemed hopeful . . .
'Thursday April 27
There is still much to clear up concerning the Stettinius visit and the whole
question of the Memoranda is still in doubt. I did a good deal of work with Falla
concerning the reports of Bowman interviews and wrote a letter to Michael
Wright sending him the general report and giving him a pat on the back. Then
Dickson [Dixon] asked for a Brief for the S. of S. to present the papers to the
Dominion Prime Ministers. There was no time to consult anybody so I wrote it
in a couple of hours in the evening.
'Friday April 28
I got the brief in by 12 o'clock as promised. I shewed it to Law who approved it
easily. In conversation he said the PM did not want any world organisation at all
but continental Leagues of Nations and a Four Power Alliance. He asked me to
write a brief against it . . .
   'I find Laws brief pretty hard to write and I have finished it at 1.30 a.m.
having written since 9.30. It is at any rate clear and incisive and I think the
arguments in the first part of the paper re 4 Power Alliance are decisive. The
second part about Europe, I am not very satisfied with.[42]
'Sunday April 30
. . . Gladwyn unexpectedly arrived. I went over and put him wise to all that had
happened. He found a slip in my revise of the covering Memoranda for the
Dominion PM's and we telephoned the correction. Guy Millard, Eden's Asst Sec,

was in his room and we went to see him about another paper for the S of S. He shewed us Edens letter to PM about the Memoranda which was very unsatisfactory for he abandoned C altogether. Gladwyn wrote a minute to him entreating him not to do this. But will he fight the PM and the General Staff . . .?
'Monday May 1
The S of S read all the papers during the weekend including my brief which Law had sent him and warmly approved. He had marked several passages in the Memoranda and seems to have worked very carefully. He asked for a brief on the difference between Hull's views and those of the PM which he described by a diagram. This I agreed to do and I have written it between 9.30 and 1.30. It was easy enough to shew that the PM's idea of 4 Power Alliance outside a world organisation [was impractical?], more difficult to deal with his vague ideas about a European Council.[43] However, I have managed to make what I think is a very convincing statement.
'Tuesday May 2
Gladwyn accepted my brief without any criticism and it was sent in. . . . Then Gladwyn sent an S.O.S. He had seen S of S for about 4 minutes and been told that the PM insisted on his own schemes and apparently S of S would not fight. Thus no papers are to be given to Dominion Premiers and consequently none to the Americans. This is a really big issue on which the fate of the world may ultimately depend. For it will look as if we had let Hull commit himself with the Senate and then let him down. This may well drive the U.S. into isolationism and leave us alone with a chaotic world and the Russians. We have got a scheme which we know the U.S. will accept, from the conversations with Bowman, and here is the PM insisting on throwing away this glorious opportunity. The S of S had asked for a short summary of the scheme made in such a way as to please PM as far as possible. Gladwyn had already done this but I was not satisfied with it and have revised it for a couple of hours this evening. It is a degrading occupation and I shall have to consider whether I can go on. But what can anyone do with the PM when the second front is so near. It is impossible to resign and he certainly won't.
'Wed May 3
I found Gladwyn had written a comment on the account of the discussion in the Cabt on the World Organisation which Bridges had sent S of S though it is not official. The PM talked the vainest nonsense advocating among other things a World Court to settle all disputes i.e. a sort of equity tribunal like the New Commonwealth of which he is President. Then regional councils with nothing to do and the 3 Powers running round first to the Council of Europe, then Asia, then Pan America. It would be exceedingly funny if it were not so tragic. I was not satisfied with Gladwyn's draft and redrafted it hastily making the P.M. in conflict with S of S and office rather than with Gladwyn himself as he had seemed to do. This and my draft was sent off to S of S late in the aft[ernoon]. Gladwyn telephoned the S of S and I went over and found that S of S was ready to stand up to P.M., wanted a draft summary without any concessions to him

and hoped to send all the papers to the Dominion PM's. So we hastily redrafted for him to get it at dinner time . . .

'Thursday May 4

I saw the minute which S of S had written PM to go with the summary "I much hope you will allow me to circulate all the papers not as committing you or any of us but as an official study." Gladwyn came to my room to see what we could do. I said I would tackle Evan Durbin and he would get in touch with Jacob. There did not seem anything more that we could do.

'Friday May 5

I had to go to see Evan at No 11 where he was tied as he had to see his master at any moment. I explained the position to him. He said only once had he stirred up his master against PM when latter tried to get away with pretending Cabinet had sanctioned German dismemberment. He could not stir him up in that way now. Indeed I did not want him to as we did not know what would happen. But I gave him the account of Bowmans visit and the Brief about necessity of acting now for general organisation . . . and suggest[ed it was] time Attlee learnt what had happened to papers his Cttee had passed.

'Sat May 6

News that PM will write a minute against the papers.

'Monday May 8

. . . In the evening we [Jebb and Webster] saw the PM's minute. It accepts our papers in principle and then puts in all the stuff about the three regions. It accepts a Council of the 4 and 3 reps from the continental regions. It ended with a terrible blurb about a united states of Europe.

'Tues May 9

I found Gladwyn had hastily written a note smashing PM's paper for S of S and had seen him for about 2 minutes. He was still confident. . . . At 3 I saw Norman Robertson the Canadian principal F.O. official. He had been at the meeting. He was much perturbed at what he considered an attempt by PM and Curtin to have Commonwealth as member of Council rather than U.K. He asked us if we were so uncertain of being a Great Power that we must so act. I said that the only 2 people I knew who questioned our position as a great power were Smuts and Halifax at which he was pleased. I tried to make him believe it was only a question of words but he could not be persuaded. He said Canada could not accept being represented by us as Commonwealth or represent us similarly. We told him our plan fully met his views and encouraged him to stick up to P.M . . . [44]

'Wed May 10

. . . Gladwyn was still a bit pessimistic about yesterday and Dick Law had been sunk in gloom but I had not been so cast down. I think the P.M. will find it hard to stop the papers being sent to U.S. which is the main thing. When I got back this evening to E[conomic] and R[econstruction Department] I found Gladwyn had been given the decision of the P.M. meeting that the papers were accepted subject to five principles which were quite innocuous. Also Jacob who had seen minutes said the P.M's ideas had been knocked out. The S of S is confident and told Gladwyn it would be all right. So I am full of hope tonight that we shall get our papers through after all . . .

'Thur May 11

[A crisis day] . . . The crisis began at tea when after I had read the minutes of Tuesday's meeting in Law's room, I & Gladwyn had tea with Law. He was very pleased with the result of today's meeting. All the P.M's he said had praised my papers,[45] looking at me and making Gladwyn I am afraid a bit jealous. The P.M. had been much taken aback at the universal opposition to his views and acceptance of ours. But some concession must be made to him. We must make some alternations in the papers to suit him. After discussion we agreed these should be in the covering note only putting forward the PM's views and explaining why they could not be given to the Americans & Russians. Gladwyn asked to be able to write a minute to the PM against his ideas. He said no one had ever challenged him properly. Law was a bit sceptical about this but said he could try a shot at it. Meanwhile he asked us to see Bridges about what had happened today.

'I wrote the paper altering the covering brief and Gladwyn wrote his shy at the PM. Bridges could not see us till 10 o'clock and we stayed with him and Laithwaite till 10.45. The story they had was very different. The PM had abandoned his United States of Europe in deference to criticism but had stuck to his idea of a 3 Power Council with no duties but maintaining order, i.e. no general organisation at all. We argued that the PM's could not have accepted this but they said they had done . . . My paper they said was completely out of date. When I said it was impossible to alter our papers in the sense of the PM's proposal Bridges talked of amour propre in not wanting to alter my beautiful symmetrical papers. I got angry at this and said I had all along said the only real point was to get US in and I did not mind about details and had no amour propre. He withdrew his remark and said if the issue was political the S of S ought to argue it. He had been talked down by the PM. No one had put the point against him. There must therefore be some alteration in our papers. When we had cooled down a bit Gladwyn said we might alter in an innocuous way and there we left it until we see the minutes. I lashed out at Bridges as I left and said never before had Britain been governed by a Dictator. He said then people must stand up to him. I said I wish they would give me half an hour with him . . .

'Friday May 12

Gladwyn & I first thing this morning made the alterations in the papers to suit PM taking care to do no harm or rather I did this while G wrote a separate minute. Then we had 3/4 hour with Cadogan who agreed generally with what we had done but reserved his final approval until he saw the completed draft. We were still without the minutes of yesterdays meeting but felt we knew enough to go on with. I got Law's sec to telephone up to urge the Secretariat to send us the minutes. They came in the afternoon. Gladwyn got hold of them first and then Dick Law. However, it took Law a good time to read our papers and while he was doing it I read the minutes twice. They in no sense confirm what Laithwaite claimed, that the D[ominion] PM's had approved a 3 power council. On the contrary they all approve our papers. But our PM got away with it at the end and summed up that alterations in emphasis should be made in our papers as well as the Brief. He withdrew his own paper, however, and according to Law was hard hit when they all preferred our papers to his . . .

'It is a lovely warm evening . . . and though I am a bit tired I feel happier than this time last night. But the old boy may still play the devil with our papers!
'Sat May 13
I wrote a letter from S of S to Fraser the New Zealand PM commenting on his speech at the D[ominion] PM meeting — of a soothing kind. Meanwhile Cadogan had got our papers and was not too happy about them but had sent them to the S of S . . .
'Sun May 14
Alarums and excursions. S of S had sent our papers back with much red ink intimating he could not back down so far, though we have given nothing away. Cadogan also says he will not go to Washington with such instructions and they can send Beaverbrook. However, later on when Cadogan had really read the papers he saw their point and telephoned S of S (who had not read them) & gave him a serious talking to. So I suppose they will go in. Gladwyn says what we need in our Dept is a psychiatrist not a diplomat! Cadogan does not seem to like the letter to Fraser & thinks it inopportune. But Dick Law ordered it! . . .
'Monday May 15
The S of S has now approved my papers of corrections though I doubt if he has read them. Cadogan made only one change in them. They will, therefore, be sent to the PM who will also probably refuse to read them. Meanwhile the days slip by and the opportunity in the United States may go and never return. If once I could get the papers to Washington I could rely on Bowman and his colleagues to throw out the obnoxious parts and if we got an agreement on the rest the PM would be hard put to it to prevent acceptance by the Commonwealth. He probably knows that and relies on preventing us from doing anything.'

On May 16 the papers were sent to the P.M. but one day later Webster learnt that Churchill refused to read them before he made a speech in the House of Commons which was to deal with that very subject. Understandably there was consternation in the Foreign Office as to the line that the Prime Minister might take in his speech and Webster and Jebb worked on a minute by which Eden might influence Churchill.

'Tues 23 May
We made another version or rather Gladwyn did and I checked it. It is not bad — but not very good. This was for S of S to give PM to get him to say something sensible instead of blowing up the whole shew. It went off to Cadogan. It is getting late to send it in. Cadogan sent it back to have it revised i.e. put first what Winston might like and second the warnings that he had been

using. Thus one might get him just to give our plan in outline and then something innocuous about a United Nations Commission for Europe which nobody minds because it does not commit the future. All this was very nice but when I saw Gladwyn at 7 o'clock I found that the S of S had turned it all down. In fact he funks it. So Winston is left to his own devices for tomorrows speech except a waffle of Cadogans which says nothing at all.

'... Z[immern] said he had met Winnipeg Free News man ... He had said Canadians came over full of suspicion of FO ... Thanks to my papers they have gone back as pleased as punch and thinking FO is straight and good. So it is on world organisation thanks to the education I have given it. Gladwyn never remembers that 18 months ago he was talking much the same nonsense as the PM is talking now. Eden never was and saw the thing properly from the beginning I think, but he wont risk a little finger for it. And he never looked at the papers which have done the trick for him until they had passed the Cabt Committee. Well we shall see what the PM says tomorrow and if the whole shew is upset.

'Wed 24 May

When I got to the office I found Winston's speech on World Organisation had arrived and was quite innocuous.[46] We only suggested altering three words. This is an immense relief and shews perhaps that the S of S knew better than any one else how to handle the old man and that if our papers had been sent in they would have only provoked opposition ...

'Sat May 27

... The PM's minute[47] has been lost in E & R but Falla got a copy in Dixon's room. I had not more than glanced at it before. It gives up everything but a "European Council" in which the 3 powers take part. This is little more than our old friend the European Commission, put across in the note of July 1, 1943 accepted as basis for <u>immediate</u> planning (as distinct from long term organisation) at the Moscow Conference. I therefore drafted a minute to the PM inserting this in Memo A and saying nothing about the covering brief which has served its purpose. Peck, the PM's P S has written to ask what we want done about our original changes and I drafted a reply which asked him to hold up the papers until we had prepared substitutes.[48] But Gladwyn wants to make changes in the "covering brief" explaining our motives and also to explain to the P.M. how absurd his "United States of Europe" idea is. This is unnecessary and will irritate ...

'May 31 Wed

Meeting in Cadogan's room to discuss note to PM. Ronald, Shannon also there with Falla as sec. Gladwyn's note was basis but he very fairly said I did not agree. In the end we had a sort of compromise, but I gained my point that no reference should be made to covering brief which could now be dropped. Gladwyn after redrafting was told by Falla that I could not be found though I was at F.O.R.D. all the time. This was unfortunate but I doubt if I would have altered the new draft much. Anyway it has gone in. Meanwhile Hull has spilled a mouthful in Washington and announced that discussions [on world organization] are to take place including China. He told Halifax that he did not want any papers. I put very strongly to Gladwyn and he agrees that we should think twice before accepting this. It may offend Russians put us in an inferior position and may prejudice and will certainly slow up the Conference.'

On June 2 Eden sent Churchill the redraft of the Foreign Office papers, which completely omitted the covering note. The only major alteration was a new paragraph in Memorandum A which referred to the establishment of a United Nations Commission for Europe, thereby allowing for the Churchillian desire for a United States of Europe.[49] Yet Cabinet endorsement was necessary before the F.O. papers could be given to the Americans and Russians. On July 3 the Foreign Secretary submitted a new Cabinet memorandum which incorporated the changes suggested in the redraft submitted to the Prime Minister on June 2.[50] The memorandum came before the Cabinet on 7 July.[51]

'Friday 7 July
Gladwyn and I coached Dick Law for 3/4 hr before the Cabinet which was at 11.30. But it was all unnecessary. The P.M. walked out, said he was not much interested and the Cabinet passed the papers without discussion! This is a real milestone I think. The papers are not yet the policy of the Govt but we are authorised to discuss in these terms and unless the Americans play the fool or the Russians are sticky, something like what I have suggested should go through. Meanwhile the S of S has got very excited over a dispatch by Duff Cooper on a Western Group which has been the round of the office.[52] It has taken nearly a month to get to him. There was a meeting today which I was not asked to attend. Cadogan & Dick Law took the view which I did that nothing should be done until after the W.O. [is] settled but it was finally decided that S of S should talk to the Ambassadors here in an innocuous way, of course stressing the W.O. Gladwyn had to draft the line to be taken which was quite all right except he talked about a permanent seat for France. I persuaded him to cut this out. I read the dispatch and the minutes for the first time. The dispatch was very wordy and uneven and in my view a poor performance. The minutes were better but shewed little imagination. I gave Gladwyn a lecture on trusting too much to the devices that might have prevented this war. We were moving into a quite new age. They should try to think up what would meet the new circs. An Alliance was all right in 1935–39 but we wanted something more concrete. He was duly attentive as he generally is, but I doubt if I made much impression on him. I think I shall have to write a paper on the evil effects of historians on peace making . . .
'Monday 10 July
The "Western Europe" idea has now degenerated into a mere pep talk between Eden and the Ambassadors [in London]. For some reason he is determined to do something – no matter what. On the other hand he was not able to

understand our A.P.W. paper on further instructions.[53] I think Gladwyn had put
up the papers badly and given an excuse for a complaint but the truth is the S of
S has very little knowledge of the original papers, which he probably has not
read through and so cannot understand developments of them. However the
Russians have now officially agreed to the Conference[54] [at Dumbarton Oaks]
and we only await Mr. Hull's date to know when we go. It seems impossible that
we have got so far at last!'

In fact it was to be some time before a final date for the opening of the
Conference was agreed. However, the British position on world organization had
now been established. Thus when the State Department presented the American
proposals on international organization to the British Embassy on July 18, it was
possible for the Foreign Office to react swiftly, the British plans being given to
the Americans on July 21.[55] The content of the American proposals was a great
surprise to the Foreign Office as Webster recorded in his diary for July 23:

'When I got to the office I found the summary of the American paper had
arrived, the third section on the Council verbatim. I at once made a study and so
far as I could see it was far better than I expected. Indeed it was simply a
reformed Covenant. France was specially mentioned to receive a permanent seat.
The only snag was territorial trusteeship several times mentioned with a section
on it not yet sent. This may prove a grave stumbling block. In my opinion the
Assembly is given too much power and the sections on armaments so far as they
can be understood need pulling together. The escape clause (given verbatim)
seems nonsense as it stands.

'At 5 Gladwyn & I met Cadogan and discussed the paper for 1½ hours. He
said he had never expected anything so good. He had already made his own
examination and we had little to teach him. Both Gladwyn & I agreed that he
was head and shoulders above all the others. As to territorial trusteeship he is to
get the S of S to see Stanley with the officials before the awful A.P.W. gets hold
of the question. Gladwyn urged that it would be criminal to give up this scheme
because of a mandates commission or something like it which after all did us
little harm. We pressed Cadogan strongly to stick up for our point of view. He
agreed with it but how far he will go I do not know ... The Russians have
appointed their Ambassador [Andrei Gromyko] at Wash[ington] [as their]
rep[resentative] — a terrible decision ... The Russians wont be there
[Washington] till the 12th. So Malkin & I will have a week to wait. It will I dare
say pass quickly ...'

Two days after his sight of the American proposals Webster sailed for the
United States with Sir William Malkin on the Queen Elizabeth. Cadogan, who
was to lead the British delegation to the conference on world organization,
followed with other members of the delegation on the Queen Mary on 5 August.
The first phase of transformation of plans to agreements was about to begin.

CHAPTER 4

Dumbarton Oaks and After

The Dumbarton Oaks conference on international organization opened in Washington on 21 August 1944. The conversations were divided into two stages. From August 21 to September 28 the British, Russian and American delegations drafted the document released to the world on October 9 as the Dumbarton Oaks Proposals.[1] During the period from September 29 to October 7 the British, American and Chinese delegations conferred, but the changes proposed by the Chinese were not incorporated into the Dumbarton Oaks Proposals, it having been agreed that they would be submitted to the general conference on international organization. Originally, the Soviet phase of the conversations was expected to begin on August 14, but a Soviet request for delay was accepted.[2] Consequently, Webster and Sir William Malkin, who had arrived in New York on July 31, were able to spend a considerable time studying the American proposals and discussing points of interest with American officials. On August 4 Webster lunched with Bowman and gained some insight into the way in which the American proposals had been drafted:

'. . . He said that not until June 15th had they any agreement by the President on the line that they were taking in the papers. Then something had to be settled because of the Convention,[3] and it was then that the President agreed to the basic proposals and gave his press conference describing them. He did not say whether it had been difficult to obtain the President's agreement, but he rather hinted that it had been so.

'He said that as a result of discussions in London they had made an absolute revision of all their territorial trusteeship paper. He had come to the conclusion that their original paper, written by young men, had been far too academic and impracticable. He said that one of them had described himself as an "idealist" and he had warned him never to use that word again. He said that the new trusteeship proposals had tried to look at the matter from our point of view. . .

'Dr. Bowman expressed considerable doubt as to what the Russians would do, and regretted that they had not been able to have the papers sooner. He said, however, that this was impossible because of all the processes that had to be gone through before the papers could be circulated.

'Lastly he said he thought that we were finding a new technique for the orderly progress of international relations in these negotiations at an official level, and that he himself was ultimately going to write a book comparing this procedure with that used during the past peace conference.[4]

'Tues Aug 8

I began and finished a memo on the U.S. plan for Collective Security. It is amazing that they have made such far reaching suggestions. I can still hardly believe it. I wish I dare have been so bold in my papers. But they would certainly have been rejected, if I had, on the plea that the United States would not consider such things! However, some of their proposals will hardly be welcomed by the smaller states including the Dominions and I have wrapped up advances nearly as great in words that would be more likely to command assent. There is more originality in my papers though I say it myself, and I hope we may keep the American substance while softening it with the kind of approach which I made to various aspects of the problem, in particular with my Objects & Principles.'[5]

During the following days Webster wrote a number of memoranda analysing the American proposals. One is of particular interest since it examined *inter alia* the point which was to become the main focus of controversy during the Dumbarton Oaks Conversations — the question of great powers on the Council voting on disputes to which they were a party. The problem was essentially one of deciding how far the veto principle should be applied. All the great powers agreed that there should be a veto, but would it be appropriate to maintain this principle even when a great power was involved in a dispute? Of the opposed arguments, one relied on equity, the other on political reality: if the veto were retained by a great power even when it was party to a dispute, then the great powers were giving themselves the right to be both judge and jury. The international organization could take no action without a great power's concurrence even if that power were guilty of aggression. But if a small power were guilty of aggression it would be unable to prevent action by the international organization. A double standard would be created. If on the other hand the great powers did not have a veto in disputes to which they were a party, then the equality of all members of the organization would be theoretically maintained. But what would be the effect of this in practice? What likelihood was there that the international organization would be able to apply sanctions against a great power aggressor in the same way that action might be taken against a small power? And what would be the effect on the organization of failure to act if it had been resolved to be necessary? These were the questions that had been considered by the planners in Moscow, London and Washington prior to the Dumbarton Oaks meeting. The Russian position was clearly stated in paragraph V (6) of their Memorandum on an International Security Organization:

> Decisions of the Council on questions pertaining to the prevention or suppression of aggression shall be taken by a majority of votes including those of all permanent representatives on the Council.[6]

The British position was diametrically opposed to the Russian view. Paragraph 13 of Memorandum B in the British proposals for a general international organization stated emphatically 'In any event, the votes of the parties to the dispute should not be taken into account'.[7] In contrast to the clear exposition of the Russian and British views, the text of the American proposals for Dumbarton Oaks was vague on this crucial point. Paragraph III.C.5 stated: 'Provisions will need to be worked out with respect to the voting procedure in the event of a dispute in which one or more of the members of the Council having continuing tenure are directly involved'.[8] Webster commented:

'As regards (d) [the explicit American reservation of the Great Powers' position] this is left open in our Memoranda. Indeed in them the Great Powers in theory come under exactly the same processes as the other states if they are parties to a dispute or threaten peace and security. We have recognised that in practice such a process could not take place without the threat of a major war between the Great Powers which the Organisation is designed to prevent.

'I am not sure that we gain by explicitly reserving the Great Powers from the general procedure. I think we may be certain that neither we nor the United States would ever consider applying sanctions against each other. But it might perhaps serve our interests, and world interests, that such powers should be held in reserve as a warning to other states that in the last resort there would be the nucleus of a world combination against them.

'Public opinion in most small countries and considerable sections of it in Britain and the United States will be shocked if the Great Powers reserve explicitly their own position.

'If, therefore, the U.S.S.R. and China were prepared to apply the procedure in theory, to the Great Powers, I do not see why we should not accept it. It would be easier to do so if the Assembly, as suggested in a separate memorandum, is not given the right to make recommendations.[9]

'In any case the United States has not yet made its position clear on this question. I imagine that there has been some controversy about it and that they have not yet been able to work out a formula. It will no doubt be one of the questions on which we shall seek explanation as soon as possible . . .'[10]

In fact, as Webster correctly surmised, there had been considerable controversy within the American delegation on the question of whether great powers might use their veto in disputes to which they were party. However, on 10 August by a vote of 11 to 4 the American delegation decided that a great power party to a dispute should retain the right to vote.[11] This new position was restated by Hackworth on 15 August when the American delegation considered the British position on this question.[12] Effectively, therefore, the Americans had moved from uncertainty to agreement with the Russian rather than the British viewpoint. Yet by 28 August the Americans had accepted the British proposal that parties to a dispute should not vote.[13] This change in the American stance between 15 August and 28 August has not been properly appreciated by many historians.[14] The Webster diary shows his role both in influencing the American delegation to reconsider their position and in sustaining the British policy.

'Tues 15 Aug
... Michael Wright took us to dine at 7.30 at his house. Dunn & Wilson [were] there. We discussed the papers for 2 hrs. The dreadful truth came out that they wish the Great Powers to take none of the obligations which the others assume. I argued against Dunn for 1 hr but Gladwyn supported him clean agst our instructions. Wilson said little & Michael Wright less than nothing. Dunn maintained what is no doubt a majority view but I am sure there is a strong minority. I had another argument with Gladwyn about it after we got home. He is quite unscrupulous about it & I see I shall have to fight hard. On other points there was not so much disagreement & in the main the papers are along the same lines. But to accept the U.S. view would disrupt the Commonwealth. I believe if we stand out we shall eventually win or make a compromise which we shall support. But I am very anxious.
'Wed 16 [Aug]
I hardly slept last night so anxious was I about the U.S. plan to refuse to take the obligations of the Organisation ... We had the first of what are to be daily Delegation meetings at 9.45 (an idea I put up) We told about the U.S. plan. Cadogan was strongly of my opinion but Gladwyn most unscrupulously backed by Col Capel Dunn tried to shew that our instructions allowed us to accept the plan. However, I was not to be put off & I think shewed the contrary. The rest of the Delegation ... said little but I think were sympathetic with me. Gladwyn & I completed our examination & then I went off to the Exec[utive] Offices in [the] East Wing of the White House to [see] Ben Cohen who took me to the Hay-Adam for lunch. I found that he was just as opposed to the US plan as I had been & we agreed to oppose it. He said that this decision about armed power without reckoning moral will would result in disaster & I agreed.
   'Then Gladwyn & I met Dunn and Pasvolsky in P's room & in 2 hrs drew up the 12 points on which our plans differed substantially. P was not nearly so insistent as Dunn had been on the plan [concerning the position of great powers voting on disputes to which they were a party] & said question [was] still open to consideration. (J denied he was weaker but he cannot be fair on this question). Later we saw Cadogan and I was able to tell him the situation. We then went to Shoreham to a cocktail party of J's in our room ... I had a long talk with Bowman about the plan. He admitted they thought only of the Senate & had never discussed effect on Commonwealth or Lat America. I said US had always stressed equality of status in Latin America & he had no reply. Grove-White is also on my side. I warned him agst Capel Dunn & J. So I have done what I could today. Prospects look brighter & I hope I shall sleep ...
'17 Aug Thursday
At the [British Delegation] meeting I told of my discussions of yesterday. J countered by saying Col Stimson and Army very much on his side and Col

Stimson was coming to Wash[ington] for talks. We had our photographs taken before meeting & result tonight is that I come out well & Gladwyn like a criminal. He is very upset about it. I lunched with Charles Murphy at the Carlton. He is an Editor of Fortune whom I had met in London . . . He had just been round the U.S. & seen how all the production had been done with so little strain on the ordinary standard of living. It is indeed a miracle but what will be the effect on the U.S. people of realising their immense power. He was a bit afraid of it but I do not think it a bad thing. It is far better than isolationism and there will always be enough moral uplift to neutralise it.

'Gore-Booth asked me to sub for J . . . I was free & so took part in a large dinner. Pasvolsky & his wife were there & the former told me that the U.S. Delegation had had a meeting today & altered their great Power position. I believe this is due to me — and Mr. Dewey[15] — more than to anyone else . . . I confirmed in a note today that our instructions were that the Great Powers were not to vote & said Capel Dunns attempts to shew otherwise "had no substance" . . .

'18 Aug 1944 Friday

I lunched with Redvers Opie to meet Pasvolsky at the University Club. We had a good discussion . . . P is clearly the dominant figure of the whole U.S. shew. I told Redvers that we had suspected his power had declined bec[ause] Bowman had come over [on the Stettinius Mission] but he said that this was because, owing to his wife, he [refused?] ocean and air travel in the war. At present P is most anxious clearly to meet our ideas and he understands . . . my papers better than anyone else who has read them. He understands the problem of peaceful change and is aware that it is unusable at present and that all we can do is to try experiments to see if mankind can work out a method.

'Cadogan sent me back my paper concerning the instructions saying he entirely agreed with me so that is settled.

'I dined with Conyers Read to meet Bill Langer, Ed Beeson, Wolfers, Ed Robinson. They attacked me immediately on what I had said to Langer about Germany. They said Germany was done for good and the real danger was now Russia. When I combatted this they tried to stir me by saying if Russia was harmless there was no need for the U.S. to take any responsibility in Europe. I said this was an old fashioned view of the world that no one knew what power would arise in the next half century. They said we had always combined against the strongest power and I said this was quite untrue, that we had never combined agst Germany from 1871 to 1900 though she was clearly the dominant power of Europe. That there was no need to combine agst Russia unless she were aggressive and that there was sign & hope that she was as peacefully minded as U.S. They brought forward Russian policy towards Poland and I asked what deductions were to be drawn from US attitude towards France. Altogether it was a pretty frank debate . . .

'Monday Aug 21

Opening of [Dumbarton Oaks] talks at 10.30. Formal sessions. Speeches by

Hull, Gromyko & Cadogan. The last largely written by Gladwyn with a few
alterations by me was much the best. He delivered it very well. Then we were
photographed ad infinitum. I found Ben Cohen disturbed so took him home to
lunch. He thought we defended the status quo at any cost bec[ause] we did not
like to enforce decisions. I think I made him see we got to the same end by a
better route. In the afternoon after a meeting of the "three" Cadogan, Gladwyn
& I discussed the Soviet plan which it had been agreed to make [the] basis of
discussion — a bad decision . . .

'Tuesday 22 Aug
Great progress on W[orld] O[rganisation]. Soviet plan taken first & expounded
resulted in decision to set up 4 Cttees.[16] Cadogan has put me on central one but
we have yet to see how its functions work out . . . Talked for ½ hr to Sobolev. He
was much exercised about right to move through a country in order to maintain
peace & security, obviously thinking of Poland. I said we had done such a thing
to Eire. Better to get powers by agreement with Council as in American plan
but in last resort must be taken. We got on well over necessity of good relations
between our 2 countries and on necessity for long peace for Russia to rebuild
her country . . .

'Wed 23 August
The flow of good news is overwhelming. Roumania has ratted & Paris is in the
hands of F[ree] F[rench] as well as Marseilles [and] Toulon probably. The U.S.
forces have reached Grenoble . . .

   'The day at Dumbarton Oaks also went well. We had to discuss the Soviet
draft in the Organisation Cttee but we got most of our points made and in spite
of Soviet caution made very distinct progress. Gromyko spoke all the time for
the Russians and shewed himself very dignified. In the Security Commission in
the afternoon things went even better and they have practically already got
agreement on all points. However such issues as [a] Great Power not voting in
disputes to wh[ich] they are a party still hang over the future. I lunched with
Hackforth & Fletcher & found out that they had intended [to have a] new
permanent seat for Brazil!! I got them to consider other methods of getting
bigger 'small' powers on to the Council . . .

'Thursday 24 August
At meeting of [the] Organisation C[ommi]ttee we made little more than
perfunctory progress & rose early. But the three delegations agreed to draw up a
list of subjects needing further consideration. Gladwyn & I made one and then
met Sobolev & Pasvolsky and drew up an agreed list, practically the same as
ours, with suggestions for how each should be treated. If the Steering Cttee
accept this tomorrow morning we may get something done. But clearly
Gromyko dare not do anything outside his instructions without first
communicating with Moscow. This is the excuse for the extraordinary jaunt
which Ed Stettinius has devised. He will take all delegates who want to go to
New York in an aeroplane for two days with shews etc. . . .'

From Friday 25 August until Sunday 27 August most of the members of the British, Russian and American delegations participated in Stettinius's 'jaunt' to New York, including Webster who much enjoyed the visit. On returning to Washington, however, Webster found that there were very real problems to be surmounted.

'Monday Aug 28
An anxious day. The U.S.S.R. has advanced its claim for the 16 republics.[17] There is little progress on fundamentals. The steering Ctee on wh Cadogan & J sit discusses all these reserved points[18] and I only see the minutes & telegrams so I cannot judge the atmosphere but it seems that it will be very hard to get a workable scheme. This morning I wrote an analysis of the Chinese plan to send to London ... I also made a draft of principles & objects.[19] At the formulation Cttee this afternoon we first decided [the] order of work and then began with the Principles & Objects, latter subsequently called Purposes. We did pretty well and got a fair draft. Instead of my respect for political independence and equality of status but not of function we took the Moscow Declaration of "sovereign equality".[20] This is less near the truth but it may cause less criticism. Sobolev could not accept any ref to int[ernational] cooper[ation] in ec[onomic] & soc[ial] [matters] but we made a clause for it in purposes with his consent if his gov does accept. We put in carrying out obligation & not employing arms except in accordance with [the] purpose of [the] organisation. We had no difficulty in knocking out [the] word "maintain" wh was in [the] US draft. All this will no doubt get much verbal amendment some day. But it is something to get the principles & objects accepted as articles of the Organisation. That was my first invention. We shall see if the others go through. Tonight I dined with Gladwyn. Late[r] Capel Dunn came in and they were even more absurdly "realistic" than usual. No doubt some of their remarks are made to draw me, but it is curious that two men of high intellectual qualities, though of course very imperfectly informed about history and political science (they are constantly committing elementary blunders) should be so foolishly crude. They remind me of the American journalists they dislike so much.
'Tues Aug 29
... We have had 5 hrs Formulation Cttee today and made good progress. Moreover what we have done has been pretty good. Sob[olev] is coming along. In spite of the language difficulty he sees all the points — often quicker than Hackforth who is sometimes quite stupid. Pasvolsky makes a very good Chairman (never having been elected) and is always on the spot. It is he and not Dunn who makes the American decisions ...

'After lunch I had a long talk with Alec [Cadogan]. He said Gromyko had given way on including Ec[onomic] & [Social] Coun[cil] and had withdrawn [the demand for the] 17 [16] Rep[ublics]. But he had dug his toes in on [the] veto of the Great Powers. The Americans were now fully on our side in this question. (This is due to me more than anyone else I think. I kept up the end the first night & since then through Ben Cohen, Fletcher, Hackforth & others I have kept up a ceaseless flow of argument on this subject but of course nothing would have been of any avail if Cadogan had not stood so firm in the Steering Cttee. Malkin has also been excellent). Alec was anxious to know what to do. I said leave it to the Ministers Conference[21] but he did not wish to do so if he could avoid it. He had an idea that there might be some formula on the first American lines that the Great Power should be asked to suspend its veto so that a dispute could be discussed. At any rate the Council should have jurisdiction to discuss even if it had not [the] right of settlement or sanctions. He asked me to consider alternatives but the task is not an easy one . . .

'Wed Aug 30

It has now become clear that the real work of the Conference is to be done in the Formulation Sub-Committee of the Organisation Sub-Committee. This is Pasvolsky, Dunn, with some assistance from Hackworth, Sobolev and an interpreter Bereskoff, Gladwyn & I with some assistance from Capel Dunn. Gerig is Secr[etary]. Notter & others listen in. We are now drafting the whole document. Today we finished the Assembly. We wasted a great deal of time but I knocked out a great deal of the fancy stuff of the Americans . . .

'Thur Aug 31

All day in Formulation [Committee]. We got little down but discussed Council a great deal. I attacked with force the U.S. idea of continuous sessions for the Council but Pasvolsky defended it so tenaciously that I think it must be his own idea. We shall have to make some compromise . . .

'Friday Sept 1

All day in Formulation Cttee. We made good progress and have completed 4/5ths of the document. Sometimes we have to take half an hour to make Comrade Sobolev understand the distinction in our minds between one form of words and another but the time is not ill spent if it enables him to grasp the fundamentals. He reserves a good deal but I hope all this will go down like the Nazi lines are going down in Europe. . .

'Sat Sept 2

Seven hours in Formulation Cttee. We have finished our draft except the most important points of all which are reserved to the Steering Cttee. After dinner we went back to [the] Embassy and an hour on the document with Malkin & Cadogan . . .

'Monday Sept 4

Labour Day and a holiday but not for us. We spent a long time in Formulation Cttee on Regulation of Armaments and gradually got something out though it is all reserved for final approval. We had some long explanations and discussions but I had little to do. However I produced the formula which got us over one hurdle and could have done more if it had not been our role at this time to let the Americans make the running. P on the whole handles all this with great skill and patience and he can, if necessary, translate into Russian when S is doubtful about the exact meaning of words. . .[22]

'Tuesday Sept 5

Weather a bit less humid. We had 5 or 6 hours in Cttee . . . We got through Ec & Soc (all in brackets[23] bec[ause] the Soviet[s] have not yet agreed to have anything at all) the Secretariat and some odds & ends. So far as we are concerned the document is now finished though there are some changes to be made here and there. Tomorrow some of the big points are to be threshed out by the Steering Cttee. If these should go well (a big 'if') we shall have made an epochmaking document which will arouse immense applause and almost as great disapproval from the US and British isolationists. But all is yet in the lap of the Gods and there may be a complete reversal of everything that we have done. Unless the Russians agree to Parties to a Dispute not voting in their own cause, much of what we have done cannot be put into force at all. We cannot get the smaller powers to accept these drastic obligations unless the great also take them, however unlikely it is that they will ever be used against any of the big three. If this is what is wanted we had better make a naked alliance but the U.S. would never sign such a document. . .

'Thur Sept 7—Sun Sept 10

The work increased so much at the end of last week that I had not time or at any rate energy to keep my diary . . . The Formulation Cttee finished its first draft after very hard work on Friday evening working late after dinner. Then telegrams had to be sent in which I helped Gladwyn. On Sat the Steering Cttee got hold of these drafts and made some progress. I waited at Dumbarton Oaks until 7.15 to get the result. There was nothing on the main question but in the course of these two days the Soviet Amb[assa]dor agreed to putting in the Ec & Soc part. We redrafted it in 1/4 hr, Pasvolsky agreeing with me in ruthlessly cutting it down . . .

'Tues Sept 12

Did little in the morning but after lunch which I had at the Oaks there was a Formulation—Steering [Committee meeting]. In the morning Gromyko had startled them so Alec told us by demanding that nothing should be done here with China. To say this at this stage with the Chinese Delegation here is idiocy. Do they mean China is not to reckon as a 'Great Power' and have no veto? Perhaps, but I do not see how U.S.A. can give way on this. The meeting in the afternoon was stupid. The Cttee is too big for drafting & the subordinates cannot talk freely in front of their masters. We discussed Regionalism, Interim [period] & Axis States & some formulae were produced, but my own impression was that these questions had not been thought out. They are vital since it may be that the Four Powers will have separate power for a long time. Are we to have another Supreme Council divorced from the Organisation? The name United Nations has now been accepted by the Russians & consequently the term 'Security Council' by the others. I hardly think this latter can remain until the end . . .

'Wed Sept 13—Sun Sept 17

I have hardly dared write in these days of crisis. On Wed we heard the news of the Soviet decision [that they refused to alter their position on retaining the right of veto when great powers were involved in a dispute]. At a Conference with A[lec] C[adogan], W[illiam] M[alkin], D[enis] C[apel] D[unn], G[ladwyn] J[ebb] and myself we discussed all alternatives. It seemed impossible to leave the question open for the Ministers to settle. There seemed no chance that they would do so. I suggested that we might make a consultative organisation and leave it to the organisation itself to work out its future but I was not very much in love with the idea myself and though we put it on our telegram it was not supported by anybody but Malkin. There was also the idea of unanimity less parties to [a] dispute for action agst a Great Power but no one thought this likely of acceptance. Everything depended on [the] view of the general situation in [the] war & as I was not informed about that I did not feel able to press a view. So we decided on a compromise leaving sanctions out [i.e. the restriction that parties to a dispute should not vote would not apply on the question of enforcement measures]. An attempt was made to get this & [the] Formulation Cttee without me or Denis, only Gladwyn going, worked this out.[24] Meanwhile A C had been sent for to Quebec.[25] I myself never thought Soviets would accept [the] compromise and did not worry too much but it was a hateful time. . . On Sat A C came back, Loxley & Capel Dunn had gone with him. He found that the compromise would not be accepted. Gromyko on being informed indicated there was no chance of his Govt accepting either. So the deadlock is complete. But I still have some hope that later we may find a way. We have got into this jam

(a) because we did not give sufficient time between our papers & the meeting. The Russians should have had at least 2 months. Nobody is to blame for this. It was impossible to get things through.

(b) because the meeting has been so advertised to suit [the] political situation.[26] We intended to meet quietly and explore. We have even advertised fact that a U.N. Conference was to follow.

(c) because we have gone far too much into detail at this stage. This is due to necessity of shewing [the] Senate exactly what everything means and we could not oppose it.

(d) because U.S. were not clear on the main point & thus encouraged the Soviets to make theirs. Our papers were clear & Sobolev told Gladwyn they knew it so but did not find point in U.S. papers and so thought they could make it.

'My immediate superiors are now convinced a W[orld] O[rganisation] is impossible and [are] thinking [in] no other terms. At a long talk with Alec & Gladwyn last night I combatted this view. I can make no impression on latter of course but former realises all that such a situation means. However much may alter in next few months and there are many expedients that may yet be considered if diplomacy is not bankrupt. But I do not think we can do much until world situation is clearer. One of the difficulties though not the main one is that a great deal has to be done which cannot be done in the W.O. It will take years before it can function adequately. It is perhaps well to recognise this fact and that was one of the reasons for my own suggestion. I expect when I get back I shall be quietly dropped from this kind of job. The unsuccessful are always wrong . . .

'. . . All the Delegation are naturally subdued but except A C & Gladwyn scarcely realise what is at stake. I am sorry for Gladwyn who has worked so zealously & skilfully. He might have had a great success & would have deserved it. As it is he will have to start again. . . .

'When I got back [from dinner] Gladwyn told me that [the] Steering Cttee had met and approved two communiqués for submission to Govts. They suggest [the] document will soon be published and [a] Conference of [the] United Nations called for Nov 15. This seems absurdly optimistic & I cannot see Soviet Gov agreeing though Gromyko seemed friendly enough to the idea.

'Monday Sept 18

. . . I had a long conversation with James Dunn & Pasvolsky, Gladwyn & Capel Dunn. The Americans were down esp[eciall]y Jimmy Dunn . . . I also talked to Ben Cohen & Bowman. They had no suggestions. I told them they had gone ahead too fast and tried to settle in 3 weeks a problem, the heir of 150 yrs of history, which needed long diplomatic preparation. I realised they had done so to try to satisfy their Senate. All this was gloomily acquiesced in. I then adumbrated my idea for a consultative organisation side by side with one with teeth of the 5 Powers + to keep Germany & Japan in order which they seemed to think deserved consideration. Meanwhile Gladwyn had written a Memo for a 5 Power [organisation] to keep Germany & Japan in order + a consultative Great Power Council + a Council & Assembly as in our project to keep small but not great powers in order. This perpetuates "sovereign inequality" and will be no more acceptable than the original compromise plan. I wrote a short note on this & sent it in for Alec to see. Capel Dunn is near my point of view but Malkin strangely enough seems to consider Gladwyn's plan worth trying. However, all these schemes are still a bit unreal . . .[27]

'Wed Sept 20

. . . Gladwyn & I . . . arrived terribly late at dinner with E. Wilson where were Fletcher, Pasvolsky & Bowman. We had a most pleasant party. The Americans were all cheerful again because Dewey had made a helpful speech. They hardly seemed to realise that U.S. may be ready to sign a document which U.S.S.R. will continue to resist unless she gets her way all round. Gladwyn & I went back to the Chancery & with Capel Dunn sent the text of the final document to London. Thus we have now an agreed text — with of course the all important question of Great Power veto on their own disputes reserved for further study. I saw Alec during the day and said I did not want to be committed to the note I had written on Gladwyn's proposal. He agreed we ought to pause & see the effects of our document when it is published. We saw him at 11.45 & talked for

an hour. He is now very disillusioned and rather bitter about the whole thing.
. . . The situation should have of course have [*sic*] been prepared diplomatically
before these all important questions were raised. But it may be that out of this
document when it is published (if the Soviet Govt allows it to be) something will
come. Alec asked me to stay on with Gladwyn and I cannot refuse. The Chinese
face must be considered and I can see I am needed. But I am going to bed with a
heavy heart.'

It was not until September 28 that the final meeting with the Soviets took place,
but the last week was largely concerned with drafting the communiqué. Cadogan
was unable to remain in Washington for the Chinese phase of the conversations
and Lord Halifax assumed charge of the British Delegation, whilst Webster
continued in his role as a member of the Joint Formulation Group. By October
7 this second phase had been completed, the Chinese having agreed that the
changes they proposed should be discussed later with the Soviets in the hope of
incorporating them in the charter at the general U.N. Conference. Two days later
the Proposals were published, together with a communiqué in which the four
governments affirmed that further study of the proposals would take place and
'they will as soon as possible take the necessary steps with a view to the
preparation of complete proposals which could then serve as a basis of discussion
at a full United Nations conference'.[28]

On returning to London Webster undertook the task of writing a commentary
on the Dumbarton Oaks Proposals.[29] He was also involved in controversy as to
the attitude to be adopted towards the major problem left unresolved by the
Washington meeting – the extent of the great power veto. The formal British
and American position when the conference ended remained that of 28 August
that no great power party to a dispute should have the right to vote. Both
Roosevelt and Churchill had rejected the Formulation Committee compromise
of 13 September which had been based on a differentiation between peaceful
settlement and enforcement measures. But as British and American officials
examined ways of bringing the great powers together on this problem the debate
amongst them swung away from the position that great powers party to a
dispute should not vote in any circumstances and towards consideration of
whether the compromise of retaining the veto on enforcement measures was
sufficient, or whether it was necessary to accept the full Russian thesis that great
powers party to a dispute should have the right of veto on peaceful settlement
procedures as well.[30] Perhaps not surprisingly Churchill reconsidered his hasty
decision at Quebec and on 4 October he informed Roosevelt 'we are pretty clear
that the only hope is that the Great Powers are agreed'.[31] The 'we' was
somewhat misplaced, in that no Cabinet decision had been taken, but it was in
this context that Webster continued his opposition to the Soviet viewpoint.

'Sat Oct 14
I worked at the Office. Gladwyn reports that everybody is now on his side and

against my view of the importance of the Great Powers accepting the same system as the smaller ones. Alec has written a memo for the P.M. urging a compromise on the lines of Gladwyn's suggestions at Washington — or so the latter says. Cripps is strongly for Russia & so now is the P.M. & S of S [and] also Dick Law. I take all this with a grain of salt. I am sure none of these wish to quarrel with Russia, as indeed I do not as much as anyone else, but I am not sure that they accept the Russian view. Still there is no doubt but that the Office is strongly of that opinion. . .

'Monday 16 Oct

. . . I finished the commentary this morning. I read Alec's Memorandum.[32] It recommends a Conciliation procedure for the Great Powers if one is a party to a dispute, leaving the rest of the system intact. I hardly think this will do. In my view the best thing now is to delay and perhaps the Americans will agree to do so once the election is over. Gladwyn agrees that some form of compromise must be sought & that we cannot simply give in to Russia.

'Tues 17 Oct

I saw Alec for about 20 mins & talked to him about the Chinese talks. . . I spoke to him also about a minute Cripps has written the P.M.,[33] strongly supporting Russia's claims but for absurd reasons as he has got the whole thing mixed up. He said we had better write a letter to Cripps explaining his mistakes and he would send a copy to the P.M. I expect I shall have to do this. I have urged Gladwyn to have a meeting of the Law Cttee to discuss the document & he has asked Nigel [Ronald] to get it done. We cannot act without him & he always takes a long time. Moreover Dick Law is not well & overwhelmed with work. I gave Gladwyn the commentary & meanwhile I wrote an account of the controversy for the summary. The Office, I am glad to say, agrees that the more discussion of the problem the better. This is a wise decision.

'Wed 18 Oct

I wrote a letter to Cripps sufficiently mellow in tone I hope. Brierly came to see me. He was in complete agreement with me on the great question. I took him to see Gladwyn but he was hardly forceful enough to impress the latter. Nevertheless, he said the smaller states could not agree [to the Russian proposal]. This is of course the crux for if Canada & Brazil do not agree the whole existence of a World Organisation is threatened and we shall have lost all the advantage of sticking to principle & gained nothing in return. . .

'Thurs 19 Oct

. . . After much thought I telephoned Lord Cecil & fixed an appointment with him. . . He agreed entirely with my point of view — indeed it was his own. We both agreed that any W O was better than none but he was sure that the smaller powers would not agree. "They cannot get away with it", he said. I told him conf[identia]lly a good deal of the whole story. I asked him to speak in our sense at his meeting at Chatham House which he will address next Thursday, taking care not to make it an anti-Russian. He said Russia was in a commanding position so long as the German war lasts but would not be so to so great an extent afterwards. He was, therefore, for delay. He said she would gradually come to understand she could not defy public opinion as she would do if she insisted on being exempt. I asked him to write to Winston [about] his views. He demurred at first but when I pointed out the possibility of the pass being sold, he said he would seriously consider it. It was a great pleasure and relief to have this talk & to find so much agreement between us. The only difference was his recipe to solve the question — a return to the Covenant's position of each state deciding for itself about sanctions, but I hardly think this will do. Anyway the great thing now is to get the public to see the issues without rousing suspicion of Russia & on this we both agree with the Office. . .

'Wed 25 Oct

. . . I found a large file of papers on the Great Power question with papers by Alec & Gladwyn. I drafted a minute which I shewed Gladwyn & have just revised at home. It urges further consideration and consultation with the US & Dominions before any decision is made. It is no use appealing to principle. The Office is all on the other side and opportunistic as usual. It has little sense of the long-term values.

'Wednesday Nov 1

Evan Durbin lunched with me. He had a number of questions about the W.O. most of them rather jejune. On the great question he said his master thought as I did but he did not expect him to oppose No 1. This is a curious position for the Deputy Prime Minister who represents the Labour Party. I warned Evan that there would be no W.O. unless the Soviet Govt joined, a position he clearly wanted to have. He said it would be difficult to argue the general case about Great Powers without attacking the Soviet Govt. It is difficult but it should be done. I told him the F.O. did not agree with me but I wanted exploration and delay. . .

'Thur Nov 2

We had a meeting in Alec's room on the great question. Ronald, Gladwyn, Malkin, Jack Ward & I. I was alone in attaching importance to principle and it would have done no good if I had reiterated my point of view. It was decided to draw up a paper for [the] A[rmistice and] P[ost] W[ar] C[ommittee]. I got Alec to accept (1) a new attempt first to get Soviets to give in (2) consultation [with] U.S.A. first (3) consultation for conciliation purposes in [the] Council rather than [the] Great Powers by themselves. This would be an Article XI for the Great Powers with 15 & 16 for little powers. This is better than some suggestions and would give the cadre of something that might develop into a better thing by & by. When I mentioned Dominions Alec said Bruce had been to see him to say Australia wanted to accept Russian view & S. Africa & N. Zealand were on that side. They admitted, however, that Canada's attitude was in doubt. However Canada will probably have an election soon and her attention will be elsewhere. Gladwyn has written the paper today so he could not come to the L[eague] of N[ations] meeting.[34] I shall see it tomorrow morning. Gladwyn wanted the 16 Republics question to be taken up but Alec said that point should be in a separate paper, I am glad to say. Gladwyn wants us to be neutral on that question or leave the opposition to the Americans. If they are not careful we shall find the State Dept getting disgusted with us & who will fight our battle in U.S.A. agst the economic departments then? . . .

'Friday Nov 3

I went through the Great Power veto paper with Gladwyn and made some alterations. But it was well written and faithfully carried out the conclusions of our meeting. It advocates first trying once more to get the Russians to accept the UK.USA position, offers 3 compromises, one of them my suggestion, & says we should not give in altogether.[35] This is better than I one time thought possible but I feel I am an accomplice in crime. . .

'10 Nov Fri

I found Geoffrey Wilson & Gladwyn in combat over the 16 Soviet Republics entering the W.O. Gladwyn is silly about this, not thinking it matters & saying leave it all to the US because of India.[36] Geoffrey Wilson, being a fervent Russianist, naturally always wants us to let the Soviet have all it desires. Gladwyn is taking the weekend off while his masters do, so it was settled that Geoffrey & I should work out a paper. . .

'Monday Nov 13

Geoffrey has written a paper on the 16 Soviet Reps & after discussion Gladwyn & I came to an agreement on it. We also arrived at conclusions on the Commentary which Paul [Falla] can now send to the Printer & on the Veto Paper. I have still some more to do on the 16 Republics but we have a line. It is a difficult subject to handle for a Cabinet Paper because nobody knows what Russia really would do if she is refused. I believe a lot of her demand was a bluff to stop the US getting her own original members in the W.O. She certainly succeeded in blocking "Associated" Nations.[37]

'Tuesday Nov 14

. . . Gladwyn had tried to get S of S interested in W.O. but he had refused to read the paper on voting, said it was too long. Jack Ward who was there said the S of S boasted at not having read a single one of our Dumbarton Oaks telegrams. He made Gladwyn write up W.O. for a Leamington speech literally in 20 mins — and pretty mash it was. Yet everyone thinks of him as a devoted servant of the state! When he becomes P.M. as I suppose he may he will be as bad as his old master Baldwin. . .

'Tues Nov 21

Gladwyn told me this morning that he had seen the S of S about the Great Power voting paper. He had said that it was an able paper but that he himself was more inclined to agree to the whole Soviet thesis. He did not argue the point but said the paper must be sent in to the A.P.W. Cttee in Alec's name not in his. This will leave him free to say what he likes at the Cttee. Since Dick Law & Hall have also this point of view it would seem that all the politicals are agreed. Gladwyn who has always preferred an alliance, which is, however, impossible as he knows, says that the S of S goes further than he would go himself. But I do

not think either of them have yet fully estimated the difficulties in the way of
such a course or the difficulties of getting the World Organisation any real
backing if they did manage to get it through by "Great Power" bullying. . .'

The tortuous efforts to reach agreement on policy concerning great powers
involved in disputes was stimulated on December 5 by a telegram from President
Roosevelt to Stalin and Churchill.[38] Webster recorded his feelings in his diary:

'The President has sent Stalin a long wire urging settlement of the voting
question right on lines of Dumbarton Oaks compromise. A conference of
officials to settle it. He did not consult us first. This except for the manner in
which it has been done is probably the best that can be got. But will U.S.S.R.
give way. And would it not have been better to hold this step in reserve to be
made after [the] meeting [at Yalta] had begun discussion.'

On December 20 the Cabinet considered the question of great power voting.[39]
Eden recommended that whilst there was merit in the compromise formula, it
was necessary to consult the Dominions and that no decision should be sent to
the Russians before indications had been received of Stalin's attitude. This was
agreed. Naturally Webster was concerned about the outcome of the debate in
Cabinet:

'Thur Dec 21
Knowing that the Cabinet had taken the W O papers last night and Gladwyn
being away I saw Cadogan and got the frightful story. The old man [Churchill]
had put local govt first & they took nearly 2 hours over it. Only S of S insistence
got our papers discussed at all. No one knew anything about them. All that
could be done was to decide to ask opinion of Dominions. It is really amazing
how we are governed. Truth is P.M. who will read nothing is always talking of
the plans of these mediocre officials. All he has read is Cripps foolish paper & he
will not read the reply which I wrote & Alec signed though it was in print before
him.[40] But we will get it through. Alec was very angry in stirring up S of S.
Meanwhile I have sent my preamble to Will [Malkin][41] . . .
'Thur Dec 28
. . . There has been a Prisec cable from Washington saying the Americans think
the Russians have accepted their plan and, if so, they will summon a United
Nations Conference by March 1st. It will take us all our time to get the necessary
decisions by then. We shall have to have a Minister. Will Dick Law be allowed to
go? Will it be left to Halifax who would probably do it as well as anyone?'

This information from Washington stiffened Eden's resolve to press for a
favourable decision on the Americans' formula.[42] He prevailed upon the Prime
Minister to allow the Armistice and Post-War Committee to consider the voting
question. On 4 January 1945 the Committee agreed to accept the American
compromise, subject to Dominion agreement.[43] This decision was endorsed by

the Cabinet and on January 13 the government's acceptance of the American proposal was sent to Washington.[44] However, the news that the Soviets still adhered to their voting position[45] shattered the fragile unity of the Cabinet, and on the eve of the Yalta conference Churchill adamantly maintained that he would support the compromise only if it was acceptable to the Russians.[46] Fortunately there had been less controversy over the Soviet demand for membership of the 16 Republics. In view of the anomalous position of India[47] the British Government agreed to allow the Americans to bear the burden of opposing the Soviets, whilst providing as much support as possible. Webster was most upset by the lack of resolve on both sides of the Atlantic and was apprehensive of the outcome of the Yalta conference.

'Monday Jan 22
. . . Meanwhile the Vandenberg & Connally proposals[48] are flying about and bedevilling things. Gladwyn had gone so far in a minute as to say that if we got a treaty with U.S. about Germany & Japan he did not care about a World organisation at all, but he cut this out when I expostulated. The P M has said he does not want to back the President over the Great Power veto but simply accept the Russian proposal and the President has told Halifax he is ready to barter the veto agst the 16 Republics.[49] All this is expediency & trickery and there is no principle amongst these men who have held power until they are unable to make decent and honest judgments. Gladwyn, I must say, in face of all this has stuck to his guns & still wants to put up the compromise. . .
'Thur 1 Feb
. . . Things are indeed in a great mess. Alec has gone out [to Yalta] in a most defeatist mood and anything may happen to the Dumbarton Oaks Proposals. If they are scrapped and Gladwyn follows his new hare to the exclusion of the other it will be time for me to go.'

To Webster's great relief the Yalta conference seemed to resolve the disagreements about the Dumbarton Oaks proposals.

'Thur Feb 8
. . . News has come in that the Russians have accepted the compromise on the Veto. This is very important and I have high hopes the D.O. [Proposals] may go through. They have reduced their 16 Republics to Lithuania White Russia and Ukraine. The P.M. wants the Cabinet to let him promise to support Stalin on this at the Conference but Moley [Orme Sargent] & Christopher Warner think we should keep in step with U.S.A. They are right . . .
'Fri Feb 9
Good and bad news from the Black sea. The Russians have not only accepted the compromise but reduced the republics to two [—] White Russia & Ukraine. The Foreign Ministers have agreed all this and decided that the United Nations

Conference will meet in the United States on April 25th. The date must have
been selected by Gladwyn for our birthdays . . .
'Tuesday Feb 13

. . . Gladwyn arrived back. He had had a temperature of 102° . . . but he says he
is all right and is very bucked at all he has done. He has some right to be pleased.
He said we would have done even better if the P.M. had not given way on
admitting the two Soviet republics after Stalin had said he would not press the
matter. The Russians gave way easily on the Veto question after it had been
explained to them. Gladwyn had talk with Maisky about it. The P.M. also gave
way on the Mandates question thus overthrowing all Stanley's arguments. He
said Stanley was a defeatist . . .
'Wed Feb 14

. . . Gladwyn gave a very amusing account of Yalta, including the discomforts of
living, one room for all the F.O. to work in including 3 typists and bugs in the
bed. P.M. had gone to the voting question Conference with only Stafford Cripps
idiotic memo in front of him but Alec changed places with Eden and seems to
have coached him in three minutes. For he made quite a good speech and Stalin
said he would reflect and next day gave way. The truth is that the Russians had
never understood the question as I always thought. Neither Clark Kerr nor
Harriman ever understood it either, so how could they? On the Trusteeship
question the P.M. made a great speech about not liquidating the Empire etc.
Whereupon the Americans said their suggestion only applied to mandated
territories and P.M. said that was all right without any reference to Col. Stanleys
Memo. The latter, whom Gladwyn saw this afternoon, is naturally furious and
says his memo is now no use. The Colonial Office do not know how they will do
another in time. On the republics as I have already noted P.M. made a similar
hash . . .'

On 20 March Webster received formal notification that he was to be a member
of the group of officials attending the founding conference of the world
organization opening at San Francisco on 25 April. In the weeks before the
conference, however, there were increasing signs of great power disunity. The
Yalta agreement on the question of the membership of the two Soviet Republics
was open to differing interpretations. The Russians believed that the two Soviet
Republics should automatically attend the conference,[50] and they also
requested that the Lublin Poles should receive an invitation.[51] When the
Americans rejected these proposals[52] the Russians ominously omitted Molotov
from their delegation to San Francisco.[53] Only after the death of President
Roosevelt did they relent, authorizing Molotov's attendance.[54] These growing
signs of great power disunity did not augur well for the San Francisco
conference. In these same weeks, Webster was intimately involved in discussions
among British Commonwealth representatives in London, 4—13 April.[55]

'Monday April 8—Sunday April 15
This has been a gruelling week. I insisted that I must attend the Conference if I was to act efficiently and Alec agreed at once. So I have been in every session this week. I have had to brief our ministers and carry on the other work as well . . .

'My principal excursion into the limelight was on the question of a Preamble. Smuts had drawn up rather a terrible document. Cranborne said very rashly that the F.Ô. had prepared one. This was one I had drawn up three months ago & failed to get anyone much interested in it. This was given to Smuts & it was suggested he should revise his draft after seeing it. Accordingly I went over to him [on April 11] & he recognised me & talked of Paris 1919 days. He asked me to prepare a revise & see him in the morning. I had intended to take Will but the hour of [the] meeting was changed and I had to be at Hyde Park Hotel at 9.45. far too early for Will. However Alec agreed that it would be good for me to do what I could. So after 10 pm I made a plan and amalgamated his document much shortened and mine. I pulled Nora out of bed at 12 o'clock to type it which she did very nicely. When I saw the Field Marshal he had also prepared a draft somewhat in the same d[w?]ay, but his, typed by secretaries, was not ready. Accordingly he looked at mine and with one or two minor changes accepted it.[56] I hastened in his car to take it to Laithwaite who got it roneoed & it was on the table by 10.35 [12 April]. The Field Marshal gave me all the credit & to my horror said I had prepared the Preamble to the Covenant (which was written by Pres. Wilson). However, I altered the notes in the minutes. The Conference was fairly well disposed to the paper. . .'[57]

The consultation with Commonwealth representatives marked the final stage of British preparation for the San Francisco conference. As the world organization meeting was to reveal, there was by no means a complete identity of view within the Commonwealth. From Webster's personal point of view, however, the meeting had given him the opportunity to make one further contribution to the creation of the United Nations in the draft preamble which later formed the basis for the Preamble to the Charter. Eight days after this draft had been agreed by the Commonwealth representatives Webster took off from Northfleet aerodrome for San Francisco.

CHAPTER 5

The San Francisco Conference

Delegates from some fifty states attended the founding conference of the United Nations Organization which opened at San Francisco on 25 April 1945. Not surprisingly, the organization of such a large conference was complex. A Steering Committee composed of the heads of each delegation was the main directing body, though the size of this committee necessitated the formation of a smaller Executive Committee of fourteen heads of delegation.[1] Day-to-day control of the conference was vested in the Executive Committee. However, most of the work of the conference took place in twelve technical committees. These operated under four general commissions, each responsible for drafting a particular section of the Charter. During the conference, the committees were described by their abbreviated numerical designations as set out below:

Commission I — General Provisions
    Committee I/1 — Preamble, Purposes and Principles
    Committee I/2 — Membership, Amendments and Secretariat.
Commission II — General Assembly
    Committee II/1 — General Assembly; Structure and Procedures
    Committee II/2 — Political and Security Functions
    Committee II/3 — Economic and Social Cooperation
    Committee II/4 — Trusteeship System.
Commission III — Security Council
    Committee III/1 — Security Council; Structure and Procedures
    Committee III/2 — Peaceful Settlement
    Committee III/3 — Enforcement Arrangements
    Committee III/4 — Regional Arrangements.
Commission IV — Judicial Organization
    Committee IV/1 — International Court of Justice
    Committee IV/2 — Legal Problems.

In addition to the formal structure of the conference, there evolved what Webster later described as 'a great power conference inside the larger conference'.[2] This consisted of a 'Big Five' committee of the leaders of the great power delegations and a 'Little Five' committee composed of officials of the great powers who were responsible for the technical problems of drafting.

The all-party British delegation at San Francisco was led by Anthony Eden and was divided into full and assistant delegates. The former consisted of ministers of Cabinet rank, Eden, Cranborne, and Halifax (Conservative) and Attlee (Labour). The assistant delegates were junior ministers, Miss Horsbrugh (Conservative), Tomlinson and Miss Wilkinson (Labour), Mabane (National Liberal) and Foot (Liberal). In practice the division meant little: its purpose, in courtesy to the United States, was not to have more delegates than the host country.[3] The British delegates were each assigned responsibility for presenting the British viewpoint at specific technical committees. The officials were assigned in a similar way to provide support for the respective British delegate. Originally, Webster was listed as being responsible, with certain other officials, for no less than eight of the twelve technical committees, including all the committees of Commission III dealing with the Security Council. As the conference evolved, however, Webster spent most of his time working on the Security Council committees, particularly Committee III/1, and Committee II/2 on the political and security functions of the General Assembly. Webster also participated in the unofficial 'Big Five' and 'Little Five' committees.

The San Francisco conference began inauspiciously. The growing differences among the great powers that had marked the run-up to the conference seemed to continue unabated during the first week of the conference. Disputes over the Presidency of the conference, and over the seating of the Polish Provisional Government and Argentina,[4] belied the great power unity that was postulated as the basis of the new organization. Yet at a less publicized level there was concrete evidence of great power co-operation in the meetings of the five powers between 2 May and 4 May which resulted in the submission of joint sponsoring power amendments to the Dumbarton Oaks Proposals.[5] The extracts from Webster's diary which follow deal largely with two of the most crucial issues considered at the conference — the relationship of regional organizations to the world body and the question of the great power veto on the Security Council. Both revealed the strengths and weaknesses of great power co-operation, though it is to be noted that Webster himself did not believe that San Francisco exemplified the break-down of great power co-operation.

'Thurs May 10
[After dinner] G[ladwyn] & I ... and Hadow discussed the Regional treaty question. The Latin Americans demand the Act of Chapultepec.[6] G has written a good paper and we resolved to go for a French amendment wh is in fact para 7 of Art XV of the Covenant.[7] G dictated a long and rambling minute for the S of S & I wrote a short & clear one which I hope will [be] substituted for it ...
'Friday May 11
... the US delegation spend all their time in Delegation meetings. Senator Connally did not come to Cttee III.1 until the very end and their speech had to be made by an official. If they spent a fragment of the energy devoted to quarrelling amongst themselves and trying to run things from a hotel bedroom to

seeing that the little powers were rounded up. We could always get a vote to prevent the Dumbarton Oaks text from being amended . . .

'One thing G told me is simply unbelievable. The U.S. want to write the Act of Chapultepec into the Charter to please the South Americans. It is of course not a treaty and it is absurd to suggest any such thing. But to add to the absurdity they do not intend to turn [it] into a treaty! For duplicity this beats Col. House. The S of S was diverted from support of the French amendment which we had recommended by Ivan Macdonald [Iverach McDonald], the nice Times correspondent, who is, however, not too clever. However the asininity of the Americans brought him back to it and that attitude was I think clinched by the Dominion meeting where all the Dominion ministers supported it.

'Sat May 12

I got up at 7.15 and was down early in order to get the heat turned on to Cttee III.1. I sent for Capt Holt to see Alec at 9 and also Hadow. I was with Alec myself and we sent him to round up the Arab states and especially Saudi Arabia whose delegates are under instructions to vote with us . . . At the Cttee I conferred with Mike Pearson, Norway['s] Raestadt, the Uruguayan Delegate and of course the USSR & USA. Blaisdell of USA who this time had brought Senator Connally with him was sure of Nicaragua and Honduras. This gave us more than the 16 votes necessary to beat any amendment to the text.[8] But as the debate began it was seen that the turning on of the heat had produced a terrific effect. Delegate after delegate got up to say that he would withdraw his amendment or vote as the sponsoring powers desired for the sake of unanimity. The final result was 36 to 0 with 6 abstentions. Saudi Arabia, I regret to say, never turned up and should be smacked. This shews, what I have always said, that if the Great Powers are united they can overcome all opposition. It was an example of good teamwork. Each big power had rounded up those who could be influenced by it. No doubt U.S.A. did most to influence Lat[in] American States but we contributed.

'I lunched with the Norwegians . . . I slacked after lunch being very tired, though if I had been a bit earlier I might have gone to a 5 Power meeting. This discussed the regional amendment all afternoon. Alec and G did a fine piece of work and nearly got agreement on a good formula. Senator Connally, however, bitterly complained that the British had as usual put it across the simple Americans and it is by no means certain that the battle is gained . . .

'Sun May 13

. . . I went with G to the informal official Cttee of the 5 . . . We discussed concessions on the Voting [in the Security Council] Pasvolsky proposed that we should agree that the first sentence of VIII.A [empowering the Security Council to investigate any dispute] should be under procedural voting. Sobelev [*sic*] said that the Soviet Govt thought procedural voting should be confined to Section D of Chap[ter] VI [which dealt specifically with matters of procedure in the Security Council]. This has a far wider application than he realises. Anyway it was agreed that nothing should prevent a case being brought before the Security Council under procedure . . .

'Tues May 15
I spent all morning in the 5 Power official Cttee considering amendments. We
made good progress . . .

'I discussed tomorrow's agenda for the 5 Power meeting [with Gladwyn] until
12 o'clock as I shall not be able to go. It is a pity as there are some tricky ones.
At a hastily summoned 5 Power high level meeting this aft[ernoon] at which I
was not present, they settled a formula for regionalism which is substantially a
great victory for us. We have kept the dominance of the central Organisation and
got out all reference to the Act of Chapultepec. The Latin Americans will be
furious — and Nelson Rockefeller also I should imagine.
'Wed May 16
. . . The Big Five meeting was about the Regional amendment. This was agreed
to at a hastily summoned meeting of the 5 from which the Russians were absent.
Nevertheless the U.S. held a Press Conference and gave out the text of the
amendments. The Russians cannot agree without the consent of their Govt and
rightly refuse to allow the Americans to go ahead in Cttee until at least they
know where they are. As Nelson Rockefeller agreed with me after the meeting
the method adopted by his Govt is fantastic.[9] The Soviet Ambassador might
have vigorously protested. I thought he behaved with restraint and dignity. We
spent 2½ hours in the officials 5 power official Cttee trying to convince Sobelev
[*sic*] that the regional proposal did not add anything new to Dumbarton Oaks. He
was not convinced but I think we made him see why the Latin Americans had
accepted this amendment. This subject is by far the most difficult at the
Conference because it had already made a breach in the logical unity of the
Proposals by Chap XII. However it represents a tendency which has to be
recognised . . .
'Thur May 17
. . . Then to III.1 Cttee where we began the momentous question of the veto.
Alec made a speech after Fraser answering some of his questions on which Fraser
asked that it should be circulated.[10] This has caused difficulty for it is agst the
rules & the Sect rightly dont wish to encourage a procedure which would lead to
much extra work. It was not until 10.45 that we got the transcript. I found one
mistake (which I had noticed at the time of delivery) and Will [Malkin] another.
I insisted that Evatts speech which followed should not be circulated . . .
'Fri May 18
. . . Meanwhile Alec & I went to Committee I of Commission III where the
debate on the Veto went on. Fraser delivered another waffling speech & to my
delight Alec at my suggestion got up and delivered a delicious broadside . . .
Canada attacked the veto because of course her own amendment[11] is not agreed
& some Lat American powers. Then Colombia moved a sub committee for
clarification and to suggest amendments. Alec immediately got up & said he
would clarify but would not sit on any Cttee which tried to amend. Senator
Connally said ditto. China (Wellington Koo) also defended the Yalta agreement.
The Soviet spoke first (Gromyko) and intimated pretty clearly that it would not

join any organisation except under the voting rules. This impressive demonstration of Great Power unity produced, I think, immense effect.

'Sat May 19

... I had a pleasant lunch with Halifax, Alec, Dingle Foot & Gladwyn. Then we had a meeting of the big 5 in Stettinius flat to receive the Russian answer on the new regional amendment. It turned out to be surprisingly good. The alterations which it suggested were only drafting. I told Nelson Rockefeller that he need have no hesitation in accepting it. I have no doubt we will. But there is to be a meeting tomorrow to do so. Meanwhile it was considered and slightly redrafted in our 5 power meeting [of] officials . . .

'. . . I had to keep the Press right when I got back from the 5 Power meeting. There was no one else to do it. Alec who had turned the tables on the small powers in the "clarifying" sub-cttee by asking them to "clarify" their questions was in high good humour[12] . . .

'Sunday May 20

... At 5 we went to an (officials) 5 power meeting. Sob[olev] was a bit difficult on the new draft and insisted on the omission of the word "restoration". In my opinion it made very little difference either way . . . However eventually [in the Big 5 meeting] it was agreed to leave it out and thus a most important agreement was completed.[13] It is in my opinion a victory for the global as against the regional point of view . . .

'Monday May 21

The discussion on the veto continued this morning its dreary way. The Philippine Delegate delivered a sort of revival speech lasting 22 mins. Several other insignificant states took part but also regrettably Brazil & Argentine who supported the Australian amendment which is quite impossible.[14] The small powers are ganging up though they know in their hearts they can accomplish nothing. As the Russian Ambassador [Gromyko] said to me when we left "they forget that if they had their way there would be no Organisation at all." . . .

'Tuesday May 22

... Committee III.1 got in a terrible mess. At the end no one knew what had been decided so I claimed to know with great firmness and the Sect just wrote down what I said. It was as easy as that. The great hurdles in this Cttee are still to be taken. We have now got the questionnaire & tonight we decide on the answers . . .

'Wed May 23[15]

It is nearly two o'clock. I have had Cttee II.2 this morning and III.1 after dinner . . . After this meeting [of III.1] at 11.30 p.m. we had a meeting with Pasvolsky, Gromyko, Sobolev, G, Alec & I to discuss the Canadian amendment. Gromyko indicated he would accept it but only if Canada and the other Dominions and Argentine & Brazil accepted the Yalta formula. We tried to shew him that we could not make a bargain openly in this way but that all the five powers were ready to stand on the Yalta formula and that the others would thus have to accept if there were to be any Organisation at all. Sobolev shewed clearly that he

thought that US & Britain had contemplated giving way on the formula but I
hope the Russians were reassured on this point. They simply do not realise that
we must make some concessions of form to the Dominions and other states to
save their faces . . .

'Friday May 25

A fairly hard day. We had a pretty good morning in III.1 and finished the sixth
Chapter except for the voting section. Considering the immense importance of
these clauses we have got them through with very little trouble. Certainly with
no change of importance in the Dumbarton Oaks text . . . This afternoon we had
a meeting of the 5 officials to decide the answer to the voting formula. G had
done another redraft which read pretty well though it contained some mistakes.
But we had to take another US text, better than the one discarded which tasted
like cotton wool. Sobolev scrutinised the new text with his usual suspicion and
ability but eventually we got a new text drafted. This I have just seen and it
seems moderately good. Its real value, however, lies in the last sentence which
states uncompromisingly that the sponsoring powers cannot depart in any way
from the Yalta formula . . .

'Sat May 26

Something of a crisis has arisen. The officials of the 5 met to decide on the final
draft on the answer to the questions. All went well on the statement preceding
the answers and we thought that we had obtained complete agreement. But
when we came to the questions themselves there was the absurd question which
I suppose Evatt or one of his officials raised as to whether the question of what
is procedure is decided by a procedural vote.[16] For some time I argued alone
that it was while Sobolev fiercely said it would allow the small powers to alter
the whole constitution, an absurd contention. G would not support me, a great
mistake on his part at this stage, whatever the final issue, and Leo [Pasvolsky]
and Liang were strongly on Sob[olev]'s side. I had to abandon the struggle but
shortly afterwards Fouques-Duparc asked to reverse his judgment. Just as the
Great Powers would distrust one answer so the little powers would distrust the
other. But of course Sob would not give way though Leo was shaken and the
question remained unanswered. But this affected the introductory paper where
it was stated that a procedural vote governed the question of a dispute being
considered and discussed by the Security Council. I went over before G to
explain the situation to Alec so that he could coach Lord Halifax before the big
five meeting at 9.15. He was very perturbed and saw my point of view
immediately. Our cocktail party to the Soviet Delegation was already due. It was
a great success but Alec spent most of his time talking to Gromyko who, he told
me later, had shewn signs of not agreeing that matters must be automatically
discussed if brought before the S[ecurity] C[ouncil] . . .

'At the Big Five [meeting] Lord H allowed Alec to make the running and he
established clearly that the words in the statement were not enough if the Soviet
answer to the question on procedure was accepted.[17] I also told him & he
accepted that the statement was not enough but that the Charter must be altered

to make the statement true if the Soviet interpretation of voting as to procedure was accepted. Gromyko's attitude was most ominous. Dulles tried to shew that there was nothing in the difference but failed. Halifax suggested to trade our conception of the right to discuss [in the Security Council] against the Soviet interpretation of the question of what is procedure. But Alec thought it unwise to throw such an idea into an already confused meeting & I am sure he was right. Moreover the question needed examination before we could decide. So we decided nothing and the officials are to meet tomorrow Alec replacing G who is off to golf. We tried to explain it all to the poor Lord in his room over a whisky & soda afterwards but I doubt if he has got the point or thinks it very important if he has. What he wants is a settlement at any cost. It is true that all this will probably signify little in the days to come when the Charter is in force. But they signify a great deal now – perhaps the signing of the Charter.

'Tuesday May 29

A strenuous day. We had a 5 Power Cttee in the morning which led to over 2 hrs of painful discussion. It was called to discuss a French amendment clarifying Art XII . . . The rest of the morning was spent in Stettinius urging speed . . . This was an endeavour to get the heat put on the Russians I suppose but it had little effect. Gromyko said it was better to make a good Charter than a hasty one and the suggestions of a time limit and reference of everything to the Steering Cttee was turned down by everyone as likely to increase rather than diminish delay . . .

'Wed May 30

I had no Cttee after the Brit Delegation meeting this morning and it was a blessed relief to have a little time to think. I worked out exactly what I wanted on the Veto and got it approved by Alec & Will as watertight. The former is all for standing up to the Russians and we have the approval of the S of S, which has come so quickly that he must just have decided it himself. In the afternoon . . . I was left alone with the little 5 . . . Sobolev produced a new text which to my surprise involved an alteration in the Yalta formula.[18] He wanted, however, to leave everything else out e.g. words to safeguard discuss and consider in Section A of [Chapter] VIII. Of course I made it quite clear that we could not accept this & Leo backed me up. Liang was more than usually tiresomely clever but Fouques-Duparc put in an effective plea for not asking more from the little states. We could do no more than record our differences and the Big 5 must decide. . .

'. . . I dined with Alec & G and heard that the Dominions meeting had decided for a Convention[19] in 10 yrs without the veto. I voiced my indignation in no uncertain terms and Alec could only defend himself with casuistry. He did not believe what he said and was only defending for Protocols sake. I do not believe that the project can be carried out but even to ventilate it will do harm in the present state of our relations with the USSR . . .

'Thur May 31

I have had a most anxious day which has resulted, I hope, in the most evil

consequences of the Dominion meeting being averted. I woke up this morning early oppressed by the thought that we had initiated or promised to initiate a move to revise the Great Power veto after a term of years in a Conference. The telegram which I saw on entering the office confirmed my worst fears as it was a definite recommendation to London to accept that point of view. I, therefore, asked Alec if he would object to me making a protest when the point came up at the Delegation meeting. He gave his consent readily and I, therefore, made a strong and, perhaps, too emotional protest which, however, produced considerable effect. Lord Cranborne had gone but, of the others, Mabane supported me while Dingle Foot opposed. (I later tackled him on this in an inconclusive conversation) Still perturbed and fortunately with a morning free from Cttees I composed a minute stating my view as effectively as I could to Lord Halifax. Again I consulted Alec who agreed that I should send it direct to Lord Halifax. I gave copies to him and G. and no one else.[20] At 5 o'clock Lord Halifax sent for me. He had been much impressed and suggested that a second telegram should be sent expressing my views and alluding to me by name and at the same time saying that he himself, though not entirely agreeing, would act most cautiously. I saw Alec and he agreed with me that my name should not be used. Meanwhile Lord Halifax asked me & Alec to dinner & cinema, (Wuthering Heights which turned out to be very good) and said that he Alec & I could settle the telegram when we got back if I would draft it. I drafted it while all the rest of the Delegation was attending cocktail parties (which I thus escaped with a good conscience) We had a delightful dinner . . . We then conferred on my draft. It was accepted in principle and some alterations made which improved it and brought out my points even more clearly. I feel that Lord H & Alec acted as great gentlemen. They had taken an all-important decision without due consideration of all the possible consequences and they shewed no resentment when I pointed these out. They in fact eat their own words in a most unequivocal way. I hope the telegram will reach London in time.[21] It is being ciphered as I write this. I hope that I have done the right thing. The action proposed would have immediately caused the greatest suspicion in the mind of the Soviet Union & have thrown confusion into the ranks of the United States Delegation. If it were to be implemented it would open the way, under circumstances which cannot be foreseen, for the U.S. to withdraw at the behest of an isolationist minority, give the Soviet Govt a legitimate excuse to refuse real cooperation in the new organisation and turn everyone's thoughts to revising the Charter instead of making it work. If I have prevented this I have done good work and though Lord H & Alec do not agree with me as to the probability of these things happening, they admit that it is quite possible they will happen . . .
'Fri June 1st & Sat June 2nd
The crisis of the Conference has arrived and with such violence that it hardly seems possible that it can survive and bring the Charter into existence. Yesterday we learnt that Sobolev was going to Moscow i.e. he had been recalled. How ominous this was was seen when the 5 Power meeting met after dinner when

Gromyko produced a new version of the statement in answer to the questionnaire which stated with great clarity that the Soviets refused to accept the interpretations that a dispute brought to the Security Council could at least be received and considered i.e. discussed without any power, whether party to a dispute or not, being able to stop the process. The statement, indeed, argued that in some circumstances even consideration & discussion might be dangerous as leading to further steps, and, therefore, must be subjected to a veto.[22] We did no more than receive this statement and passed on to other items . . .

'Alec, G & I discussed this with Halifax after our return. Alec was very gloomy. We decided that the Soviet proposition was absolutely unacceptable. No other course was possible after the attitude taken up by us and announced publicly by the S of S. When the big 5 met this morning first Stettinius said that the US had announced their opinion 4 or 5 months ago and that they could not sign a Charter with the Soviet interpretation. Halifax said it was quite "unacceptable" to us and that the Soviet position could not be justified. Koo inclined to the same side though he dared not speak right out. M. Paul-Boncour said that though he had not yet [received] a French translation of the Soviet statement he was on the same side so far. These two latter statements might have been expected to be "waffling". But the British and American statements were completely forthright and as strong as those of Gromyko himself. The latter could only say he would transmit to his Govt. But he held out no hope of a change . . .

'Senator Vandenberg said the Senate would never pass such a treaty & Senator Connally said they probably would not.

'. . . We did not meet after dinner where the British eat sturdily and with forced cheerfulness. We have already evolved various expedients to try to save something from the wreck. Perhaps we shall. Perhaps a way will be found to have a real Charter. But at present it seems almost impossible to get out of this deadlock. The small powers & in particular Mr. Evatt have succeeded in driving a wedge between the Soviet Govt & the other Great Powers. Whether they will be pleased when they do not get a Charter at all, I have my doubts. In fact it is quite likely they will set up a howl trying to throw the responsibility on some one else. The first responsibility rests on the Soviet Govt. But those who have for 5 or 6 weeks shewn how they mistrusted her and have used every expedient to force inconvenient questions into the foreground have a very large share in the responsibility . . .

'Sunday June 3rd

. . . G & I dined with Ham Armstrong & Isaiah Bowman at Jacks. It was a most pleasant dinner. It is delightful to be able to say what one likes as we can do to people we know so well as these two . . . We reviewed the extraordinary events of the past week and especially the proceedings of the Big Five Committees . . . I hope the alarm and despondency of the smaller powers will grow and that they will begin to realise that their manoeuvres threaten to wreck the whole scheme. The prospect of a completely lawless world must make them pause — or must it? as so many of them seem to have no sense of responsibility at all. At the end of our discussions I put forward a view that we might find a solution by the other four powers putting forward a different interpretation of one para of the Russian draft i.e. substituting a para of their own. Then they should frankly state the difference and say that it does not much matter. This did not receive much favour from the other three but I have since I got back made a draft and it does not look so very bad. I doubt if the Russians would accept it but it might be worth trying. I will explore the matter further tomorrow.

'Monday June 4

No progress has been made on the main issue. Lord H had a meeting with Stettinius this morning with Alec, G & Neville [Butler] and Pasvolsky & Jimmy Dunn. It seems to have been an inconclusive discussion. S quite rightly is very anxious to get a Charter signed even with reservations. It was agreed to stand fast on the principle. P had an idea that discussion should only be vetoed by a unanimous Great Power vote which Alec & G thought a good idea. I am not so certain as it departs from the principle that discussion is automatic but it may be used as a face saving device. G has strongly opposed my own idea of a joint statement with separate explanations of the discussion question. Alec thinks it may cause delay. Hardly more I think than any other method but I have not pressed it . . . Meanwhile the facts are really all known, especially in Scottie [James] Reston's articles in the N.Y. Times. I shall not be sorry if some alarm and despondency is aroused in the smaller powers. It may serve to shew them the dangerous game they have been playing. But a number, I dare say, hate Russia so much, that they would like a break in the hope of getting an Organisation without her. They seem to have no idea of what such a situation would mean and how unlikely it would be to preserve the peace . . .

'Tues 5 June

There are no signs of any settlement of the major question and this makes efforts for much minor affairs a very hard thing to do with any enthusiasm . . .

'Wed June 6

A good day! Just before dinner there was a fresh telegram from Moscow saying Stalin had agreed with us. If so all obstacles to the signing of the Charter are removed. The others believe it. I am just a little dubious but the behaviour of Gromyko at the Five Power meeting today certainly confirmed it . . .

'Thur June 7

This has been a great day! I found telegrams in my room this morning assuring us that instructions had been sent to Gromyko to accept our interpretation of the Veto as a result of Harry Hopkins interview with Stalin who swept all Molotov's objections aside as petty in comparison with the final result to be achieved. Our P.M. had also prepared a fine appeal to Stalin but I do not know if this reached the latter and contributed to the result.[2 3]

'I was not present at the meeting of the Big Five at which the news was announced as I had a Committee to attend in which I had to obtain a result. But several of those there described it to me. The Americans were all very emotional except Leo who made a rather pedantic statement (missing said Ham Armstrong excitedly the psychological moment). Anyway everyone was very pleased. The Steering Cttee was told afterwards at a meeting called for other purposes and there was also a wave of emotion. This should augur well for the passing of the veto clauses. I am sure I was right in doing my best to spread alarm at the final result & the threatened loss of the Charter among the smaller powers so that they would be more likely to accept the unanimous opinion of the Five Great Powers when that was obtained . . .[24]

'Saturday June 9

An exhausting day, battling with Mr. Evatt. I am afraid that I have gone too far in my speech this evening and very likely I shall get hauled over the coals for it but I think it was worth it anyway . . .[25]

'At the evening meeting [of Committee III.1] Senator Connally made an oration at the beginning which was not very successful. It was all thunder and said no great power was seeking territorial extension which was not true. Evatt made a long speech and circulated a paper alluding to Alec's interpretation as different to the statement of the sponsoring powers . . . In my speech I attacked Evatt for saying unanimity would be a return to the system of the Dark Ages saying I did not know that he had been born in the Dark Ages. I said that we had been surprised to find the veto of the permanent powers non parties to a dispute challenged at all. It was part of the system of the world in which we lived . . .

'Then I attacked Evatt's remarks about a veto on conciliation by shewing the importance of the decisions e.g. a decision as to whether a matter was essentially one of domestic jurisdiction. (Perhaps I ought not to have said this.) He also said that the Great Powers had chosen themselves & I pointed out that they had been elected by a unanimous vote of this Cttee & that they had won their position by blood sweat & tears & would save others as well as themselves. Evatt interrupted me here.

'I received a good many congrats but think my speech was on the whole a failure & probably I had better waited till Monday & let Koo speak . . .

'Wed June 13

A day of triumph — and defeat. The Yalta voting formula was passed in III.1 this morning by 30 to 2, 15 abstentions & 3 absentees (inc[luding] Saudi Arabia). The result is not quite so good as I had hoped since the majority is not 2/3rd over the 2 + 15. Still it is better than we had at one time hoped . . .

'One bad thing happened today. At the meeting this morning Cranborne raised the question of voting for the Australian amendment which removes domestic jurisdiction entirely out of the survey of the Organisation except for enforcement action. He wanted to vote & speak for it. Both G & I strongly protested. I said it would make much harder the task of dealing with any future persecution of the Jews. Lord H said we must do evil for the sake of conciliating Australian opinion. I heard tonight that Evatt had won hands down by 30—3 . . .'[26]

Although the decisive vote on the voting formula had been taken, there was continued controversy over the rapporteur's report on the action taken in Committee III.1. The Soviets complained that the report revealed a bias against approval of the Yalta formula. On 19 June Committee III.1 unanimously accepted the report (which had been redrafted twice) and it was sent to Commission III for final approval. In the debate the apprehensions of the smaller powers were readily apparent, but finally the future article 27 of the Charter was adopted without objection by the Commission. Thus Webster was able to write:

'Wed June 20
A decisive day. All the issues of the Conference are now decided and the day for the signature of the Charter finally fixed. Barring some quite unforeseeable event the purpose of the Conference has been achieved. Moreover in all essentials the Dumbarton Oaks Plan stands. Nothing has really been added to it but verbiage. The most important additions are in the Purposes and Principles but we had already agreed to the main addition "justice" during the Chinese phase of the conversations [at Dumbarton Oaks]. Chapter VI, the heart of the Charter,[27] has only received those amendments we ourselves inserted plus a couple of technical ones of no great importance . . .
'Sat June 23rd
. . . at 4.45 I went with Lord H to the Steering [Committee]. G was there & Will came after ½ an hour. The room was crowded. The discussions were farcical. A new draft of the Preamble was distributed which A[rchibald] MacLeish had done with Smuts. But it left out respect for treaties & was challenged by Chile, Peru and Gromyko. Smuts made a good defence, but G succeeded in getting only the original draft sent to the Coord[ination] Cttee. Mackenzie King who has come back for the signature made some sensible drafting suggestions. The result was that we did these in the last Coordination Cttee[28] after the Steering [Committee] & that is the end of the Preamble. It still bears a good deal of trace of my early draft but it is not a very good document. However it is not as bad as some people say, who would like the glory of drafting one for themselves.
    'Then the Charter was approved by a unanimous vote of 50. This was a momentous decision, though already foregone, and I could not help feeling a little sentimental about it. The ratifications have still to come, but I think my job is ended. I have certainly never before had so much influence on a great event . . .
'Tuesday June 26
Today has been the culmination of all my hopes (and fears) since I got back from the United States nearly three years ago and I can scarcely bring myself to realise all that has been accomplished. The Charter has been signed today by 50 nations. Each signed separately and I was present as a witness at the signature by the U.K. . . .
    'All [speakers in the final plenary session] said the Charter was imperfect as of course it is. It is an Alliance of the Great Powers embedded in a universal organisation as the Covenant also was. But this fact is more clearly denoted

because of the fact that sanctions cannot even theoretically be put on a Great Power as it could in the Covenant. This is a great blot and I wish it were not there. Otherwise there is little I would do to alter the Charter, except of course clear away some of the verbiage which has accumulated round it during these 9 weeks. Its new ideas come mainly from me, if I may so record without undue egoism. The Purpose & Principles, the promise to settle all disputes, the acceptance of primary responsibility by the S[ecurity] Council, the promise of the other states to obey it — all come from my original paper before it was even submitted to the Law Cttee. Some of the phraseology has come right through.

'The separation of the Ec & Soc [Council] from the Sec Council comes from the U.S. though something not unlike it was in our first paper D, derived as the U.S. idea from the Bruce Cttee. But we would have had more final control by the S C over such matters and I believe we were right. However the S C can always intervene if the maintenance of peace & security is threatened. The Soviet desire to leave out Ec & Soc matters altogether and the new functional organisation also tended to keep the two things separate — also the U.S. desire to give the small powers one place where there was real "equality" — in theory.

'The Trusteeship sections are, of course, entirely new and I have had little to do with them except to encourage David Owen in his early negotiations with the Colonial Office. They have been worked out by Cranborne and Stassen on the advice of Poynton and Gerig. They have been meant to enable the U.S. to obtain the Pacific islands innocent of all control except by a body on which she has a veto. We have allowed our mandates to go on under the new control, but for the rest the matter remains exactly as before except that there is a sort of machinery if states desire to put their colonial territories under it. We have no such intention and I am sure no other power has. Nevertheless the fact that the machinery is there is important.

'The Preamble has been a dreadful struggle. In its final form it still contains one or two sentences deriving from my original draft. Indeed about ½ of it is so derived though the words are changed a good deal. The rest is Smuts much amended. The final result is not so bad as those who wished to substitute their own words pretend to believe.

'The statute of the Court is conservative. It is a pity the old statute could not have been adopted but no great harm has been done.

'The P.M. has sent a telegram of congratulation to Lord H and I think the British Delegation deserves it. But we must be careful not to claim too much paternity for the ideas in the Charter. We must let U.S. have credit and let the Soviets believe they have got all their own way. But some day, I dare say, the truth will be known. If the Charter succeeds, I shall have made a greater contribution to history than I ever thought it possible that I could do.

'That I have been able to do so has largely been due to Gladwyn Jebb. It was he who brought me in to the centre of the machine. He is not aware how much his own ideas have changed under my influence. He was quite ignorant of his subject when he became head of the Reconstruction Dept. He had all the ideas of his generation and distrusted and disliked the League. Of course both Eden and Cadogan took a very different view, and, if they had not done so, my efforts would have been of no avail. But it was I who found the new methods of harmonising the Great Power Alliance theory and the League theory. It was I also who got the checks of the Purposes & Principles so that the new authority conferred on the S Council was not to be arbitrarily executed, yet there was no such rigid procedure as in the Covenant. The decision by majority voting came from other sources, — American mainly but it may be very important, though as it is at present combined with Great Power unanimity in the S C it is not really much different from the Covenant. Its use in the Gen Assembly may also turn out to be very important.

'The Chinese got "justice" in at Dumbarton Oaks. It has been much embroidered since then. We have gone a little too far for the truth. But my phrases have been kept in the Preamble — not to achieve justice but conditions under which justice may be achieved. It is all we can do as yet.

'The fight with the smaller powers was inevitable but it would have been much better conducted if it had not been for the energy and imagination of Evatt. He was the ablest of the statesmen of the smaller powers — and a really malignant man. He obviously hates us ... This egoistical and ambitious Australian has overplayed his hand. He has got nothing but his domestic jurisdiction clause, which he could have got anyhow (& which he only of course got with our assistance) while he has offended both U.S. and U.S.S.R. on whom Australia must rely for protection agst a yellow peril if it ever exists as it certainly does not at present. He tried to get rid of the U.K. veto, which is his greatest protection ... He has also been the advocate of the greatest possible extension of power to the Gen Ass while at the same time fighting perversely to limit it by domestic jurisdiction. This latter is now the only gap in the Charter, if indeed such a gap really exists ...

The Latin Americans have frothed but they were ultimately under U.S. control and have done little harm and I think accept the Charter quite happily. They have got regional protection. But this in the long run works out to no more than I always gave in my papers. The region is completely subordinate to the centre unless the Great Powers quarrel.

'The French have emphasised the exemption of the treaties agst the enemy states. This is a necessary stage. But it can be absorbed in the Charter when the Great Powers desire, i.e. when the new Locarno (without Germany this time) comes and the S C takes responsibility for the maintenance of p[eace] & s[ecurity] everywhere. When & if this does come, the new Organisation will really have been founded firmly ...

'The smaller European powers Belgium & Nether[lands], have behaved rather foolishly. But that is largely due to personalities & weakness of Govts at home. The Soviet satellites have of course done as they were told, though Masaryk has preserved the dignity of Czechoslovakia. Norway has of her own free will behaved splendidly & seen the full implications of the Charter.

'Lord H had a farewell meeting of the Brit Delegation, calling in the girls and making an excellent speech of thanks. He has done excellently. He has seen nearly all things in proper proportion. He is a very clever though rather lazy man. He has no principles about mundane things. His intervention in III.1 Cttee and as regards amendments were splendidly timed and most effective. Lord Cranborne has been absorbed in Trusteeship & not in good health. He is a delightful person to work with and his wife is as nice as he.

'Of the others Miss Horsbrugh did excellently. Mabane was effective but not liked. Dingle Foot, I now think, was not as good as I at first judged. He was too parliamentary and I have had to undo some of his rather easily made concessions. Geo Tomlinson went a round about way to get the I.L.O. objectives — but that was due to Bevin.

'Anthony Eden was excellent while he was here — but on edge and uncomfortable. His inside was already worrying him and he shewed great courage in going on so long.[29] He was as quick as a needle — much quicker at grasping things than Lord H. He had generous ideas and was altogether on the right lines. He was too hasty and weak on detail sometimes, especially in his famous press conference . . .[30]

'We have seen most of the Americans & the Chinese. Our relations with each have been nearly perfect. We understand & work with each other. The Americans tried to pinch credit which is not always theirs, but what does that matter? I personally have seen a great deal of the two Senators in my two Cttees. Connally is the most trustworthy. Vandenberg the cleverest. The latter is now genuinely on our side. It would not pay him to be otherwise. They have both treated me in the nicest possible way. Their principal advisers Blaisdell in III.1 & Cordier in II.2 have been pretty good but a bit heavy handed.

'Leo, like G, has been absorbed by the central [machinery]. He tired & was less effective than I had hoped . . .

'Ed [Stettinius] was magnificent. I doubt if he yet knows what the Charter is all about. But he is a genuine & sincere man and combines a certain dignity in public session with immense friendliness in private. A cleverer or more egoistic Sec of State might have ruined everything.

'Dulles has had a great deal of influence. He is too legally and ecclesiastically-minded but he helped in a number of ways.

'Ham Armstrong did very well and was the best American exponent of the Great Power thing which he thoroughly understood.

'As to the Chinese . . . T. V. Soong had really no interest in the Charter. Wellington Koo is a little ineffective but a really sincere and likeable man. Liang worked hard and was only tiresome at times. (He gave G & me a farewell lunch today). Victor Hoo is a bit of a tough but clever and he did not do much harm.

'The French were rather pathetic and must have had some nasty moments. Their officials were excellent and amongst the clearest minded at the Conference. They were anxious to be on the best of terms with us . . .

'The Russians were & remain an enigma. When Molotov was here they could negotiate. After he had gone Gromyko could do little on his own responsibility. That was one of our main difficulties. Sobolev tried to overcome it — and I am afraid fell from favour ... I can't help liking the Russians even the toughs. I believe we ought to get on with them if we try hard enough, though I don't pretend it will be easy.

'On this last thing depends the future of the United Nations Organisation even more than on the shape we have given to it. But the machinery which we have made should make such agreement possible if it is desired. And if it is not desired, no machinery will be any good.

'I have no illusions about the Charter I think. But it has registered a definite advance in the relations between states — and especially great powers — which the change in technique has made possible.'

CHAPTER 6

Special Adviser to the Minister of State

On returning to London from San Francisco Webster submitted his resignation. The European War had ended, the framework of the world organization had been established and Webster believed that it was time to return to his duties at the London School of Economics. However, the Foreign Office prevailed upon him to stay, Jebb emphasizing that he should at least remain to see the Charter through the House of Commons. This Webster did whilst also drafting 'A Commentary on the Charter of the United Nations'.[1] Yet many practical problems remained. A Preparatory Commission had been established at San Francisco to prepare for the first meeting of the new organization and an Executive Committee had been appointed to consider the detailed problems. The first Executive meeting took place in London on 16 August 1945 and as the host nation the Secretaryship of the Committee was given to a British official – Gladwyn Jebb. Temporarily, therefore, Jebb became an international civil servant. The loss of Jebb together with the demands made on the Foreign Office from other quarters had severely depleted the personnel available for dealing with United Nations affairs. The new Labour government had decided to give the United Nations high priority and fortunately the Minister of State dealing with the United Nations – Philip Noel-Baker – had great experience and knowledge of the League. However, expert support was needed and Webster was thus designated a Special Adviser to the Minister of State on United Nations Affairs.[2]

The meetings of the Executive Committee and Preparatory Commission continued in London throughout 1945. They were conducted against a background of deteriorating relations among the great powers. At Potsdam it had been agreed that there should be periodic meetings of Foreign Ministers. The first such meeting was held in London from 11 September to 2 October. The main business was the question of peace treaties for Finland, Hungary, Roumania and Bulgaria. However, the powers could not agree and the meeting ended without even reaching agreement on the formulation of a public communiqué. The wisdom of divorcing the establishment of the United Nations from the consideration of peace treaties was again apparent.

The Executive Committee of the Preparatory Commission that met in London consisted of the representatives from the same fourteen states which had formed the Executive Committee at San Francisco.[3] Their task was to consider the arrangements for the first sessions of the various organs of the United Nations. To facilitate this work the Committee decided to establish ten committees to concentrate on specific areas.[4] Among the many problems dealt with by the Executive Committee and later the Preparatory Commission itself, Webster's diary reflects an overriding interest in the site of the new organization and the selection of a Secretary-General.

'Mon Sept 3
... when Stettinius came to see Phil [Noel-Baker] , I was present at my request, and as he brought NOYES with him I stayed the whole time . . . [Stettinius] told us about Grom[yko]'s offer to agree on San Francisco if U.S. offered it & said China was also keen. Phil said he had not consulted his S of S & could only speak tentatively but that many of his officials thought it ought to be in Europe. Stettinius said, if so, it could only be at Geneva & Phil agreed and talked about the enclave. He also said we must stand up to the Russians. Stettinius was I think, putting all his cards on the table. I doubt if he himself wants San Francisco which would reduce his own personal position. I think European affairs might escape from the U.N. until a first class crisis occurred. Still there is something to be said for it, if it keeps the U.S. interested. The Organisation on their own soil is bound up with their prestige. The principle is, however, a bad one . . .
'Tues Sept 11
I have been too busy to write since last Tuesday except on Sunday and then I was too slack. We have had a great debate on the whole of the work of the Executive Cttee and the Preparatory Commission as a result of Stettinius desire to get the United Nations into operation as soon as possible.[5] Phil both last Friday, Tuesday and today has argued very well. He accepted the object but shewed how difficult it was to work out in detail. Thus we have already got the Prep Comm to about Nov 12 and as there will have to be an interval after it, it looks as if the 1st Genl Assembly could not meet until the beginning of Jan. That is what we want as it leaves time for the League business which the Soviet Govt wants to stop . . .[6]
'Sunday Sept 16
... On Thursday [September 13] at the Ritz Phil, G & I met Stettinius, Winant and Stephenson [*sic*] ... We had some good talk during dinner ... Ed again practically threatened that if we did not agree to Dec [for the General Assembly meeting] he would move for U.S. in Jan. We took no notice of this but there is force in [the] argument that states should not have to send twice delegates to London, once for P[reparatory] C[ommission] & once for Gen Assembly. He was not satisfactory on the Organs going on in London after 1st meeting of Gen Ass. Said no one would agree. I think we ought to have pressed him on this but I dare say we can get it. I have a suspicion, however, that Ed wants to take the

whole shew over to the U.S. where he would be more comfortable. He does not really care for the efficiency of the whole. It might of course be more efficient but I am afraid of it getting into a very unreal existence. On the site he was not much better. But Winant who had been with him 100% on all the previous points, even including backing Ed's fantastic notion of taking the Organs and the second meeting of the General Assembly to the Bahamas. But on the site while Ed was still in his old position Winant was much nearer us in desiring Europe. We argued Europe not Geneva but everyone knew it meant Geneva. I think Ed wants San Francisco and means to get it. Here again we can do little if the U.S. Govt really wants it. But a large number of important men in the Govt are too wise to want it. That is the only hope . . .

'Monday Sept 17

. . . I went with Phil to Stettinius flat for tea for a "Big Five" meeting. Phil could only stay for ½ hour & I took on. Massigli, Grom & Victor Hoo were there. The Sec Genl was the most important item. I agreed the Big Five must agree on that point soon. Even Phil[7] can't really refuse to do that since by the Charter each of them has a veto . . .

'Tuesday Sept 18

At the Executive Committee meeting this morning Stettinius said to me that it looked as if the first meeting would have to take place in January after all. This is as complete a reversal as Gromyko's yesterday [when Gromyko advocated January]. I told Phil & Gladwyn who were much amused . . . We have now warned the Govts about December and we will see what the response is. But I think, as I told Stettinius, there are so many different snags that January is likely. We have always thought so but did not want to force him to the conclusion but let him find out for himself . . .

'Wed Sept 19

I had no Committees nor had Phil so that I was able to have some quite long talks with him to discuss important matters. One was the Sect General and I urged him to get Alec to come in. He at last did so and we talked very frankly. Phil said Stettinius had suggested Gladwyn but both Alec & I agreed with him that he was not suitable. Alec said he was unpopular which I said was due to his desire to get things done. But I could not say that he had the necessary qualities of judgment in a crisis. He is too much up or down. Phil put Winant above Eisenhower but Alec like me was strongly for the opposite. We urged him to see Stettinius about it as soon as possible . . .

'. . . I could not talk much to Ben [Cohen] at dinner but went up to his room afterwards and talked very freely. I broached the site and the Sect Genl. I urged Europe but he did not give much away on this. On the Sec Genl he was all for Eisenhower but also thought Winant would do very well. I forgot to say Phil had put his 3 names, Eisenhower, Stassen and Winant to the last who had said we will take it meaning himself. But later he had urged Eisenhower . . .

'Thurs Sept 20

. . . Stevenson dined with me at the Club . . . He suggested Mike Pearson for Sec

Genl and I said ought to be an American which seemed to surprise him. He said
not Great Power but I said that did not matter while Great Power did matter for
site which would be permanent. I said Mike very good but not quite good
enough. We discussed time table and necessity for 5 power talks. He said they
wanted to keep in close touch with Phil but found it difficult if he refused
intimate talks. I said he was prepared to discuss Sec Genl & other questions but
not to bind himself. He wanted to discuss this matter of Sec Genl intimately with
Stett. Altogether I think we got along & I have prepared the way for Phils talks.
'Tues Sept 25
While I was at the F.O. meeting Tahourdin came for me. Stet had brought
Stevenson and two others so I sat in with Phil. We had a fair talk . . . Stet raised
Sec Genl which led to site and frank discussion of Geneva by Phil. We got
nowhere but I think the talk has done good. Unfortunately as Phil told me
yesterday Bevin is not only against Winant but against Eisenhower as well. He
had even suggested Moley! [Orme Sargent] . . . Phil will of course have none of
it or of G for the job, but it makes our talk with the Americans difficult . . .
'Wed Sept 26
There was a 5 Power meeting at Park Lane Hótel at Gromyko's room . . . After
some silly discussion of unimportant points we got on to the Sect & Seat. As
regards the first the only point was that he should not be a national of same
state as seat. But all did not agree this wise though they thought probable. Then we
went on to the Seat and each stated their views. Philip began and — unwisely I
thought — defended Geneva as well as Europe, Koo plumped for U.S.A., Massigli
made a moving appeal for Europe, Grom refused Geneva point blank and asked
for U.S.A. Stettinius said [they] w[oul]d do what majority wished. As we went
out I congratulated Massigli on his speech. He said in a moving tone. "If the seat
is in the New World, it is the end of Europe." Note that it was U.S. not San
Francisco which was advocated. Stevenson says it will not be San F. but East of
the Rockies . . .
'Friday Sept 28
. . . I lunched with TURGEON, Canadian Ambdr to Belgium now head of their
Delegation at the Dorchester. Escot Reid, Gerig, Stevenson and David Owen
were there and Stettinius, who, though this [was] at a lower level, was very
forthcoming. We discussed the seat very frankly and Stet told the situation as
envisaged in our 5 Power meeting. I explained that we were in no way
committed. We also had over again the old discussion on the nature of the
S[ecurity] C[ouncil]. Stet attacked again our idea of quarterly meetings of the
Foreign Secretaries. I told him that we did not necessarily think the U.S. should
do as we did because the President had different powers to a Cabinet . . . But he
said he would put the seat at San Francisco to <u>prevent</u> the Foreign Secs from
going! He dreads being superseded in a crisis, yet, that is inevitable if the S.C. is
to do its work properly . . .
'Wed Oct 3
. . . [The Executive meeting] went very badly. Gromyko had evidently prepared

the way with skill. China led off (Victor Hoo) attacking Geneva & plumping for
U.S. Massigli made a good reply, stressing that a Great Power should not have the
seat. Evatt then strongly supported San Francisco, though I had warned him
that if the seat was in the U.S. it would probably not be San Francisco. Phil then
made a passionate defence of Geneva and of Europe, using the geographical
argument with effect. Gromyko then stated baldly Russia's preference for U.S.
After the Nether[lands] had supported Europe briefly Jugoslavia supported her
[the Soviet Union] naturally. After tea the Latin Americans Chile, Mexico,
Brazil supported U.S. but with no enthusiasm . . . Then Grom insisted on a vote
after Stettinius had said U.S. did not seek but would accept . . . Then [the] roll
call vote. Aus, Braz, Chile, Czech, Mexico, Iran, USSR, Jugoslavia, China (9)
voted for U.S. U.K., France, Neth agst. U.S. & Canada abstained. Then in a
vote on Europe Aus, Braz, Chile, Czech, USSR, Jug & China (7) voted agst
U.K., France, Nether for. U.S., Canada, Iran and Mexico abstained . . . It was
decided to publish the vote at once . . .

'The battle is not yet over. The U.S. will decide. The East U.S. will anyway
probably defeat the West. But Europe is feeble and divided and it cannot have
the seat unless the U.S. decides for it, which, while Stettinius is there, will not be
done. The effect on the Organisation will be great. As Phil hinted in his speech it
will increase regionalism. I am inclined to think we may get many organs
meeting in Europe. Geneva should be kept for that purpose. But we shall see. I
do not take the result as tragically as Phil. Nevertheless it is a Russian victory for
it will mean that the United Nations will have less to do with Europe.[8]

'Thur Oct 4
I made all preparations for turning on the heat this morning after an interview
with Phil . . . Then Phil went to the Cabinet and when he came back he was
considerably deflated. The Cabinet had refused to make a fuss though they still
adhered to Europe. But they did not want at this juncture, after the For[eign]
Ministers flop, a row with U.S and USSR. So I called the preparations off. The
Cabinet said let it "simmer". Simmering will mean congealing and unless the U.S
itself acts I consider the question of the site pretty well settled . . .

'Mon Oct 8
. . . Meanwhile Ed had demanded a Five Power meeting. Phil agreed but said he
would go late and I must represent him at the beginning. Subsequently he told
me he would not go at all [and] said I must stall on everything as he had not
discussed Sec Genl with Bevin. The latter had, however, told him at lunch time
that Byrnes had said he did not want the UNO in the United States and he did
not think the President did either . . . My task at Stettinius flat in Claridges was,
therefore, an ungrateful one. Ed had three things.
(1) Sec Genl on which he produced 5 names (all small power) . . . Two
Canadians, Pearson & Robertson, 1 Venezuelan, Parra Perez, 1 Australian, Bruce
and 1 Dutchman, Van Royen [sic] were his 5. His others include Dick Law,
Eden and Lord Cranborne as well as Wellington Koo and Tsiang. It was an
irresponsible performance. Massigli replied superbly creating just the right

atmosphere of subtle contempt for these methods and refusing to go so far. I had little to do but associate myself with him. The other two, therefore, made no contributions either.

(2) Place of the site in U.S. Ed now said U.S. wanted U.N. to decide where. This is a complete reversal of his previous position as I pointed out. Again Massigli & I refused to consider question. The other two welcomed it. The talk, however, shewed difficulties. Massigli said necs to know if U.S. accepted conditions of U.N.O. for seat. We said West Europe cities might also offer etc. Ed. suggested a Sec[retaria]t Commission to visit U.S. It all petered out in desultory talk but he might bring the proposition up at the Exec . . .'

On 27 October the Executive Committee of the Preparatory Commission completed its report, which included the recommendation that the permanent headquarters of the U.N. should be in the United States.[9] Some three days earlier the U.S.S.R. had deposited its ratification of the Charter thereby bringing the Charter into force. The second meeting of the full Preparatory Commission took place at Church House on 24 November. Deliberations continued until 23 December. Eight technical committees were established, each charged with considering the appropriate chapters of the Charter and the relevant sections of the Executive Committee Report.[10] The Report played an indispensable part in the preparatory process, but the Commission did not in all cases adopt the recommendations and proposals of the Executive Committee. Indeed, even where the proposals of the Report were accepted they were sometimes strongly challenged in the Commission. This was true of the choice of a permanent site for the United Nations. The British in particular were prepared to wage a rearguard battle against the United States being designated as the site of the organization.

'Sunday December 9 1945
For nearly three weeks I have been too busy and exhausted to write up my diary. The worst is not yet over but I have taken today off . . . and I will try to summarise some of the main trends.

'. . . In the Committees [of the Preparatory Commission] all general attention is focussed on the site. We are in the middle of the battle and the issue is very doubtful. I can count 20 votes agst [the] U.S.A. which would be enough to block a decision, but some of these are very doubtful. The U.S. is now awakening to the fact that the majority of the world does not want the Headquarters in America. It is a great shock and though Byrnes himself would not really wish it there the Truman Administration is now thinking it will be politically bad for them if the seat is established elsewhere. So they are beginning to turn the heat on and Brazil which had promised to vote Europe has gone back to U.S.A. Phil, Spaak, Massigli with Fouque[s]-Duparc and myself had a meeting to decide tactics. But I cannot get them to decide on a place, though Geneva is definitely out, and Belgium-Luxembourg the most popular. Spaak decided to rest on the Great Power issue . . . The debate has so far gone well.

After a protracted struggle on procedure which shewed the difficulties of the problem the main debate began two days ago. The first day produced a sensation in Poland plumping firmly for Europe. The Philippine Delegate made a terrible speech in favour of the USA which did his cause much harm. On the second day Spaak made a great oration which should have great effect. But votes are not settled by arguments but on interests and power. If we can get a secret vote we should win but I doubt if we can win on an open vote for a secret vote. . . . The Arabs hold the key votes. They can decide the result since the Latin Americans, Australia, China & USSR and stooges will vote USA and the rest Europe . . .

'Wed Dec 12

. . . The debate on the site yesterday was rather tame. The tension is growing and many of our officials are losing their nerve as the U.S. gets more & more demanding. Both the House [of Representative] & the Senate have passed resolutions inviting the U.N.O. to go there. It may be that these signs of wounded pride will carry the day in their favour, for no one wants to offend the only nation with the power to give. It is scandalous that the U.S. should dream of using this power . . .

'Sunday 16 Dec

During the last hectic four days I have got back at midnight or after too tired and worn to write this diary. The great question of the site of U.N.O. has been settled.[11] The tactics of the winning side were far the cleverer. They had not only the recommendation of the Exec[utive] Cttee [of the Preparatory Commission] but a compact Lat American vote and the Soviet satellites easily handled. Nevertheless if there had been a secret vote they would have lost though no other site could have won. They succeeded in preventing the secret vote because the U.S.A. declared against it. Indeed for the last fortnight the U.S.A. has been working hard in secret. On Saturday [December 15] they were forced into the open. They can never say that the site was forced on them by a world which did not know what else to do. The vote on the secret vote and the vote on Europe shewed that the majority of the nations of the world wished the site to be outside the U.S. Ten European nations were unrepresented. Five votes were controlled by USSR and Czechoslovakia made no secret of the fact that it voted by force.

'. . . The US was determined to have the site as a matter of prestige. I always told my United States colleagues that they would settle the question. If they really maintained their pretended indifference they would not get the seat. If they pressed for it they would get it because they were the strongest power in the world. They did so . . .

'But the final result justifies the action of the Minister of State. By his courageous stand he has justified us in the eyes of Europe. Moreover, by forcing the U.S. to shew its hand and seek for the seat he has produced more important political results. As Stevenson confessed in his speech the U.S. can no longer pretend that a special responsibility for the success of the UNO does not lie upon her by the fact that she has the seat. She sought it . . .

'Wed 26 Dec

I worked until Xmas day at the same sort of pace and then I felt pretty washed out . . . I will try to sum up these last ten days sitting in a dressing gown before my bedroom stove.

'The chief incident has been the decision to put the seat in the East [ern U.S.] On the Friday while we were still discussing the qualifications and procedures Phil had little time to spare. He came & went having much F.O. business. I had thus to speak a good deal since we were still the leaders in the matter . . . as the question of the East or West of U.S. had already been raised I said that if the East was not chosen after the narrow vote on Europe & the seat placed 3000 miles further away, "I should consider not only sound judgment but chivalry dead in the world". Freitas Valle, Nervo and Zulueta the President of Precom [Prep. Commission], approached me in the tea interval and said we could carry a vote for the East now, when firm instructions had not been given and there was sympathy with Europe over her narrow defeat. Why did I not get [the] U.S.S.R. to agree? I said that if I approached Gromyko he would make conditions about other things e.g. the Sec Genl. They said they could win anyway. I telephoned Phil and persuaded him to agree. Freitas Valle proposed that the East be chosen, Nervo supported. Aus & China of course attacked. Phil came & supported. The vote was left over until Sat. Then there was a long wrangle about procedure. I was very anxious as to the result because if we did not succeed we should be much worse off. But the Soviet bloc came to our support — without bargaining. Manuilsky, clever man, proposed we should vote first on the West, thus reversing the unfair procedure when we were forced to vote first on Europe. The only snag was the French who opposed taking a vote because they had no instructions. I argued with them angrily . . . However this made little difference for France by her conduct has lost all influence. We had an overwhelming vote for the East so overwhelming that in the Plenary Session it was not disputed at all.[1][2] This as I explained in a telegram I sent to the S of S from Phil (without his seeing it) was a great point gained . . .

'On Monday Gromyko gave a farewell lunch at the Savoy to about 20 of the most important delegates. Phil could not go. I sat next to Sobolev who indicated that the Russians were well satisfied with the results of [the] Precom. At any rate Grom was in his most benignant mood. Afterwards he summoned Koo & Hoo, Stevenson, & myself to his room . . . The French were absent. We discussed the Sec Genl. He had previously told me and Stevenson that he wanted Simitch [Stanoje Simic], the Yugoslav Ambdr at Washington. By agreement with Stevenson I advocated Spaak first and Mike Pearson second. We demolished Simitch. Stevenson put up a number of U.K. names including Sir John Anderson, Sir A. Salter & Eden. Also Monnet. I would have none of these. But I insisted that, despite the seat in the US, Eisenhower was still the best choice &

would be received by the whole world with acclamation. Stevenson promised to consult his Govt but was sure the result would be negative.'

With the preparatory work concluded Webster was able to attend the first meetings of the General Assembly and the Security Council on 10 January and 19 January 1946 respectively. In his diary entry for 30 December Webster recorded with pleasure that Cadogan had agreed to devote all his time to the General Assembly whilst Orme Sargent looked after the Office. This meant that Webster did not have to carry a burden of work similar to that during the Preparatory Commission. Nevertheless, Webster was drawn into the fray more than he had hoped, writing numerous speeches and, among other things, negotiating with Stevenson and Gromyko over the election of states to the Security Council. The question of the election of a Secretary-General still remained outstanding. For a time the Americans toyed with the idea of having Anthony Eden as Secretary-General. This Webster opposed. The idea was finally killed by Ernest Bevin.[13] Instead the British and Americans agreed on Lester Pearson as their candidate. However, the Russians were unalterably opposed to Pearson though they indicated that they would accept Norway's Trygve Lie. It was difficult for the British and Americans to oppose such a qualified West European and Lie was finally appointed as a compromise candidate on 1 February 1946. Webster was not entirely happy with this choice and confided to his diary that 'Gladwyn would have done a far better job'.[14]

After these first meetings of the United Nations Webster provided his assessment of them in a letter to Isaiah Bowman: 'The General Assembly is now over and on the whole I am very satisfied with the result. The Security Council gave also a very remarkable performance. If it has not, like the infant Hercules actually strangled serpents in its cradle it has at least sent them back to their nests with a tin can tied to their tails.'[15] In April he attended the final meeting of the League of Nations. Ill health and a desire to return to academic life had, however, already led him to the conclusion that he should retire from the Foreign Office. At the age of sixty, having been awarded a K.C.M.G. in the New Year's Honours List, he ended his period of official service.[16]

CONCLUSION

The Historian as Diplomat

When asked to describe their role, members of the Foreign and Commonwealth Office (as it now is) speak with a common voice. Sir Alexander Cadogan's version of this orthodoxy, as expressed in a letter to Martin Gilbert, was:

> ... an Ambassador, or for that matter any Civil Servant ... [is] not 'hired' (as an American would say) to formulate policy: his duty is to supply his chief not only with all the relative facts that may help the latter in coming to his decision but also his own recommendations as to what should be done.[1]

One of Cadogan's successors as Permanent Under-Secretary of State, Lord Gore-Booth, writes similarly, '. . . the Permanent Under-Secretary, like all his colleagues, is a counsellor and not a courtier' and '. . . generally speaking the task of a government is to decide and the task of a diplomat at any level is to try to make the decisions work'.[2]

Contrast the words of Richard Crossman, reflecting on his experience as a Cabinet Minister:

> The really big thing I completely failed to notice was that in addition to the Cabinet Committees which only Ministers normally attend, there is a full network of official committees; and the work of the Ministers is therefore strictly and completely paralleled at the official level. This means that very often the whole job is pre-cooked in the official committee to a point from which it is extremely difficult to reach any other conclusion than that already determined by the officials in advance; and if agreement is reached at the lower level of a Cabinet Committee, only formal approval is needed from the full Cabinet. This is the way in which Whitehall ensures that the Cabinet system is relatively harmless.[3]

The description in an earlier chapter[4] of the passing of the Webster and Jebb memoranda, first through the interdepartmental committee under Richard Law, then through the Armistice and Post-War Committee under Clement Attlee, and then through the War Cabinet under Churchill, seems amply to illustrate the Crossman thesis, until one recalls Webster's extreme agitation about what might happen to the papers when the Cabinet, and particularly the Prime Minister, got hold of them. Clearly neither the Cadogan–Gore-Booth orthodoxy, nor the Crossman doctrine, expresses more than a facet of the truth, which, as always, is many-sided. In attempting to develop a somewhat rounder version of the truth than is offered by the foregoing extracts, there are perhaps some half-a-dozen variables that need to be identified and considered, and it is proposed to discuss these in the light of the illumination afforded by Webster's diary. Before doing this, however, it is necessary to examine the notion of rational choice, or decision, a theme that is now familiar enough to the scholar, but is rarely contemplated by the practitioner, at least in his descriptions of his activity.

In his justly-acclaimed book on the Cuban missile crisis, Graham Allison considered three approaches to decision-making, which he called models, the rational choice, the organizational process, and the bureaucratic politics models.[5] It is the first of these that is in question here. Historians and analysts of foreign policy have long employed, implicitly or explicitly, variants of this model. It assumes that in relation to a defined objective all possible courses of action are scanned, their respective consequences are assessed, and that course of action is selected which will go furthest towards achievement of the objective. Sometimes a refinement is introduced, whereby the course choice is seen as being affected not only by the degree of advance towards the objective that may be achieved, but also by the degree of probability that the postulated advance will be achieved: thus a course with a greater probability of achieving advance may be selected in preference to another which is less likely to achieve advance even though the advance, if achieved, would be greater.

The fallacies of this model as applied to practice are easily identified. In the first place there are always several objectives, never just one. In the memorandum 'The Four Power Plan', presented to the War Cabinet on 8 November 1942, it was stated: 'We have to maintain our position as an Empire and a Commonwealth. If we fail to do so we cannot exist as a World Power. And we have to accept our full share of responsibility for the future of Europe. If we fail to do that we shall have fought this war to no purpose . . .'[6] It rapidly became apparent after the war that action directed towards the maintenance of one of these objectives (such as keeping substantial forces east of Suez) might be incompatible with measures necessary for advancing the second (such as guaranteeing to keep a certain number of land and air forces on the mainland of Europe). And it is not merely with hindsight that this problem is identifiable: already before the war British policy had fallen between the two stools of half-hearted resistance to Japan in the Far East and half-hearted resistance to Germany and Italy in Europe. Recognizing that these objectives could not be realized by Britain alone, the Four Power Plan concluded that the fullest possible co-operation would be necessary after the war among Britain, the United States, the Soviet Union and China; but it did not point out that there would be no co-operation from the United States on the maintenance of the Empire, as Churchill's brushes with Roosevelt over India had already shown. So a further incompatibility of objectives existed. This is the typical situation in which foreign policy-makers have to work. The rational choice model has nothing to say about the assessment of course choices in relation to a variety of conflicting objectives.

Even if decision-makers were in agreement on a hierarchy of objectives (which they will usually not be) there would be no rational way by which preference could be determined for course choice alpha, with A_1 advantage and B_1 disadvantage in relation to objective 1, and A_2 advantage and B_2 disadvantage in relation to objective 2, over course choice beta, with M_1 advantage and N_1 disadvantage in relation to objective 1, and M_2 advantage and N_2 disadvantage in relation to objective 2. This formal illustration of complexity points to the second weakness of the rational choice model — that it postulates a completeness of information that in practice can never be realized. Choice can be made only among those courses of action that are seen to exist and to be feasible; but the information available may fail to reveal some possible courses of action, or may make others seem wholly impracticable. In addition, and more important, the calculation of the respective consequences of various choices can never be based on more than partial information, much of it intuitive: indeed it may well be the case that the response of decision-makers in state B to a particular action by state A will not be known by B's decision-makers themselves until they are confronted by the action in question. So there is no way in which A's decision-makers can assess with exactness the consequences of any course of action, and the preferring of one course to another must therefore be based in part upon judgment and intuition as well as upon calculation. This is so in relation to a single objective; it is even more so in those cases where decision-makers have the range, the capacity and the time to consider the implications of actions in relation to several objectives.

One further point is usually not considered. At what level is the model supposed to apply, or is it taken to apply at all levels? In the case of the world organization planning, the number of levels that might be identified include the Webster—Jebb level, the Cadogan level, the Secretary of State level, the Prime Minister level, the Cabinet Committee and War Cabinet levels, and the inter-state level. The rational choice model evidently has different degrees of relevance at different levels. Webster and Jebb had time to think and plan (an unusual situation in matters of foreign policy). Presumably at this level the greatest number of course choices could be identified and scanned. But what was the objective? To preserve Britain's world influence, which was seen as entailing preservation of the Empire? To restore and maintain the 'freedom' of Europe? To provide means for the maintenance of international peace and security? To construct a form of international organization that would ensure continued United States participation in the post-war world? These objectives were evidently by no means unrelated, but it was equally clear that action chosen to serve one of them might not always be helpful in relation to the others. So in making decisions (in this case formulating proposals for the new world organization), Webster and Jebb consciously or unconsciously gave priority to one rather than another among these objectives. Moreover, even at this level, as the foregoing chapters have clearly shown, there was not complete agreement: Webster, the historian and outside expert with the longer and more detached view but the less practical experience, naturally tended to see the third of the objectives as dominating the others (though he gave high priority to the fourth), whereas Jebb's primary concern was with the first. Moreover, both were fully aware of the political context within which they had to work and, as the genuflexions to Churchillian regionalism show, their scanning of course options was affected by this consideration as well as by their varying views about objectives.

At the Cadogan level the interplay among expertise, multiplicity of objectives, and context of operation was perhaps most clearly seen. Cadogan was exceedingly well-informed on the world organization question, not merely because he was a highly efficient Permanent Under-Secretary and a very rapid worker, but because he had spent ten years as head of the League of Nations section of the Foreign Office and saw very clearly not only the failures of Geneva but also the potential importance of an international organization of some kind. But Cadogan was also deeply involved in the complexity of interrelationships among separated and various problems: his interest was in policy (he was irritated by problems of organization and administration), and he regularly attended the War Cabinet and travelled extensively with Eden and with Churchill. From these continuous personal contacts with the highest political figures, he derived a lively, and sometimes impatient, awareness of the limits of political possibility. His choices in relation to the questions of world organization were thus influenced not just by the objectives of British policy that might be served by such an organization, but by a sensitive perception of what kind of an organization might be fitted into the pattern of Britain's external relations and internal political leadership.

As one moves towards the political level, the aspect worn by rational choice changes again. Eden, in Webster's opinion, 'saw the thing properly from the beginning I think' but '. . . he never looked at the papers which have done the trick for him until they had passed the Cabt Committee'.[7] Churchill had very firm, if not very clear ideas about the way the world ought to be run after the war, and he paid almost no attention to the information, proposals and recommendations prepared in the Foreign Office until he was forced to do so, partly by Eden, but mainly by the Dominion Prime Ministers. To apply the word 'rational' to the decisions at this level, in relation to any of the objectives that the world organization was intended to serve, would deprive the word of all meaning. It was a case of prejudgments, unmodified by consideration of alternative possibilities, overridden because of the political necessity not to be split from the Dominions. It is perhaps fair to note that the issue in question is an untypical one, and the political context unusual: long-range planning is not the activity in which the Foreign Office is normally engaged, and Churchill's authority, derived from his position as war leader and from his temperament and personality, was enormously greater than a Prime Minister can normally enjoy; but in these circumstances the rational choice model serves as a means not of describing how decisions were actually made but rather of identifying divergencies from a theoretical and idealized procedure.

The formulation of the British proposals for a new world organization was not, then, the result of rational choices, at least in the sense described above.[8] The proposals emerged from an interplay among individuals and groups, playing various roles, with varying interests and objectives. Critical components of this interplay were the time-scale, the type of issue in question, the relationship between the Foreign Office as an institution and the outside expert, the possession and diffusion of information and expertise, the political context and the role of Ministers, and the involvement of other interests, domestic and external.

International crisis is normally defined in terms of the magnitude of the issues seen to be at stake, the shortness of time within which decisions have to be taken, and sometimes the element of surprise in the events to which responses are seen to be necessary. Decision-making in crises is usually characterized by reduced ability to perceive a variety of possible courses of action, by intensifying commitment to a course once chosen, and so by small ability to modify or reverse a line of policy once it has been adopted. Thus the role of the official is likely to be reduced. The time-scale within which Webster and Jebb were operating was for a foreign policy question unusually long. The first paper on a future world organization was presented to the War Cabinet on 8 November 1942; the stimulus to action came from the Quebec and Moscow conferences in September and October 1943 when the three major allies recognized 'the necessity of establishing at the earliest practicable date a general international organization, based on the principle of the sovereign equality of all peace-loving states, and open to membership by all such states, large and small, for the maintenance of international peace and security';[9] the British memoranda prepared in accordance with this declaration were drafted and discussed in March and April 1944; Dumbarton Oaks was in August and September, and San Francisco in April, May and June 1945. The Charter was therefore in gestation over a period of more than two and a half years. Of course within that period there were times of intense activity — June 1943, April 1944, and the two great conferences — but the time-scale in general was such that the planners were able to explore and examine in depth the range and nature of the problem and, not less important, assess the extent to which particular solutions would be internationally acceptable, especially by the United States, the Dominions, and the smaller European powers.

The position of Webster and Jebb thus became exceptionally strong. The time at their disposal meant not merely that they were able to develop a deeper theoretical understanding of the problem than anyone else in the Office or the government, but that they knew what was likely to be acceptable to Britain's major partners. Thus the April 1944 memoranda, which contributed much to Dumbarton Oaks, and so to the Charter, were able to be drafted on the basis of earlier work in a very short time and in such a form that, though more general in language, they closely paralleled the United States proposals, and were generally acceptable to the Dominions.[10] But when Webster refers to his having educated

Jebb and the Foreign Office, and to the memoranda as being 'my plan', he perhaps underestimates the influence upon himself of the environment in which he worked. The United States and British proposals emerged with their similar ideas as a result of early talks among their respective authors, in which a high measure of agreement on fundamentals was discovered, and the whole of this process was critically governed by the time available for consideration of the problem.

This availability of time, which so strengthened the position of the experts, derived of course from the nature of the issue. It was not a question on which 'action this day' was called for: on the contrary, Churchill frequently complained about being required to consider the future of the world when he was wholly immersed in the effort of trying to ensure that there would be any future at all worth living in. Moreover it was not the kind of issue with which a foreign office in the normal course of business habitually deals. The work to which diplomats are accustomed, and in which they become skilled, consists in very large part of receiving and assessing information about developments outside their country, of formulating recommendations about (or sometimes deciding) what responses should be made, and of giving or carrying out instructions for the implementation of these responses. The nature of the responses may of course vary very widely, from conversations with another official, or with a foreign politician, to launching or carrying forward a commercial negotiation, to mobilizing a show of force; but overwhelmingly the activity relates to the handling of immediate issues as expeditiously as may be, usually under considerable time pressure, and with as much regard as possible to the likely effect of the responses on a wide range of not very precisely formulated interests or objectives.

The world organization planning was a matter of quite a different kind. It involved looking beyond pressing day-to-day problems to the imagining of future global constellations. (Roosevelt's determination to include China as one of the permanent members of the Security Council was in part politically motivated, but Britain's reluctance to acquiesce perhaps reflected poorer foresight – though had Roosevelt foreseen the nature of the China that was to emerge in 1949 he might, rightly or wrongly, have been less insistent.) It required an insight into the deep underlying trends and tendencies in the onward march of world history – not merely which states would rise and which decline, but how the quality and structure of the economic, strategic, technological, social and cultural relationships among peoples were developing and evolving, and what consequences were implied for institutional arrangements. In the context of these trends it was then necessary to consider what kind of compromise might best be made between the arrangements that might be most appropriate and the arrangements to which the significant world political leaderships might be prepared to agree. The problem therefore lacked sharp limits, not only in time but also in range: it involved all parts of the world and all states in the world, and in this respect also was untypical for foreign offices, which are commonly organized mainly in regional divisions. Finally, the relative newness of the question meant that there was no long-established and deeply-entrenched traditional method of dealing with it and attitude towards it, nor were there many members of the Office who considered this to be the area in which their primary expertise lay.

These were conditions in which it was easier for the experts to write what they believed than may normally be the case, provided they perceived with sufficient accuracy the political limits, external and internal, of what might be possible. The statement in this form is however over-simplified. There may have been few in the Office who saw this subject as their own, but had there been an ill-informed or inflexible Permanent Under-Secretary, the extent to which Webster's ideas could have come through must have been significantly reduced. Cadogan's diary in the Dilks edition records no concern with the world organization planning before the issue was broached with the Americans in April 1944 when the planners had already given many months of thought to the problem; but his speed of assimilation and his previous experience were such that Webster could record when the United States proposals were received in July, 'Gladwyn & I met Cadogan and discussed the paper for 1½ hours . . . He had already made his own examination and we had little to teach him. Both Gladwyn & I agreed that he was head and shoulders above all the others';[11] and in his summing-up on the day of signature of the Charter Webster records his own opinion that without Cadogan (and Eden) 'my efforts would have been of no avail'.[12]

In addition one must repeat the point that, although many of the ideas and some of the actual language in the Charter accord with Webster's own in the April 1944 memoranda, none the less these ideas and the words in which they were formulated resulted from discussions and interplay among persons and groups within and outside the Office and the United Kingdom, and they cannot rightly be seen as springing fully-fledged from the mind of Webster like Aphrodite from the sea-foam. Moreover, the much more detailed and formal nature of the United States proposals meant that although the Soviet draft was accepted as the initial basis of discussion, much more of the language of the American submission came through in the Dumbarton Oaks plan than of the British or the Soviet. Gerig's summary of the respective contributions made by the three is illuminating,[13] but the summary is not complete, for he does not notice, for instance, how it was the Soviet draft that explicitly laid down that Security Council decisions should be binding on all members of the Organization, and that Chapter II, paragraph 4 of Dumbarton Oaks (which became Article 2 (3) of the Charter, 'All members shall settle their international disputes by peaceful means in such a manner that international peace and security, and justice, are not endangered') almost exactly reproduces the language of Webster's Memorandum B, paragraph 44 (i), with the exception of 'justice' added at Chinese insistence in the second phase of the Dumbarton Oaks conversations. Even with a commentary written immediately after the events to which it refers, and with an intimate day-to-day record such as the Webster diary, it is thus not possible precisely to delineate the source of ideas and their development.

The longer the time-scale, and the more unusual or specialized the issue, the more influence the expert or the official is likely to have. But, as the previous paragraphs have suggested, the validity of these statements is conditioned by the institutional context within which the activity takes place. Like all organizations, though in varying degrees, the Foreign Office was (and is) characterized by a hierarchical structure, by standard operating procedures, by a traditional ethos, and by a strong *esprit de corps*. The effect of the hierarchical structure is to some extent modified by the operating procedure by which (except in times of acute crisis) business is first handled by a relatively junior officer and is passed with his recommendations up the hierarchy to whatever level is deemed appropriate for the matter to be determined. The apparent degree of freedom and initiative that this confers, however, is evidently affected by the extent to which junior officers are aware of, or feel the need to respond to, the expectations of their seniors, by the effectiveness of the organization's socialization processes, and by the strength of its ethos. Webster is repeatedly illuminating on these matters.

In terms of technical skills the Foreign Office clearly ranks high. Among these skills is drafting. Anyone who has sat on a committee composed of persons with varying expertise and levels of knowledge, with differing personal objectives and conceptions of the committee's objective, and respectively commanding prestige or authority not necessarily related to their knowledge of the committee's business, will be aware of the vital importance of the part played by the person recording the discussion and the resulting decisions, or drafting the instructions flowing from them. Cadogan notes on 4 March 1941: 'Completely confused discussion, ending in instruction to me to reconcile everything in draft telegram to Washington!'[14] Webster records on 22 May 1945: '. . . Committee III.1 got in a terrible mess. At the end no one knew what had been decided so I claimed to know with great firmness and the Sect just wrote down what I said. It was as easy as that.'[15] Perhaps more subtly, the result of the Cabinet meeting on 16 June 1943 was, in Webster's words, '. . . not so bad . . . The result which I suspect due to Bridges drafting as much as to anything else . . .'[16] And finally, see Webster's account[17] of the wide disagreements between the recollections of participants in the Dominion Prime Ministers' meeting of 11 May 1944, and the official account of that meeting as recorded in the minutes.

Of course the force of these points should not be exaggerated. The last of these examples shows the overriding authority of Ministers, for Bridges simply assumed that, irrespective of any merits of the case, the world organization papers would have to be revised because the Dominion Prime Ministers had accepted Churchill's position. That he was wrong in his recollection does not alter the fact of his attitude. So the conclusions one would draw from these instances about the importance of drafting would be something like the following:

well-drafted papers will be likely to carry if they are designed to accord with the opinions of significant members of the approving body (note Zimmern's report[18] of Canadian satisfaction with the world organization papers); a clearly formulated and agreed opinion in a political approving body will be decisive over an official view; frequently in all kinds of committee there will not be general agreement, or an opinion will not be clearly formulated — in those cases the form of the record, and the precise nature of the action that is thereafter seen to be necessary, are likely to be of critical importance. At the very least it is clear that the official contribution to policy-making (which includes the carrying out of a decision as well as the determination of it) will often be substantially greater than orthodoxy suggests.

It is in this context that the significance of Webster as an outside expert is perhaps particularly to be noted. The principle that peace is an interest of the whole of mankind was seen by Webster not as the abstract statement of an ideal, but as a foundation upon which, with due regard to the hard reality of political relationships, institutional structures could be built. Such principles were not commonly held among members of the Foreign Office — at least not if they were seen as carrying practical implications for policy. The world was as E. H. Carr (formerly one of their number) had described it — one in which international government was impossible since power, an essential condition of government, was organized nationally, and in this condition of anarchy issues would be settled primarily (if not quite solely) by the power of the respective protagonists. The League, or any successor to it, might be useful as an additional mechanism through which Britain's power might be deployed to further British interests, but was not to be contemplated as an expression of airy-fairy notions about collective interest which were remote from reality. Such an ethos in the Office was natural. For a century Britain had with remarkable success (and having unique capabilities) followed Palmerston's maxim that Britain had no permanent allies but only permanent interests; the organizational structure, the method of working, and the flow of business in a Foreign Office mean that issues tend to be seen within a limited framework and have to be handled according to the immediate pressures and within the means immediately available; and the experience of officials who had lived through the terrible years of the 1930s could not but confirm the belief that power was ultimately decisive. As the foregoing pages have shown, Webster, idealist in his realism, frequently felt profound irritation at this prevailing ethos in the Office: '. . . the young men became a little less hard boiled. But they are immersed in this nauseous atmosphere and look on every negotiation as an intrigue.'[19] 'It is no use appealing to principle. The Office is all on the other side and opportunistic as usual. It has little sense of the long-term values.'[20] 'Gladwyn never remembers that 18 months ago he was talking much the same nonsense as the P.M. is talking now.'[21]

This last quotation makes the point sharply. Comparison of Appendices A and B with Appendix C shows how far opinions had moved. Jebb, a man of strong personality and high intelligence, was able over the months of partnership with Webster to develop a broader view than is usually possible for the normal career official – though this is not of course to say that Webster's outlook prevailed over his own, as their disagreements over the voting question at Dumbarton Oaks and after sufficiently show. It took a man as big as Jebb to be able partially to transcend his experience and his training; but it must at least be open to doubt whether this could have happened had he not brought into the Office a man with thirty years' experience outside it, with a personality not much less strong than his own, and with a mind less incisive than his but deeply versed in the history and the theory of the subject.

Their collaboration meant that Eden's predilections could be served. Before he became Secretary of State, Eden, first as Under-Secretary and then as Minister for League of Nations Affairs, had acquired extensive experience of international organization. The failure of the League experiment with which he had been associated caused him not to abandon his belief that some form of global peace-keeping institution was necessary, but to recognize that only a new type of structure, accepting the fact of inequality of power, might be able to be successful. Without Eden, and Cadogan, as Webster recognized, his work and that of Jebb would probably have been abortive; but without them Eden would not have seen the Dominion Prime Ministers mobilized against Churchill, and the brief for the British delegation at Dumbarton Oaks would have been unlikely to have been so close to the Americans' as, to the great advantage of the negotiations, in fact was the case. The crucial components of the amalgam were Eden, Cadogan, the Office as refracted through Jebb, and the outside expert.

But the case illustrates admirably the thesis of Ray Tanter that 'influencing policy involves seeking out an organization or individual whose preferences require the particular model or research findings that a scholar has to offer'.[22] Webster did not consciously use these tactics within the Office, but was lucky in having a Secretary of State for whom they were in fact appropriate. He saw their value at a different level, however, as shown by his frustration at being unable to get the memoranda transmitted to Washington, because he had correctly assessed the extent to which they would be acceptable in the United States, and once support for them had been demonstrated in that quarter their future would be assured. The Tanter point is obvious enough; but it is an alert practitioner who will act by instinct in accordance with it if the principle has not been spelled out to him, and it appears that it was more by good fortune than by deliberate intent that the influential British hands that received the world organization papers were predisposed to receive them with approval.

The fourth of the interacting variables that affects the degree of influence exerted by the official has already been touched upon. Choices of courses of action can be made only among those that are seen to exist. Confidence in rejecting an official recommendation will be affected by the degree of technicality of the question.[23] Information is thus critical. The amount of information received in a large organization like a foreign office is far more than can be assimilated and acted upon by persons at the head of the organization, so at successive stages of communication information is selected for onward transmission, the selections being influenced by expectations, values and beliefs, and by assessments of significance deriving from conceptions of task and knowledge of the situation (or occasionally according to beliefs about what the recipient of the information desires to hear). The significance of information may be missed by an agent if he is inadequately informed about a situation, but the requirements of secrecy and confidentiality impose restrictions upon wide dissemination of information. Moreover, established procedures for the circulation or classification of information will determine the extent to which relevant information reaches appropriate destinations in good time. Some information will never enter the system at all. Finally, understanding of information will be affected by the degree of scientific, economic, strategic or other specialist content that it may have.

For all these reasons no system is ever completely informed, and none can ensure accurate appreciation and effective co-ordination of that information which is received by the system. Thus the alternatives that are seen to be open emerge from a succession of previous judgments, from unconscious value-filtering, and from the operation of routinized procedures, and this is one of the main reasons for seeing policy-making as a process in which it will frequently not be possible to determine quite how and when the issue came to be resolved in the way it was.

The world organization case is again not typical in this regard. There was only a small flow of information about the subject from foreign representatives at listening-posts round the world. The activity related to the state of the world at some unknown future time and in some unknown condition. The skills that bore upon it seemed therefore to be historical, theoretical and prophetic, and in skills such as these the politician – particularly one such as Churchill – was likely to see himself as the expert. As Webster recorded: 'He would never even organise a small commando raid without taking some expert advice even if he did not follow it. But here he is trying to shape the whole of the future without saying a word to his Cabt, For Sec or their officials.'[24]

But in fact there was information that was relevant and expertise that was critical, and ultimately these counted. The exposition of Churchill's ideas against which Webster was expostulating in the previous extract was to a group of Americans in Washington including the Vice-President, Wallace, the Secretary of War, Stimson, the Secretary of the Interior, Ickes, the chairman of the Senate Foreign Relations Committee, Connally, and the Under-Secretary of State, Welles. According to Churchill, they all said 'that they had been thinking on more or less the lines which I had propounded, and thought that it was not impossible that American opinion would accept them or something like them.'[25] The information that Churchill perceived to have been conveyed to him by this meeting was ill-founded. It was soon to become clear that two of the fundamental elements of Churchill's position – a continuing and overt

Anglo-American alliance, and United States membership of a Council for Europe — were in fact unlikely to be acceptable in Washington, and Webster had a better understanding of this from his American contacts. The better quality of his information was clearly shown when Stettinius arrived in London in April 1944, and discussions with Isaiah Bowman confirmed how close were most of the essential assumptions about the post-war organization in the minds of the two sets of planners on either side of the Atlantic. Likewise the information in the Office about the attitude of the Dominions, and their natural opposition to a Council of the Big Four to run the world, was even more strikingly confirmed at the May Dominion Prime Ministers' meeting, much to Churchill's surprise and chagrin.

The technical skill that was relevant was to devise some coherent scheme which would be politically acceptable and would reconcile the objectives of on the one hand universality and on the other concentration of authority in the hands of those with the resources and so the responsibility for the exercise of power. The striking difference between the Webster memoranda and the United States proposals is the argumentation, political, philosophical and historical, in the former, and the drafting precision of the latter. 'I wish I dare have been so bold in my papers', wrote Webster, 'But they would certainly have been rejected, if I had, on the plea that the United States would not consider such things!'[26] There may in this have been some rationalization of regretful recognition by Webster that what he had written looked long-winded and woolly against the detail of the American provisions; but beneath the generalities the essential technical issues were there.

Jebb, like his Prime Minister, was a 'Great Power' man. So was Webster — which was one of the reasons why Jebb asked for him to be transferred to his department rather than Toynbee or any other of the Foreign Research and Press Service.[27] But the historian Webster had a deep understanding of the Concert of Europe and the effects of its behaviour on the smaller states and peoples of the continent. He had extensive knowledge of the special importance to Britain of relations with small powers, buttressed by his recent research on Palmerston, and by his understanding of the significance of the emergence of the Dominions as fully independent states. Further, he perceived in some degree the growing unity of the world at least in economic and strategic terms (as the first world war had demonstrated, and the second was even more strikingly confirming). For reasons such as these the perspective in which Webster saw the world organization problem was different from that of his Foreign Office colleagues, and indeed of most of the Americans. It is difficult to imagine Webster, even under the stress of the seemingly fatal disagreement with the Soviet Union over voting procedure in the Security Council, ever, like Jebb, contemplating writing in a minute 'if we got a treaty with U.S. about Germany & Japan he did not care about a World organisation at all'.[28] The problem was to reconcile the fact of great power resources (and their consequent natural and proper concern that direction of these resources could not be in any hands other than their own), and the no less proper desire of the smaller powers to ensure that their interests and aspirations were safeguarded and could not be overridden by great power combination or mutual connivance. The problem was expressed on the one hand in the Soviet determination to have unanimity among the four (or five) great powers in all Security Council business, and on the other in the smaller powers' efforts at San Francisco to weaken the 'veto'; while United States uncertainty appeared in the unhappy sentence in their proposals, 'Provisions will need to be worked out with respect to the voting procedure in the event of a dispute in which one or more of the members of the council having continuing tenure are directly involved.'[29]

The particular solution found for this problem (that of the broad political issue that lay behind the dispute, not of the mechanics of the voting formula) reflected the particular skills and outlook that Webster possessed. All accounts confirm that it was the British delegation that laid special stress on the Purposes and Principles set out in Chapter I of the Charter, and it is this Chapter which more than any other reproduces or contains the essence of the language of Webster's April 1944 memoranda. This was the technical mechanism — exercise of authority by the great powers, but only within the framework of agreed principles of international conduct — by which what Webster called the Great Power Alliance theory and the League theory were harmonized, and the particular nature of the solution reflects his expertise. It is hardly to be doubted that a solution to the problem of one kind or another would have been found, but it is certain that the nature of the argument at San Francisco, and possible that its outcome, and probable that the degree of world-wide acceptance of the outcome, would all have been different had the solution proposed been of a different kind.

From the foregoing discussion it might appear that the facet of the truth represented by Crossman's statement about the role that Ministers are able to play is the most important one. This will not always be the case. It is common in Britain for Ministers to change office frequently while the governments of which they are members stay in office for some years (contrasting with the situation in the French Third and Fourth Republics, where Ministries changed frequently but the same Minister often reappeared at the same post in successive governments: especially was this the case at the Quai d'Orsay). But a Minister who does hold the same office for a number of years (Denis Healey at Defence from 1964—70 is a recent example) may develop an expert knowledge that will alter the character of his relations with his office. Eden had become a junior minister at the Foreign Office in 1931, and was Foreign Secretary from 1935 to 1938. He returned to the same office in 1940, and for the third time from 1951 to 1955. By the middle of the war his experience in the office was considerable, and he had acquired high technical skill, good understanding and extensive knowledge. Moreover, part of that experience, as mentioned previously, was in a specially created office for dealing with League of Nations affairs. This reflected his interest, and his orientation towards world politics.

In normal times a problem that relates to a Minister's special skills and interests will be likely to attract a disproportionate amount of his attention. During the planning period for the new world organization, however, Eden as a member of the War Cabinet was deeply involved in the general prosecution of the war, he was believed to command the special confidence of Churchill, he travelled extensively both with Churchill and on his own account, and he served at the same time as Leader of the House of Commons. Cadogan in his diary refers repeatedly to the difficulties of conducting policy when the responsible Ministerial head was so much away from the office. From the point of view of the officials the difficulty was aggravated by Eden's determination to get away to the country as often as possible at week-ends, and Webster at one point irascibly noted: 'Eden is sulking in the country and even Dick Law suggested he might go away for the weekend when he heard Cadogan would attend [the Armistice and Post-War Committee]. ... The irresponsibility of Ministers is almost beyond belief but I have had so much opportunity of seeing it in my official life that I have now come to expect it. No wonder that the Civil Service which, whatever else it is, is conscientious often comes to despise them.'[30]

In this extract, like Cadogan in his frequent outbursts, Webster was perhaps insufficiently allowing for the variety of roles that a Minister has to play, and this again affects the influence of the official. What division of his time he makes between Parliament and his department is always a difficult decision for a Minister, and Eden's Leadership of the House throughout this period aggravated the problem. Had he not obtained from his absences from London regular relief from the pressure of heavy responsibility and multifarious roles his judgment would almost certainly in time have suffered. But equally the only intermittent attention that he was able to give to the affairs of the Office might have had serious consequences with a less effective Permanent Under-Secretary than Cadogan. These were conditions, however, to maximize official influence, given the satisfaction of one further condition, namely the status of the Minister in Cabinet.

A Minister without strong opinions and clear judgment is likely more readily to accept official recommendations. But such a Minister may not exercise much influence in Cabinet unless he has a strong personal political base. On the other hand, a Minister who has status and authority in the Cabinet is likely also to be able to view official papers critically. The conditions in which the influence of officials on major policy-making is likely to be greatest are those in which they 'know the Minister's mind' and thus can present proposals of a kind and in a manner that he will approve, in which the Minister commands influence in Cabinet, in which he plays many roles and thus can devote only a portion of his attention to any one, in which the subject is one of interest to the Minister and which he therefore desires to promote, in which there is a degree of technicality sufficient to give the Minister an advantage over his colleagues but not so great as to make it difficult for him to master the subject in the limited time at his disposal, and in which there are few or no immediate political implications that might disturb other members of the government. All these conditions were satisfied in the matter of world organization planning, but there was one further element in the policy process – the Prime Minister.

The diary sufficiently chronicles the ups and downs in the officials' struggle to overcome this obstacle, and there is no need to repeat it here. Suffice it to recall Webster's despair at Eden's seeming unwillingness to do battle with the Premier, his generous recognition that perhaps the Secretary of State knew all along the best way of handling the Old Man, and the perfunctory attention given by the Cabinet once Churchill had given way. Even at the first consideration of the papers by the Armistice and Post-War Committee the 'covering brief and papers & Jebb's on Security [were] all passed with small alterations of no consequence. . . . Flemings paper on the other hand on coordination of economic and political organisation has foundered. . . . Cadogan who was present at the Cabt Cttee said they did not know what they were doing.'[31] On 7 July 1944 the Cabinet passed the papers without discussion, leaving a few points for further consideration by the Armistice and Post-War Committee, Churchill having walked out; on 4 August, after Webster and Malkin had sailed, the papers that formed the instructions for Dumbarton Oaks were finally approved by the Cabinet, Churchill being 'cynically jocular' and at 11.55 saying 'There now: in 25 mins. we've settled the future of the World. Who can say that we aren't efficient';[32] while on 21 December, when policy decisions on the crisis over the voting formula were urgently required, 'The old man had put local govt first & they took nearly 2 hours over it. Only S of S insistence got our papers discussed at all. No-one knew anything about them . . . It is really amazing how we are governed.'[33] As Cadogan said about the same occasion, 'Then World Organisation! A complete madhouse – P.M. knows *nothing* about it . . . we want to have a mind of our *own* and no one will give any attention to it.'[34]

The factor that caused the Prime Minister grudgingly and with ill-grace to give way (not to change his mind) was of course the external context, and this is the final variable of which account should be taken. At the top political level, with the tide of battle beginning to run their way, but with the magnitude of the threat from German and Japanese military might still dominating their minds, it was natural for Stalin, Roosevelt and Churchill to think in terms of retaining in their own hands the ability to ensure that no such threat should again be allowed to develop. For Stalin this determination was reinforced by his conviction of the ineluctable hostility of capitalist-controlled states (whatever aspects of friendliness expediency might cause them from time to time to wear), so the defence of Soviet sovereignty and the exploitation of new-won power to increase Soviet security was a central tenet of his policy. For Roosevelt the United States' historical experience of relative isolation from external pressures was not now to be reversed when American capabilities were at their zenith, and in any case, even if he had not himself been determined to maintain the sovereign authority of the United States, his memory of the Senate's rejection of Woodrow Wilson and the League of Nations was vivid enough to sustain his resolution. For Churchill, dreaming of a united imperial system with Britain at its head, the prospect of Britain as one of three (or four) world policemen supervising local police forces to maintain order round the world fitted both his sense of British greatness and his judgment of what was feasible and practical.

But for two of the big three, influences from both their domestic and their external environments called these images into question. The United States planners, some drafted academics, like Webster in Britain, others career foreign servants, had from the early days thought in similar terms to Webster, and by the time of Stettinius's visit to London in April 1944 Roosevelt had accepted principles for an organization basically similar to those being developed in London. His care not to get too far ahead of Congress and opinion at times led him to perhaps excessive caution: it was not until after Governor Dewey, his Republican opponent for the Presidency, had expressed concern at reports that the four participants at Dumbarton Oaks were planning to subject the other nations of the world to their coercive power[35] that the President approved the principle that great powers party to a dispute should not vote in the Security Council. His Secretary of State, Cordell Hull, had from the early days of 1942—3 opposed Roosevelt's Churchill-like ideas of regional organizations with a World Council, rather than a world organization;[36] and Hull maintained this position consistently with his planning advisers and in his discussions with Congressional leaders. The arguments mobilized to persuade the President referred to the danger that conflicts among regional organizations might develop which the world council would be unable to control; to the dominance over a region that a great power might inevitably establish, a dominance that the Latin Americans in the western hemisphere would certainly wish to avoid (although in fact in 1945 the Latin Americans surprisingly became most ardent advocates of the Monroe Doctrine); to the undesirability both of European or Asiatic states participating in a western hemisphere council, and of United States participation in a European council; to the consequent probability that regional organization would lead to a recrudescence of United States isolationism.

These were the arguments that Webster and Jebb had identified in their discussions with the United States planners. The arguments persuaded Roosevelt and he remained firm in his conviction. They left Churchill unmoved. He believed, not without reason, that only states with a major interest in a dispute would make the efforts necessary to bring it to a conclusion, and from this he deduced that peace-keeping must be based on regional organs. He believed, secondly, and again not without reason, that many of the world's recent troubles had grown out of the disunity of Europe, and movement towards confederal (if not federal) arrangements in Europe was desirable. Thirdly, he was profoundly convinced that only if the big three could continue to work together after the war could peace be preserved, partly because differences among them would permanently threaten peace, and partly because they alone would have the resources to maintain peace, and so should carry the responsibility and the authority for doing so.[37]

None of these principles was without merit. But they were inconsistent with each other, and they reflected a lack of understanding of Britain's environment. Such lack of understanding is not uncommon, and many foreign policy failures result. In this case the internal and external pressures were sufficient to avert such a consequence. The reasons that gave the Foreign Office planners unusual influence have already been analysed. To their proposals, and their manoeuvrings as described by Webster, were added the facts of Britain's strategic situation. The strategic interconnections of one theatre with another were daily being demonstrated, and it made small strategic sense, particularly for an island state heavily dependent on open world-wide trading routes, to try to draw strategic boundaries round geographically-defined regions. The arguments were summarized in Memorandum C of the papers prepared for the Dominion Prime Ministers in May 1944 and submitted to the War Cabinet in July:[38] this Memorandum was written by Jebb with some assistance from Webster, but it was no more than an edited version of two papers that had been accepted by the Chiefs of Staff as suitable to be used as a basis for discussion.[39] The Chiefs did not, indeed, hold any brief for the planners' proposals (on the contrary they agreed with Churchill in disliking giving time to thinking about the post-war period when they were deeply engaged in trying to win the war); and as the diary shows they were by no means firm in adhering to their acceptance in principle of the papers on which Jebb's Memorandum C had been based. The strategic facts could, however, not be gainsaid.

To the role played by the Chiefs must be added the attitudes of other Ministers. They were divided. Cripps, and probably Beaverbrook, agreed with the Prime Minister's assessment of the problem, and with the essentials of his solution to it. Eden, as has been shown, took a strongly different view, and Attlee, though not well versed in the details of the question, had long been interested in world government and so was much closer to the position of Eden than to that of Churchill. The papers of Attlee's closest associate, Bevin, reveal interest in the I.L.O. and the functional aspect of the U.N. rather than in general principles, and it is probable that Cranborne (later Lord Salisbury), who had resigned from the Foreign Office with Eden in February 1938, broadly agreed with his former chief. The composition of the Cabinet committee that under the chairmanship of Attlee first considered the memoranda in April 1944 was thus likely to result in a favourable verdict on them, as in fact happened with the exception of the economic machinery paper. Had the membership of this committee, and its chairmanship, been different, the reception of the memoranda might well have been less favourable also, and as Crossman recorded in the passage quoted at the beginning of this chapter, once a Cabinet committee has reached a conclusion only formal approval is likely to be required at Cabinet level. Who happens to be on a particular body to which business happens to be routed is always liable to be a matter of major significance.

So by the end of April 1944 the tide was running against the Prime Minister, though he had as yet by no means become aware of its strength. The *coup de grâce* was administered by the Dominion Prime Ministers. One of the two major inconsistencies in Churchill's objectives was his wish to see Britain as one of three (or four) world policemen in a World Council while at the same time remaining (or becoming) head of an imperial system. Indeed, the justification for Britain's claiming such a world role could be found only in her position as the centre of a world empire. But the Dominions, their full independence but recently legalized in the Statute of Westminster in 1931 and re-emphasized by the contributions they had made to the war effort, were wholly unwilling to consider either a renewed centralization of authority in London, or a world system in which four powers would be given superior status, and their status, with that of others, would be subordinate. So the imperial system, which alone could justify the role that Churchill saw for Britain, would be destroyed if the structure within which that role might be played were created. Webster had appreciated this problem from the start, taking account not merely of the attitude of the Dominions but of smaller states generally, with many of whom Britain had been historically associated. The matching of the Jebb—Webster proposals to the aspirations of the Dominions, on good relations with whom Britain's influence depended, thus ensured their acceptance despite the powerful irritation of the Prime Minister.

The final critical component of Britain's external environment was, of course, the United States. The other main inconsistency in Churchill's objectives lay in his desire to preserve an Anglo-American alliance and to have the United States as a member of his Council of Europe. The long-standing United States tradition of holding aloof from the affairs of squabbling Europe made it virtually certain that if the world were regionally organized the United States would expect a major role in the western hemisphere, and might accept one in the Pacific, but would wish to get back out of Europe. But the major purpose of an Anglo-American alliance for Churchill was precisely to make certain that the United States should associate herself with Britain in trying to ensure that the mainland of Europe should not again be threatened with domination by a single power, whether that power was the Soviet Union or Germany. By the time the United States and British proposals were exchanged in July the Prime Minister had been defeated in London, but knowledge of the United States views, as conveyed by Stettinius and Bowman in the previous April, converged with the attitudes of the Dominion Prime Ministers to make Churchill's position virtually untenable.

So it came about that the ideas that had been developed largely by Webster out of his historical knowledge and insight, his friendship with influential Americans, his close partnership with Jebb, and his fifteen months' experience in the Office, eventually formed the basis for the instructions to the group of British negotiators at Dumbarton Oaks. With instructions of the kind that Churchill wanted, Cadogan, so he asserted, would not have agreed to lead the delegation,[40] but he was happy with those that the major members of the delegation had themselves drafted (as Castlereagh wrote his own instructions for the Congress of Vienna).[41] The carrying out of instructions in international negotiations, however, requires different techniques from those needed to achieve a desired policy outcome, and operates under rather different influences from those in the policy-determination process. The concluding sections of this chapter consider these techniques and influences in the light of Webster's diary record.

It is difficult to imagine any human interaction the structure of which is zero-sum — in which, that is to say, the gains of one party are precisely equivalent to the losses of the other party. The typical situation is one in which any outcome involves some advantage and some disadvantage for each participant, though the balance of advantage over disadvantage is likely to be much greater for some than for others. In most situations participants will have shared common interests (in which by co-operation they can advance a shared purpose), complementary interests (in which by exchange they can derive mutual advantage) and opposed interests (in which the gratification of one will involve the denial of the other). International negotiations are almost always of this nature, not necessarily in the issue itself around which the negotiation is conducted, but in the issue together with its context. Thus the dispute with the Soviets at Dumbarton Oaks and after on voting procedure in the Security Council involved the common interest of maintaining peace through agreement on institutional arrangements, the complementary interest of mutually exchanging some loss of future freedom of action, and the opposed interests of facilitating or hindering the spread of communism.

The number of variables affecting the outcome of a negotiation is very large. Those that are reflected in the Webster diary (and they are among the most significant) are the general international and domestic context within which the negotiation is taking place; the participants' various perceptions of the capabilities both of themselves and of others; the nature and range of the issue and the scope for trade-offs or compromise; the degree and nature of communication among the parties and, allied to this, the degree of participation of the parties; and the protagonists' perceptions of their own objectives and those of others, and of the nature of the problem. Some analysts of mediation have suggested a divorce between one type of mediatory technique for settling issues (when a mediator has authoritative support, is skilful in suggesting solutions, and produces settlements, if at all, usually in the form of a compromise) and another type of technique (when solutions emerge from the parties themselves, the task of a mediator being so to widen perceptions of the issue and of objectives that alternative goals or means appear).[42] The former may be called conflict settlement, the latter conflict resolution. The process of trade-off as against re-evaluation can occur without mediation, and both types of process appear in the Dumbarton Oaks—San Francisco negotiations. The major issues in dispute with which Webster was concerned were the Security Council voting formula (raised at Dumbarton Oaks, settled at Yalta, re-emergent at San Francisco, resolved in Moscow), the representation of the 16 republics of the

Soviet Union (raised at Dumbarton Oaks and settled at Yalta), and regionalism versus universalism (resurrected — after its decease in London — and resolved in San Francisco).

When the Dumbarton Oaks conference assembled in August 1944 the military situation was seen as being sufficiently favourable for virtual certainty that Germany would be eventually defeated, and Japan would surely follow. The respective contributions of the major allies to those impending defeats were, however, very different. The long-awaited Anglo-American landing in northern France had taken place on 6 June, and had been successfully consolidated with the clearing of the Cherbourg peninsula and the move into Brittany and towards Paris, but eastward movement out of the secured territory towards the French Channel ports and Belgium had not begun; the decision to press ahead with the southern France landing and so to withdraw from Alexander the landing-craft and aircraft he needed to press home his Italy offensive had only just been finally taken; the Italian offensive, mainly for this reason, was about to be halted by the Germans on the Gothic line between Florence and Bologna; while in the Far Eastern theatre the Japanese were being hard pressed in Burma and in the Pacific by the American navy, but no decisive blows had yet been struck, and the Soviets were still neutral. The Anglo-American forces were stretched to the limit, and although they were able to maintain their offensives, they needed all the possible support they could find. The Soviets in contrast, their hands in the east being free, had just launched their massive summer offensives over the whole of their western front. These offensives were on the point of bringing about the withdrawal from the war of Finland in the north and Bulgaria and Roumania in the south. They had brought the Soviet armies deep into southern Poland and soon to the frontiers of Hungary; and they had stimulated the Polish resistance to rise against the Germans in Warsaw, a rising which the Russians felt strong enough coldly to allow the Germans to destroy, so that the Polish government in London would have no power base from which they could resist the Soviet imposition of a government for Poland dominated by members of the Polish communist party.

How long the reach of Soviet military power into Europe would be thus remained very uncertain, but in the extremities of war the speed and size of the Soviet victories could be matters only for rejoicing, tempered though it might be by fears about growing Soviet strength, and by bitter feelings about Warsaw. The lesson of the successes of Stalin's commanders for the British and Americans, however, was to drive home the necessity of maintaining good relations with the Soviet Union if there were to be any chance for peace after the war, and for these reasons the bargaining position of the U.S.S.R. was very powerful from the midsummer of 1944 onwards. Even after the collapse of Germany in May 1945, and before the dropping of the first atomic bomb on Hiroshima in August, the desirability of hastening the end of the war against Japan by persuading the Soviet Union to lend her weight sustained the bargaining power that Moscow commanded.

These were the external conditions in which the Dumbarton Oaks conversations, and their sequel, had to be conducted. It was fortunate that there was substantial agreement among the three, and later with China, on the main structure that a new organization might take. On minor disputed questions, such as whether or not at the Dumbarton Oaks stage to include arrangements for economic and social questions, the Soviets did not press their position too hard. But on two major questions — membership of the organization by the 16 republics of the Soviet Union, and voting in the Security Council by parties to a dispute — they refused to compromise, and Webster's diary sufficiently records the grave anxiety that this firmness created. Nothing in the international situation changed to cause the Soviet Union to be more cautious or flexible: indeed by Yalta the Soviets had occupied East Prussia, had moved through Poland over the German frontier, and had nearly completed the conquest of Hungary, while in Italy Alexander was halted, and in the west the British and Americans had barely begun to recover from the shock of the Ardennes offensive and were still four weeks from the Rhine. It was for other reasons, then, that settlement of the first disputed question, and seeming settlement of the second, became possible at Yalta.

Summit conferences are sometimes hazardous proceedings. Private meetings of the main protagonists may be imprecisely recorded or recalled and so lead to future recrimination or accusations of bad faith. Personal dislike between an ambassador and a foreign minister is likely to be less damaging than personal dislike, if such develops, between two heads of government. Misjudgments of personality, of strength or weakness, of intention, of integrity, are likely to be more firmly adhered to if made by a head of government personally. Adequate briefing, and mastery of questions at issue, may be difficult for a head of government to achieve with his multifarious concerns. As Cadogan noted: 'The P.M. got rather off the rails. Silly old man — without a word of warning to Anthony or me, he plunged into a long harangue about World Organization, knowing nothing whatever of what he was talking about and making complete nonsense of the whole thing. The worst of it was that what he said was completely contrary to the line already agreed with the Americans!'[43]

What summit conferences will do is to change the perceptions of the protagonists, whether for good or ill. This seems in at least one respect to have occurred at Yalta, and mainly because of this the settlement of the two issues became possible. Webster's diary records rumours and reports about the way individual attitudes in London on the voting question shifted under the influence of mounting Soviet success in the war, and in his deep concern he gives the impression that almost he alone (and Professor Brierly and Lord Cecil, outside the policy-making process) wished to stand firm on the principle that the great powers could not put themselves outside the obligations of United Nations membership by retaining the right to vote (and so to exercise a veto) in disputes to which they were a party. This impression is confirmed by Churchill's telegram to Roosevelt on 4 October: '. . . we are pretty clear that the only hope is that

the Great Powers are agreed [i.e. unanimous]. It is with regret that I have come
to this conclusion, contrary to my first thought.'[44] But at least at this early time
it appears that Churchill's implication of agreement on the issue in London
misrepresented the views of his Foreign Secretary, and Cadogan clearly
recognized the importance of the principle, while becoming increasingly
pessimistic about the possibility of getting it accepted. The steady drift against
the adherents to the principle, a drift that seems to have carried Eden along, was
abruptly checked by the news of Washington's advocacy in a telegram to
Moscow (without consultation with London) of the compromise sketched at
Dumbarton Oaks by Jebb and Cadogan (and also claimed by the Americans to
have been thought of by them), but eventual Cabinet and Dominions agreement
to support Washington was again undermined with news of Moscow's continued
resistance. It was in these circumstances that Churchill, in the face of the Soviet
objection, said he would not back Roosevelt, and Roosevelt began considering
settlement procedures: '. . . the President has told Halifax he is ready to barter
the veto agst the 16 republics. All this is expediency & trickery and there is no
principle amongst these men who have held power until they are unable to make
decent and honest judgments.'[45]

The available evidence on the Yalta conference does not show whether the
barter that Webster found so outrageous in fact took place. It is perhaps
significant, however, that immediately after Stalin on 7 February 1945
announced Soviet acceptance of the compromise on the voting formula Molotov
raised the question of membership of the world organization by the Soviet
republics and said that the Soviets would not now press for membership of all
sixteen, but would be satisfied with the admission of three, or at the minimum
two, to which Roosevelt replied that the foreign ministers should study this new
proposal, and Churchill stated that he had great sympathy with the Soviet
request.[46] It is not possible to tell whether there had been private discussions
before the plenary, or whether the modification of the previous Anglo-American
opposition to the sixteen republics proposal was an instantaneous response in
relief at the Soviet acceptance of the voting formula. But at the very least one
can say that the disputes over the two questions were settled in immediate
succession after a concession was made on one of them.

It is, however, the Soviet position in relation to the formula that is perhaps of
greater interest. Throughout the Dumbarton Oaks conversations, as is shown by
the Webster diary and by the United States records of the discussions, Gromyko
was courteous and co-operative in discussion, accepted many compromises and
made many concessions, and only on the voting question (with the sixteen
republics issue not pressed but held in reserve) did he remain, after explicit
reference to Moscow, wholly unwilling to accept any formulation of the
principle that the great powers should abstain from voting in disputes to which
they were a party. There can clearly be detected in the diary the common
process whereby as disputed issues in a complex negotiation are successively
settled but one problem remains intractable, so this problem comes to loom ever

larger and the commitment of the parties to their respective positions becomes intensified. So the initial Webster position, 'I am not sure that we gain by explicitly reserving the Great Powers from the general procedure',[47] becomes 'I hardly slept last night so anxious was I about the U.S. plan to refuse to take the obligations of the Organisation',[48] and, after the United States had moved to the Cadogan—Webster position, 'Unless the Russians agree to Parties to a Dispute not voting in their own cause, much of what we have done cannot be put into force at all',[49] and, after unwilling recognition that full acceptance of the principle was not possible, participation in the search for a compromise produces the comment 'This is better than I one time thought possible but I feel I am an accomplice in crime'.[50]

It is not unreasonable to suppose that a similar process took place in Moscow. Within the context of the world organization negotiation in isolation, settlement of the disagreement became impossible. The shift of the Soviets to acceptance of the United States compromise proposal can be interpreted in three ways, none of them incompatible with the others. It may have been, as in the purely speculative earlier suggestion, a simple trade-off against partial acceptance of the sixteen republics proposal. It may have been that Gromyko and/or Molotov had not understood or explained the proposal to Stalin with sufficient clarity for him to have understood its precise implications: Stettinius records that after his exposition of the effect of the formula Churchill privately stated to him that 'he — and he thought Stalin — really understood it for the first time'.[51] On the basis of Stalin's precise and pertinent comments and questions immediately after Stettinius's presentation, however, the latter's own opinion was that, whether Churchill had understood it previously or not, Stalin's own understanding was very clear.[52] The third possible interpretation of the change in the Soviet attitude is to be found in the altered perceptions by the Soviets of their own interests and objectives and of those of Britain and the United States in the wider perspective created by the range of the Yalta discussions. That the United States proposal was a compromise representing a retreat from the original strict formulation of principle was the first step, the partial acceptance of the sixteen republics proposal was a second, but it seems unlikely that agreement would have been reached if the salience of the issue had not been reduced by its being considered as one among many world-wide problems.

The persuasiveness of this interpretation is increased by the subsequent history of the question. The Webster record shows quite clearly how close to collapse the whole plan was seen to be coming at San Francisco when the smaller powers, under the leadership of Evatt, succeeded in breaking the unity of the great powers. Napoleon's principle that constitutions should be short and obscure had already been breached by the length and detail of the drafting of the Charter: Evatt's pressure for exact specification of the implications of the voting formula, and in particular for determination whether the question whether or not a matter was procedural (and so not subject to the veto) should itself be regarded as procedural, had caused the Soviets for the first time to perceive (or at least to adopt a position on) a new question — whether a great power could prevent discussion of a question in the Security Council. The Soviet proposition, confirmed from Moscow, that the right to prevent discussion must exist, was totally unacceptable to all the other four major powers, and for five days the fate of the Charter hung in the balance. On this occasion, too, resolution was achieved when the issue was placed in the wider context of the general state of United States–Soviet relations: growing concern on the part of President Truman about United States–Soviet relations generally led him to send Harry Hopkins to Moscow in May as his personal emissary, and after a number of meetings in which much progress was made on several questions Hopkins raised the issue of the veto on discussion in the Security Council. Despite vigorous argument by Molotov that the Soviet position was based squarely on the Yalta decision, Stalin overruled him after a discussion in Russian in which, Hopkins noted, 'it was clear that the Marshal had not understood the issues involved and had not had them explained to him'.[53] In Webster's record, Stalin 'swept all Molotov's objections aside as petty in comparison with the final result to be achieved'.[54] The consequence of the small powers' intervention was that the inapplicability of the veto to discussion of any matter was made explicit, but on the other hand the question whether or not a matter was procedural was placed under veto,[55] an interpretation that might well have gone the other way if it had been left to be decided by practice and convention. Many entries in the diary quoted in earlier pages show Webster's constant concern to establish principles which would be better interpreted by practice in the context of a United Nations in being, rather than by specification in the abstract through negotiation among suspicious powers; but the point that is relevant to the discussion here is that resolution of this gravely disputed question was achieved by changing the perception of one of the disputants and widening the context within which the issue was set.

The other major dispute to which the diary adverts was the resurrected issue of regionalism, although in a rather different form. The diary entries in this case are much less explicit, partly because Webster did not participate in the sessions when the major issues in contention were resolved, and it is therefore much more difficult to analyse the negotiation process. The point of principle for the British delegation remained unchanged — whether such arrangements as were made for enforcement action by regional agencies should or should not be firmly under the ultimate control of the Security Council (as stated in the Dumbarton Oaks proposals), and thus the fundamental universalist character of the organization be preserved. The French and the Soviets wished to exclude action under the Franco-Soviet alliance of 1944 from Security Council control, and the Soviets were similarly concerned for the operation of their other alliances with Britain, Czechoslovakia, Yugoslavia and Poland. The Franco-Soviet demand led the Latin Americans to press for the inclusion of the Act of Chapultepec in the Charter, on the grounds that the Monroe Doctrine would otherwise be infringed, and the United States delegation allowed itself to be persuaded to support this.

This proposal rightly seemed to Webster absurd, for Chapultepec was not a mutual assistance treaty, and acceptance of it would so mock the universalist principle as to destroy the heart of the Charter. The British delegation, though not wholly disinterested (because of the Anglo-Soviet alliance), was the least deeply involved of the four major powers, and was therefore able to play a key role in clarifying priorities among objectives. As the diary shows, Cadogan and Jebb conducted the discussions, Webster's part being limited to contributions in preliminary talks to the formulation of the British position. With an exact sense of timing the French made a critical intervention proposing an amendment which, as Webster put it, 'is in fact para 7 of Art XV of the Covenant'.[56] With this proposal to build on, Cadogan and Jebb were able to devise a formula amending Chapter VIII, Section C, paragraph 2 of Dumbarton Oaks so as to exclude from control of the Security Council any regional arrangements directed against renewal of aggressive policy by an enemy state (of the second world war) 'until such time as the Organization may, on request of the Governments concerned, be charged with the responsibility for preventing further aggression by such a state' (Article 53 of the Charter). Having thereby satisfied the Soviet Union, they were able to persuade the Americans that the French proposed amendment (which became Article 51 of the Charter) was sufficient to safeguard the Monroe Doctrine.

This was a settlement resulting from power, timing, and diplomatic skill. Senator Tom Connally felt in his bones that the British had once again put something over on the Americans, but he could find no effective ground for arguing against the formula. The French timing, together with the British brokerage, had so fully satisfied the Soviets that they made no fuss about the extraordinary American procedure in publicly announcing the formula after its determination in a meeting at which the Soviets were not present. The Latin Americans, whose pressure resulted at least in part (like the smaller powers' pressure on the veto at San Francisco) from the fact that they had not been participants in the original drafting process, to the results of which they were now being asked to subscribe, were simply overridden by the United States, and had to be content with what appeared at the time to be the crumbs of Article 51. As Webster presciently noted, however, these fiercely-contested debates and crises at San Francisco all came in time to signify little — but certainly no-one anticipated that Article 51 would swiftly become one of the most crucial articles of the Charter, and among those most frequently referred to.

The purpose of this book has been twofold: first, in a historical and biographical sense, to illustrate from his own record the contribution made by Charles Webster to the framing of the Charter of the United Nations; and secondly, more analytically, to comment on the processes through which British policy towards the creation of a new world organization after the second world war came to be formulated, and on the structure of the negotiations and the international context within which the attempt was made to implement the policy. The latter was more a commentary than a theoretical exercise, because illustrative data were drawn very largely from a single source, the Webster diary, in order not to stray too far from the former purpose. It is possible, therefore, that in a broader and more rounded frame the role of Webster might seem to bulk less large.

It is none the less true that the Charter's approach to the three great problems of world organization in 1945 — preservation of the *status quo* versus peaceful change, sovereign equality of states versus world unity, and limited or regional alliances versus universalism — reflects a great deal of Webster's thinking. On the first, he believed that no formula could be found that would be both generally acceptable and adequate for future changing circumstances and interests and power relationships, and he therefore advocated the formulation of principles that should govern action, not the definition of conditions in which action should be taken. On the second, he desired an explicit statement of equality of status, but not of function, thereby differentiating the legal (and widely-valued) principle of sovereignty from the political fact that the universal interest in peace, which is indivisible, could be served only by those with the resources to preserve it: this was not agreed at Dumbarton Oaks in form, but it was in fact enshrined in the authority given to the Security Council and in the voting procedures eventually determined. On the third, regional enforcement action appeared to be firmly held within the control of the Security Council as the expression of universalism, but the importance of the loophole created (or recognized) by Article 51 was by no means clearly seen. It was therefore perhaps more than formality when Gladwyn Jebb wrote to Webster in July 1945: '. . . Do let me say — because it is somehow easier to say these kind of things on paper — how conscious we all are here of the immense contribution you have made, not only to this country, but to the whole organisation. It must be an abiding satisfaction to you to see so many of your own ideas taking form & substance & after all that is the only real satisfaction we can have in this life — the memory of work well done.'[57] To Webster himself, his gladness at having been able, as he believed, to have contributed so much was deep and unfeigned, and it was surely this thought that was in his mind when on his death-bed he was heard to mutter, 'I haven't done so badly.'[58]

Notes

INTRODUCTION, pp. 1–3

1. References in the notes to the Webster Papers represent the provisional classification given when they were first received at the LSE. The papers are now in the process of being comprehensively catalogued, but we believe that sufficient detail has been included in the notes to enable easy identification of the relevant documents even when the new cataloguing system is complete.
2. The monograph was published in 1919 under the title *The Congress of Vienna*, reissued in 1934, 1937, 1945 and 1950, and reprinted by Thames & Hudson in 1963.
3. For a fuller account of Webster's life and career see S. T. Bindoff and G. N. Clark, 'Charles Kingsley Webster 1886–1961', *Proceedings of the British Academy*, Vol. XLVIII.

CHAPTER 1, pp. 5–12

1. For a fuller exposition of Churchill's views see W. S. Churchill, *The Second World War*, Vol. IV (Cassell, 1951) pp. 717–22.
2. H. G. Nicholas, *The United Nations as a Political Institution* (O.U.P. 3rd ed., 1967) p. 3.

CHAPTER 2, pp. 13–17

1. The Director of the F.R.P.S. was Professor Arnold Toynbee. Other members of the staff included Professors J. L. Brierly, Denis Brogan, David Mitrany, Bernard Pares, R. W. Seton-Watson, and Sir Alfred Zimmern.
2. Webster *Papers*, Webster 2, Letters 5, 28 August 1939. The Webster Papers are deposited at the London School of Economics and Political Science.
3. The Cabinet Committee on War Aims was established in August 1940 with Attlee as chairman. PRO Cab 65/8 W M 233 (40), 23 August 1940. The Cabinet Committee on Reconstruction was formed in February 1941 with Arthur Greenwood as chairman. PRO Cab 67/9 W P (G) (41)24, 21 February 1941. For examples of the background work undertaken see *Papers*, Webster 1, Misc. 3.
4. PRO FO 371 WI2528/110/50 File 25234, Minute by R. A. Butler, 29 November 1940.
5. PRO FO 371 W9695/110/50 File 25234, Minute by R. A. Butler, 21 August 1940.
6. *Papers*, 3 Webster A, File 22, 11 June 1941.
7. On 8 January 1940 the State Department had established the Advisory Committee on Problems of Foreign Relations. However, the committee soon became embroiled in current policy rather than dealing with post-war preparations as originally planned. One of its problems was the lack of an adequate research staff. To overcome this a Division of Special Research was established in February 1941 under Pasvolsky's direction.
8. The Smoot-Hawley tariff was a strongly protectionist tariff imposed by the United States in June 1930. It occasioned much European criticism.

9. *Papers*, Misc. 1, File 213, Letter Webster to Lord Halifax, 16 June 1941. Lord Halifax was then British Ambassador in Washington, having been Foreign Secretary from 1938 to 1940.

10. *Papers*, Misc. 3.

11. Webster accepted this job with Foreign Office blessing. PRO FO 371 W9396/426/49 File 28902, Minute by R. A. Butler, 25 July 1941.

12. This Conference of some 50 Europeans and North Americans, meeting after the proclamation of the Atlantic Charter, but while the United States was still neutral, had as its purposes the consideration of ways in which co-operation against Nazism could be made effective, and the formulation of ideas about post-war international organization. It was private and unpublicized, because many of the members held official or semi-official positions. The British participants included William Courtenay, Geoffrey Crowther, L. K. Elmhirst, Professor H. Lauterpacht, Ivison Macadam, Sir Andrew MacFadyean, Gerald Palmer M.P., Sir Frederick Whyte and Webster himself.

13. *Papers*, Webster 1, Misc. 1.

14. *Papers*, Webster 1, Misc. 1.

15. *Diary*, 9, 22, 28, 31 August & 5 September 1942.

16. Though Cripps was not solely responsible for the establishment of the Economic and Reconstruction Department in the Foreign Office, his letter to Eden of 18 May 1942 proposing a committee to plan post-war external policy had been an important influence. PRO FO 371 U1903/1903/70 File 31538, Sir Stafford Cripps to Anthony Eden. The Economic and Reconstruction Department under H. M. G. Jebb (later Lord Gladwyn) was formed on 26 June 1942. PRO FO 371 U15/12/73 File 31501, Office Circular No 121.

17. Arnold Toynbee had accompanied the Parliamentary Under-Secretary of State, Richard Law, on a visit to the United States.

18. *Diary*, 24 September 1942. PRO FO 371 U1019/26/72 File 31499, Minute by Gladwyn Jebb, 25 September 1942.

19. PRO FO 371 U1774/10/72 File 35260, Letter Anthony Eden to Viscount Astor, 7 December 1942; Viscount Astor to Anthony Eden 9 December 1942.

CHAPTER 3, pp. 18—38

1. PRO FO 371 U1045/111/70 File 31518, Circular of 28 October 1942.

2. *The Memoirs of Lord Gladwyn* (Weidenfeld & Nicolson, 1972) p. 109.

3. PRO FO 371 U2112/10/72 File 35260, Minute by Nigel Ronald, 4 May 1943.

4. *Ibid.*, Minute by Arnold Toynbee, 30 April 1943.

5. *Papers*, Webster 1, Misc. 2. In an undated letter written after the war Webster explained that the first paper had been written by Jordan and revised by him; that he wrote the third paper, but that Jordan had written the rest 'without much contribution from me'. Webster wanted W. M. Jordan, who was one of his former doctoral students, to join him at the L.S.E. after the war, but Jordan decided to accept a post in the United Nations Secretariat in New York, where he rose to be director of the political affairs division in the Department of Political and Security Council Affairs, before his early death in 1966.

6. *Papers*, Webster 1, Misc. 2.

7. PRO FO 371 U2907/25/70 File 35320.

8. PRO Cab 66/30 W P (42) 516, 8 November 1942; Cab 66/33 W P (43) 31, 16 January 1943. For the second of these see Appendix A.

9. PRO FO 371 U1823/402/70 File 35396, Draft memorandum by Gladwyn Jebb; Cab 66/38 W P (43) 300, 7 July 1943. See Appendix B. cf. Gladwyn, *op. cit.*, p. 128.

10. PRO FO 371 U2066/402/70 File 35396. No date.

11. PRO Cab 66/38 W P (43) 300, 7 July 1943.

12. PRO Prem 4/30/2, 30 January 1943; Cab 66/37 W P (43) 233, 10 June 1943. See also W. S. Churchill, *The Second World War*, Vol. IV (Cassell, 1951) pp. 636—37 and pp. 717—21; and E. J. Hughes, 'Winston Churchill and the Formation of the United Nations Organisation', *Journal of Contemporary History*, Vol. 9, October 1974.

13. At the Mansion House on 10 November 1942 Churchill had declared: 'I have not become the King's First Minister in order to preside over the liquidation of the British Empire.'

14. The 'Armistice terms' is a reference to a Foreign Office paper which proposed that the three major allies should begin co-operation on this subject. PRO Cab 66/37 W P (43) 217, 25 May 1943.

15. The decision to form a Cabinet Committee on Post-War Settlement had been agreed at Cabinet on 29 July 1943. PRO Cab 65/35 W M 107 (43). Attlee was chairman and in addition to those named in the diary entry other members were Eden, Captain H. F. C. Crookshank, Postmaster-General, and G. Tomlinson. The first meeting of the Committee was on 5 August 1943. PRO Cab 87/65 P S (43) 1st Meeting.

16. The Bruce Committee under the chairmanship of the Australian High Commissioner in London studied the reform of the League of Nations. Its report of August 1939 recommended the establishment of a Central Committee for Economic and Social Questions, which would exercise control over all the economic and social agencies of the League.

17. A reference to Webster's paper on 'The Political and Procedural Problems of the Armistices of 1918', 31 January 1943. PRO FO 371 U417/25/70 File 35320.

18. The United States draft, given to Eden on 21 August is printed in *Foreign Relations of the United States (FRUS). The Conferences at Washington and Quebec. 1943* (Washington D.C., Government Printing Office, 1970) p. 925.

19. PRO FO 371 U3654/3653/70 File 35461, Minute by Nigel Ronald, 1 August 1943; Prem 4/30/5, Sir R. I. Campbell to S/S Foreign Affairs, Tel No 3, 15 August 1943 and Gladwyn, *op.cit.* pp. 129–30.

20. E. Ll. Woodward, *British Foreign Policy in the Second World War* (abridged version, H.M.S.O., 1962) pp. 243–4.

21. PRO Cab 87/65 P S (43) 11, 1 September 1943. The main objective of the proposed United Nations Commission for Europe was to prevent renewed German attempts to dominate the Continent in the post-war world. Since it was expected that the European war would end well before that in the Far East, the U.N. Commission was to concern itself with the general problems of carrying out the terms of surrender in the Axis countries and of taking decisions on questions such as the possible outbreak of civil wars. However the paper emphasized that the Commission would be under the ultimate authority of the world organization. The proposed membership of the Commission at the outset was to be the U.S.A., the U.S.S.R., the U.K., and 'possibly France'.

22. *Ibid.* The Foreign Office line was that the concept of an international police force was a complicated topic which was already being considered by the Chiefs of Staff and the Foreign Office. It was therefore suggested that the Attlee committee should postpone its consideration of this issue for the time being.

23. PRO Cab 87/65 P S (43) 10, 31 August 1943.

24. PRO FO 371 U 4349/1816/70 File 35440, 13 September 1943.

25. The final text of the paper on 'Confederations' as tabled at the Moscow Conference is set out in *FRUS, 1943*, Vol. I (Washington D.C., Government Printing Office, 1963) pp. 736–7. The crux of the paper was a self-denying ordinance that the great powers would '. . . not seek to create any separate areas of responsibility in Europe and will not recognize such for others, but rather affirm their common interest in the well-being of Europe as a whole.'

26. These 'principles' formed the basis of the British Joint Declaration on Joint Responsibility for Europe (see *FRUS, 1943*, Vol. I, pp. 736–7). As a subsequent diary entry shows they were not accepted at the Moscow Conference.

27. The idea of a Commission was a primary British objective at Moscow. As a result of the Conference, the European Advisory Commission was established in London. Its purpose was to deal with the settlement of Europe, excluding questions of an entirely operational military nature.

28. E. Ll. Woodward, *British Foreign Policy in the Second World War*, Vol. II (London, H.M.S.O., 1971) pp. 591–93.

29. See PRO FO 371 U6079/402/70 File 35399 for details of this exchange.

30. PRO FO 371 U6136/402/70 File 35399, Washington Tel No 5392, 29 November 1943.

31. *Ibid.*, F.O. to Washington Tel No 8463, 8 December 1943.

32. *Ibid.*, Minute by Richard Law, 7 December 1943, and PRO FO 371 U6427/402/70 File 35399, Minute by Gladwyn Jebb, 18 December 1943.

33. PRO FO 371 U1364/84/70 File 40606 B.

34. The Cairo Conference, November 1943, preceded the more important Teheran Conference. Jebb accompanied the Secretary of State to both conferences.

35. PRO Cab 87/66 A P W (44) 1st Meeting, 22 April 1944. When political and military problems were to be considered by the Committee, membership was as follows: Deputy P.M. (Chairman), Clement Attlee; Foreign Secretary, Anthony Eden and/or Minister of State, Richard Law; Minister of Labour, Ernest Bevin; Minister of Production, Oliver Lyttleton; Secretary of State for Dominion Affairs, Viscount Cranborne; Secretary of State for Air, Sir Archibald Sinclair.

36. The Committee on Preparations for the Meeting with Dominion Prime Ministers consisted of Secretary of State for Dominion Affairs (Chairman), Viscount Cranborne; Minister of Labour, Ernest Bevin; Secretary of State for India, Leopold Amery; Secretary of State for the Colonies, Oliver Stanley; Minister of State, Richard Law. Cab 99/27 D P M (44) 1, 5 February 1944.

37. PRO Prem 4/30/11, Minute by Sir Edward Bridges for the Prime Minister, 15 April 1944.

38. See Appendix C for these memoranda in their final form as approved by the War Cabinet on 7 July 1944. Amendments to the original drafts made before this final submission are shown in the Appendix.

39. Cadogan's diary comment was, 'As usual, the people who have been thinking on these things, have thought themselves into a complete fuddle and are carelessly prodigal of words. They become so prolix as to be unintelligible, but by the time they reach that stage I think they have no thought of their own. A *lot* of pruning will be required.' David Dilks (ed.) *The Diaries of Sir Alexander Cadogan* (Cassell, 1971) p. 619. As Appendix C shows, the pruning shears never got to work — indeed a few bits were added.

40. For the brief under which the memoranda were actually submitted to the Ministers see Appendix C.

41. Gladwyn Jebb was on a visit to Washington.

42. PRO FO 371 U4036/180/70 File 40691. On the question of a 4 power alliance Webster wrote '. . . there is no way to obtain the assent of the United States to a Four Power Alliance except by means of a general international organisation.' So far as continental Leagues of Nations were concerned, Webster wrote that there was no objection to groupings of states within the world organization where they could be regulated in the general interest — '. . . without it there is great danger that they will become rival alliances.' On April 30 Eden minuted 'I agree emphatically with all this.'

43. PRO FO 371 U4035/180/70 File 40691. In this brief Webster emphasized the differences between Hull's commitment to a world structure and the Prime Minister's greater emphasis on a naked four power alliance below which would be regional councils. Both men believed that great power co-operation was essential for a world organization — 'The difference between Mr. Hull and the Prime Minister lies in the methods by which the basic principle is to be established.'

44. The imprecision of early Foreign Office thinking on this question appears sharply in the United Nations Plan presented to the War Cabinet in 1943 (see Appendix A), where the third great power with the United States and the Soviet Union is named twice as the British Commonwealth, twice as the United Kingdom.

45. PRO Cab 99/28 P M M (44) 12th Meeting, 11 May 1944.

46. *Parliamentary Debates*, Fifth Series, H. of C., Vol. 400, cols. 762–786.

47. PRO Prem 4/30/7 PM Minute M583/4 PM to Foreign Secretary and Sir Edward Bridges, 21 May 1944.

48. The allusion is to a somewhat tangled skein of events. On May 15 Eden had sent the Prime Minister two documents suggesting changes to be made in the covering note of the documents on world organization and of certain passages in Memoranda A and B. These changes had been made as a result of the discussion at the Dominion Prime Ministers' meeting on May 11. On May 18, Fraser, the New Zealand Prime Minister, had written to Eden complaining about the revised versions — that they were not in accord with the sense

of the Dominion Meeting and that they reflected some Churchillian ideas which had been rejected by the meeting. Eden forwarded this letter to Churchill on May 19 evoking the PM's response of May 21. Since Churchill gave considerable ground in his minute of May 21 Peck correctly assumed that the Foreign Office would wish to change the papers on world organization.

49. PRO Prem 4/30/7 Foreign Secretary to Prime Minister. PM/44/404, 2 June 1944 and FO redraft 31 May 1944.

50. PRO Cab 66/52 W P (44) 370.

51. PRO Cab 65/43 W M (44) 88, 7 July 1944. See Appendix C.

52. This dispatch was ultimately circulated as a Cabinet paper. Cab 66/53 W P (44) 409, 25 July 1944. It was sent from Algiers on 30 May but was not received in the Foreign Office until 13 June. The dispatch analysed the state of post-war Europe, placing considerable stress on the Soviet threat. Specifically, Duff Cooper proposed 'that policy should be directed towards the formation of a group of the western democracies bound together by the most explicit terms of alliance.' Membership would consist of the U.K., France, Belgium, Holland, Norway and Denmark. Later it might be possible to include Sweden, Portugal, Spain and Italy. The Foreign Secretary's reply to Duff Cooper of 25 July 1944 stated that any world organization should be reinforced by various systems of alliances. Yet to propose an alliance against Russia would be fatal since it would lead to the end of the world organization and the hope of European recovery. Thus Eden's reply stated that a 'Western group would be welcome as part of any organisation to be set up by Britain and Russia, in the first instance, for the protection of Europe against a new German aggression' but, if directed against Russia it 'might well precipitate the evils against which it was intended to guard'. The Foreign Secretary's reply was also circulated in the Cabinet paper identified above.

53. This ultimately emerged as a memorandum by the Secretary of State for Foreign Affairs to the A.P.W. Committee. A P W (44) 45, 17 July 1944, entitled 'Future World Organisation. Points for Decision'. See PRO Cab 66/53 W P (44) 406, 24 July 1944. The memorandum considered various specific points which had not been covered in the British proposals for Dumbarton Oaks such as, *inter alia*, the exact size of the World Council, and the questions of abstention and withdrawal from the organization.

54. PRO FO 371 U6287/180/70 File 40698, Moscow to FO, 8 July 1944. Molotov had stated that the Russians would participate in the Conference.

55. *FRUS, 1944*, Vol. 1, pp. 653—69 and pp. 670—93; PRO FO 371 U6461/180/70 File 40700, FO to Washington, Tel No 6539, 21 July 1944.

CHAPTER 4, pp. 39—57

1. See Appendix D.

2. The Soviets claimed that they had not had sufficient time to study the American proposals; nor indeed had they handed over copies of their own paper when this request was made. PRO FO 371 U6756/180/70 File 40703, Washington to FO, 5 August 1944.

3. The Democratic Party Convention. 1944 was a Presidential election year.

4. *Papers*, Queries, Box 3, Memorandum No 2, 4 August 1944.

5. For the American proposals see *Foreign Relations of the United States (FRUS) 1944*, Vol. 1 (Washington D.C., Government Printing Office, 1966) pp. 653—69.

6. *FRUS, 1944*, Vol. 1, p. 710.

7. See Appendix C, p. 145.

8. *FRUS, 1944*, Vol. 1, p. 658.

9. *Papers*, Webster 1, Misc. 2, File 33, Memorandum No WD, 8 August 1944. Webster disliked the enlarged role of the Assembly in the settlement of disputes which was set out in the American paper. Specifically, Webster concluded 'That we should oppose the grant to the Assembly of powers to act on its own initiative for the settlement of disputes or the maintenance of peace and security.'

10. *Papers*, Webster 1, Misc. 2, File 33, Memorandum WC, 9 August 1944.

11. *Papers of E. R. Stettinius Jr*, Minutes of the meeting of the American Group at Dumbarton Oaks, 10 August 1944.

12. *State Department Archives*, Notter File, Box 142, Gen Minutes 9, Meeting No 9.

13. *FRUS, 1944*, Vol. 1, Informal Minutes of the Joint Steering Committee, pp. 738–43; PRO FO 371 U7098/180/70 File 40708, Washington to FO, Tel No 4634, 28 August 1944.

14. Both Ruth Russell and Harley A. Notter have incorrectly recorded that the Americans never accepted the full British position that great powers should not have the right to vote on enforcement measures when party to a dispute. See Ruth B. Russell, *A History of the United Nations Charter* (Brookings, 1958), p. 408 and Harley A. Notter, *Postwar Foreign Policy Preparation 1939–1945* (Washington D.C., Government Printing Office, 1950) p. 376. Two recent articles have examined in detail the position of the American delegation during Dumbarton Oaks, although we still lack a full and authoritative account based on all available records. See Thomas M. Campbell 'Nationalism in America's UN policy, 1944–45', *International Organisation,* Vol. 27, No. 1, Winter 1973, and Charles G. Nelson, 'Revisionism and the Security Council Veto', *International Organisation,* Vol. 28, No. 3, Summer 1974.

15. On August 16 Governor Thomas E. Dewey, Republican Presidential candidate 1944, issued a statement that he was disturbed by reports that the Dumbarton Oaks Conversations were intended to 'subject the nations of the world, great and small, permanently to the coercive power of the four nations holding this conference.'

16. An elaborate committee structure was envisaged. At first it was proposed to have (i) a Joint Steering Committee – delegation chairmen with a few senior advisers; (ii) three main subcommittees – Legal, General Questions of International Organisation, Security, attended by officials; (iii) a small Formulation Group which would work for the two main subcommittees – General Questions, Security. This elaborate structure was not utilized. The Soviets insisted that the conversations be kept informal and restricted to a small number of participants. Consequently the two formulation groups were merged into the Joint Formulation Group. This Group worked closely with the Steering Committee and eventually it replaced the subcommittees, which ceased to meet. The Formulation Group was responsible for much of the substantive discussions as well as the technical and legal drafting of the Proposals. British members of the Joint Formulation Group were Jebb, Webster, Malkin, Grove-White and Capel Dunn.

17. That each of the constituent republics of the U.S.S.R. should be a member of the world organization.

18. During the conversations a system was evolved whereby points on which all three governments were not agreed were placed in brackets. These reserved points could then be considered at a later date, thereby preserving the momentum of the conference and allowing the delegations to consult their governments over the disputed points if necessary.

19. *Papers*, Webster 1, Dumbarton Oaks, 1. Webster's paper was as follows:

The objects of the organisation will be:–

1. To maintain peace and security by the adoption of effective collective measures between members for action in the event of a threat to or breach of the peace
2. To provide means by which all disputes between states may be settled by peaceful methods
3. To furnish a centre where friendly relations between members may be promoted by the adoption of measures likely to facilitate international co-operation
4. To facilitate and promote solutions of international and social problems (including educational and cultural problems) and for this purpose to enter into relationship by mutual agreement with specialised economic and social organisations.

In carrying out these objects the Members undertake:–

1. To settle all their disputes in accordance with the obligations laid down in the basic document of the organisation
2. [Later altered to (3)] To respect each other's political independence
3. [Later altered to (2)] To fulfil towards each other the obligations which are the condition of receiving the benefits of the Organisation
4. To recognise that all members are equal in status though necessarily not in function.

20. Under paragraph 4 of the Moscow Declaration of October 1943, the U.S., the U.S.S.R. and the U.K. recognized '. . . the necessity of establishing at the earliest practicable date a general international organization, based on the principle of the sovereign equality of all peace-loving states, and open to membership by all such states, large and small, for the maintenance of international peace and security.'

21. Originally it was envisaged that there would be a Foreign Ministers' Conference after the end of the official talks at Dumbarton Oaks. North Africa was considered as a possible venue, but the meeting never materialized.

22. Leo Pasvolsky was born in Russia and spoke fluent Russian.

23. See note 18 above.

24. See *FRUS, 1944*, Vol. 1, Compromise Proposal drafted by the Formulation Group, 13 September 1944, pp. 805–6.

25. A meeting between Churchill and Roosevelt was taking place at the Citadel, Quebec.

26. The American political situation – the 1944 Presidential election.

27. See PRO FO 371 U8301/180/70 File 40723 for the Jebb and Webster minutes of September 18. Webster's main point was that '. . . If a Great Power Council existed for general matters outside the World Organisation no one would imagine that this latter body could play any real part. But if the Council and Assembly had an organic connection there would be both a chance of acceptance by the other states and some possibility of growth.'

28. See Appendix D.

29. Published as Cmd. 6571.

30. PRO FO 371 U7664/180/70 File 40719, Minute by J. G. Ward, 26 September 1944. Amongst the Americans, Breckinridge Long became a strong advocate of the Russian position. *Breckinridge Long Papers*, Diary, 19 September 1944.

31. W. S. Churchill, *The Second World War*, Vol. VI (Cassell, 1954) p. 190.

32. PRO FO 371 U7919/180/70 File 40720, Memorandum by Sir Alexander Cadogan, 4 October 1944. Cadogan's proposal was that there should be a special procedure for great powers party to a dispute. The permanent member involved could submit the dispute to the other permanent members who would constitute a 'Consultative Council'. Yet this would be solely a conciliation procedure and there would be no provision for voting. Such a system would be an improvement on the Russian proposal in that a dispute involving a great power would at least be heard.

33. PRO FO 371 U7737/180/70 File 40719, Sir Stafford Cripps to the P.M., 7 October 1944.

34. An official committee considering the winding up of the League of Nations.

35. PRO Cab 87/68 A P W (44) 117, 22 November 1944.

36. India was a member of the League of Nations even though she was not a 'sovereign state'. The British desire that she should also be a founder member of the United Nations weakened the British case against membership for the 16 Soviet Republics.

37. The 'associated states' were those states that had been invited to the various U.N. economic conferences even though they were not theoretically at war with Germany. They were Chile, Ecuador, Egypt, Iceland, Paraguay, Peru, Venezuela & Uruguay.

38. *FRUS, The Conferences at Malta and Yalta, 1945* (Washington D.C., Government Printing Office, 1955), pp. 58–60.

39. PRO Cab 65/44 W M 172 (44).

40. PRO Cab 66/58 W P (44) 667, 21 November 1944.

41. PRO FO 371 U8785 /180/70 File 40725. For this draft see Appendix E, pp. 166–7.

42. PRO Prem 4/30/10, Minute PM/44/785, 29 December 1944.

43. PRO Cab 87/69 A P W (45) 1st meeting.

44. PRO Cab 65/49 W M (45) 4, 11 January 1945; FO 371 U209/12/70 File 50670, FO to Washington, Tel No 418.

45. PRO FO 371 U425/12/70 File 50672, Washington to FO No 362, 16 January 1945.

46. PRO Prem 4/31/1, Minute M110/5, Prime Minister to Foreign Secretary, 25 January 1945.

47. PRO Cab 65/49 W M (45) 4, 11 January 1945.

48. That there should be a four power treaty between the major allies aimed at preventing any Axis resurgence.

49. PRO FO 371 U159/12/70 File 50670, Washington to FO No 97, 5 January 1945.

50. PRO FO 371 U2210/12/70 File 50690, Letter handed to Eden by Gousev on 15 March 1945.

51. *FRUS, 1945*, Vol. 1 (Washington D. C., Government Printing Office, 1967), pp. 113—4.

52. *Ibid.*, p. 150.

53. *Ibid.*, pp. 151—2.

54. *Ibid.*, pp. 289—90.

55. The Cabinet had accepted the idea of a Commonwealth Conference on 11 January 1945. PRO Cab 65/49 W M (45) 4.

56. For the text as finally drafted see Appendix E. Webster's draft typed on the night of 11 April is identical in content. Only very slight drafting changes were made. *Papers* 1, Misc. 4.

57. PRO Cab 99/30 B C M (45) 11th Meeting, 12 April 1945.

CHAPTER 5, pp. 58—73

1. The member countries were: Australia, Brazil, Canada, Chile, China, Czechoslovakia, France, Iran, Mexico, Netherlands, U.K., U.S.A., U.S.S.R., Yugoslavia.

2. Sir Charles Webster, 'The Making of the Charter of the United Nations' in *The Art and Practice of Diplomacy* (Chatto & Windus, 1961), p. 87.

3. PRO Prem 4/31/7, PM/45/93 Foreign Secretary to PM, 8 March 1945.

4. The Soviets demanded four rotating Presidents. A compromise was ultimately evolved whereby the chairmanship of the public meetings of the conference was rotated amongst the four sponsoring powers, but the U.S.A. was named as chairman of the Steering and Executive Committees. The proposed seating of the Polish Provisional Government also revealed differences between the Russians and the other sponsoring powers. Sensing his isolation, Molotov eventually accepted a formula that the establishment of a Polish government recognized by all the sponsoring powers would make it possible for Poland to participate in the conference. Under Latin American pressure the U.S. delegation pressed for Argentina's admission to the conference. The Russians were again virtually isolated as indicated in the plenary session where the voting was 31 for Argentina and 4 against.

5. *United Nations Conference on International Organization (UNCIO) Documents*, Vol III, 5 May 1945, pp. 622—28.

6. The 'Act of Chapultepec' was adopted by the Mexico City Conference, February 21—March 5, 1945. It represented the aspirations of the Latin American states for an inter-American regional system which would include a collective security treaty. The Americans were surprised by the Latin desire to institutionalize the Monroe Doctrine and insisted on a qualifying phrase in the Act whereby it was proclaimed that the inter-American regional system would be 'consistent with the purposes and principles of the general international organization when established'.

7. The Covenant paragraph referred to read: 'If the Council fails to reach a report which is unanimously agreed to by the members thereof . . . the Members of the League reserve to themselves the right to take such action as they shall consider necessary for the maintenance of right and justice.' The resemblance of this to the eventual Article 51 of the Charter is clear.

8. The question under consideration was the size of the Security Council. The smaller powers wished to increase the size of the Council from the membership of 11 agreed at Dumbarton Oaks.

9. For the text of the press conference see *US Department of State Bulletin*, Vol. 12, 20 May 1945, p. 930.

10. During his speech Cadogan expressed the tentative opinion that the veto would not be applicable to the first three paragraphs of Section VIII A of the Dumbarton Oaks Proposals, i.e. that the veto could not be used to prevent the Security Council from investigating a dispute. This was later to form part of the basis of the great power voting dispute with the Soviet Union.

11. The Canadians had proposed an amendment whereby non-members of the Security

Council would participate in meetings concerned with the use of their national forces: 'Any member of The United Nations not represented on the Security Council shall be invited to send a representative to sit as a member at any meeting of the Security Council which is discussing under paragraph 4 above the use of the forces which it has undertaken to make available to the Security Council in accordance with the special agreement or agreements provided for in paragraph 5 above.' *UNCIO*, Vol III, p. 591.

12. The discussion in Committee III.1 had resulted in a decision to set up a sub-committee to study the Yalta voting formula 'in order to clarify the doubts that have arisen'. Cadogan's 'good humour' was somewhat premature. It was the suggestion that the small powers 'clarify' their questions that led to the submission of a questionnaire of 23 items. This in turn later precipitated the great power veto crisis. The questionnaire is set out in *UNCIO*, Vol XI, pp. 699–709.

13. Ruth B. Russell, *A History of the United Nations Charter* (Brookings, 1958) pp. 702–3.

14. The Australian amendment proposed that Section VIII A of the Dumbarton Oaks Proposals on pacific settlement should not require great power unanimity, i.e. recommend- ations concerning peaceful settlement would need only a simple majority of seven.

15. On 23 May Churchill formally resigned and a general election was set for 5 July. Eden and Attlee had already left San Francisco, Lord Halifax having taken charge of the British delegation. Indeed, by the middle of May Stettinius was the only great power foreign minister still remaining at the conference. Eden, Soong, Molotov and Bidault had left. The leadership of the Chinese, Russian and French delegations was now in the hands of Wellington Koo, Gromyko and former Prime Minister Jean Paul-Boncour respectively.

16. Question 19 on the questionnaire was: 'In case a decision has to be taken as to whether a certain point is a procedural matter, is that preliminary question to be considered in itself as a procedural matter or is the veto applicable to such preliminary question?' *UNCIO*, Vol XI, p. 707.

17. Paragraph 3 of the draft statement affirmed: 'Since the Council has the right by a procedural vote to decide its own rules of procedure, it follows that no individual member of the Council can alone prevent a consideration and discussion by the Council of a dispute or situation brought to its attention.' However, since the Soviet view was that the question of whether a matter was procedural or not was subject to a veto, it followed that under the Soviet interpretation paragraph 3 meant that a veto could prevent the Council from even considering a dispute.

18. Sobolev presented the Soviet draft answer to question 19. This was as follows: 'In the opinion of the Delegations of Sponsoring Governments the decision on the question of application of one or another voting procedure from those provided by the Charter should be given to the Security Council itself as its everyday work. In those cases, when the necessity arises to vote in course of decision of such preliminary question, the Council will decide by the vote of seven members including concurring votes of the permanent members. In order to specify this provision the appropriate paragraph should be added to Section C, Chapter VI.'

19. A conference which could revise the Charter.

20. *Papers*, Queries, Box 4, Minute to Lord Halifax.

21. PRO FO 371 U4238/12/70 File 50716, UK Deleg., S.F. to FO No 533, 31 May 1945. After setting out Webster's arguments, paragraph 3 of the telegram suggested that even if Foreign Office approval were given to a Charter revision conference, Stettinius should be consulted first to see how he reacted. The Foreign Office reply of 1 June approved the course of action outlined in paragraph 3. Webster's main concern was reflected in the Charter, however. Article 109, paragraph 2 states that revisions proposed by the Charter revision conference should take effect only when ratified by 'two thirds of the members of the United Nations including all the permanent members of the Security Council'.

22. For the text of this statement see Russell, *op. cit.*, p. 731.

23. Hopkins had been asked to travel to Moscow by President Truman. For an account of his conversations with Molotov and Stalin see Robert E. Sherwood, *The White House Papers of Harry L. Hopkins*, Vol. 2, (Eyre & Spottiswoode, 1949) pp. 900–2. For the text of the proposed Churchill message see PRO Prem 4/31/7 Tel No 1122, FO to UK Deleg San Francisco, 6 June 1945. This appeal to Stalin was never sent.

24. The delight was perhaps excessive. In the excitement the origin of the crisis — whether the veto should apply to the preliminary question whether or not a matter was procedural — was forgotten and the Soviet interpretation held. What the Soviets had yielded on was their newly-proposed insistence that even discussion of a matter might be vetoed.

25. Webster baldly enunciated the great power position. The great powers had '. . . no idea that there should not be recognition of the differentiation among the powers, for history showed that it was impossible, by the vote of small powers, to require great powers to agree to take action for the maintenance of peace.' *UNCIO*, Vol XI, pp. 433—6.

26. For details of the domestic jurisdiction issue see Russell, *op. cit.*, pp. 904—10.

27. The 'heart of the Charter' to which Webster refers is Chapter V, dealing with the Security Council. This was Chapter VI in the Dumbarton Oaks proposals. See Appendices D and F, pp. 159—60 and 172—4.

28. The Coordination Committee consisted of the same fourteen countries that formed the Executive Committee. However, the individuals representing the countries were officials rather than political heads of delegations. After approval in the commissions the draft provisions were sent to the Coordination Committee, which was responsible for preparing the final draft of the Charter.

29. Anthony Eden suffered from a duodenal ulcer. On his return to London from San Francisco he was forced to take a complete rest.

30. In his press conference on 10 May 1945 Eden had said that 'no great power' had a veto, though he had meant to say that no great power party to a dispute had a veto.

CHAPTER 6, pp. 74—82

1. Published as Cmd. 6666.

2. Philip Noel-Baker had been a member of the League of Nations section of the British Delegation to the Paris Peace Conference and was a member of the League Secretariat until 1922. He was Sir Ernest Cassel Professor of International Relations at the University of London, 1924—29, and a member of the British Delegation to the 10th Assembly of the League of Nations. Webster and Noel-Baker agreed that the former should become a Special Adviser on 26 August 1945. The two had long been very good friends.

3. These were: Australia, Brazil, Canada, Chile, China, Czechoslovakia, France, Iran, Mexico, Netherlands, U.K., U.S.A., U.S.S.R. and Yugoslavia.

4. The ten committees were arranged as follows: 1. General Assembly; 2. Security Council; 3. Economic and Social Council; 4. Trusteeship Council; 5. Court & Legal Problems; 6. Arrangements for the Secretariat; 7. Financial Arrangements; 8. Relations with Specialized Agencies; 9. League of Nations; 10. General.

5. Following the end of the San Francisco Conference President Truman had appointed James Byrnes as Secretary of State. Stettinius was appointed as chief United States representative to the United Nations. Stettinius had a rather grandiose conception of the nature of this appointment, even believing that his position would be equal to that of the Secretary of State. Given these delusions he naturally wanted to bring the United Nations into operation as soon as possible. See T. M. Campbell & G. C. Herring (eds.) *The Diaries of Edward R. Stettinius Jr. 1943—1946* (New York, 1975) p. 409.

6. Having been expelled from the League of Nations the Soviets had little regard for a decent 'burial'. However, both Noel-Baker and Webster wanted the League to be wound up properly and believed that the last meeting could be held in December 1945. In fact the last meeting of the League took place in April 1946.

7. Philip Noel-Baker disliked the idea of the 'Big Five' making agreements in secret. However, it was found to be the most effective way of expediting business. See Campbell & Herring, *op. cit.*, p. 420.

8. For the verbatim record of this important meeting see the *Report by the Executive Committee to the Preparatory Commission of the United Nations*, pp. 118—132.

9. See the *Report by the Executive Committee*, pp. 15—16.

10. The eight committees were arranged as follows: 1. General Assembly; 2. Security

Council; 3. Economic & Social Council; 4. Trusteeship; 5. Court & Legal problems; 6. Administrative and Budgetary; 7. League of Nations; 8. General Questions.

11. On 15 December an amendment to the Executive Committee's Report recommending Europe in place of the United States as the site of the permanent headquarters was defeated by a vote of 25 to 3 with 2 abstentions. Following the defeat of this amendment the recommendation of the Executive Committee was carried with a vote of 30 in favour and 14 against with 6 abstentions.

12. The vote in Committee on 22 December was 22 to 6 with 12 abstentions against the West. Approval for the East was given by a vote of 25 to 5 with 10 abstentions.

13. *Diary*, 20 January 1946. See also Campbell & Herring, *op. cit.*, p. 444.

14. *Diary*, 3 February 1946.

15. *Papers* 3, File 23, 19 February 1946. The Security Council in its first session heard Iranian complaints about the failure of the Soviet Union to withdraw its troops from Iran.

16. He was proud of his K.C.M.G.; but he knew that Attlee had been strongly pressed to recommend a peerage, and this he would undoubtedly have preferred, not least because it would have given him a platform in the House of Lords from which he could from time to time have contributed to the debate on foreign policy.

CONCLUSION, pp. 83–108

1. D. Dilks, *The Diaries of Sir Alexander Cadogan* (Cassell, 1971) p. 31.
2. Paul Gore-Booth, *With Great Truth and Respect* (Constable, 1974) pp. 329 and 15.
3. Quoted from the Crossman diaries in *The Sunday Times*, 9 February 1975.
4. See pp. 26–37 above
5. Graham T. Allison, *Essence of Decision* (Little, Brown, 1971).
6. PRO Cab 66/30 W P (42) 516, 8 November 1942.
7. See p. 36 above.
8. The inescapable uncertainties of decisions in a social context have led Braybrooke and Lindblom to argue that it cannot be 'rational' to aspire to a procedure that clearly is neither operative nor operable, so the only 'rational' way of acting in social questions is by the process which they have called 'disjointed incrementalism'. See D. Braybrooke & C. E. Lindblom, *A Strategy of Decision* (Free Press, 1970).
9. Quoted in Sir Charles Webster, *The Art and Practice of Diplomacy* (Chatto & Windus, 1961) p. 75.
10. See pp. 33–6 above for the reactions of the Dominion Prime Ministers and in particular of the Canadians.
11. See p. 38 above.
12. See p. 71 above.
13. *FRUS, 1944*, Vol. I, pp. 901–15.
14. Dilks, *op. cit.*, p. 361.
15. See p. 62 above.
16. See p. 21 above.
17. See pp. 33–5 above.
18. See p. 36 above.
19. See p. 24 above.
20. See p. 52 above.
21. See p. 36 above.
22. R. Tanter, *The Policy Relevance of Models in World Politics* (International Data Archive Research Report No. 7, University of Michigan, 1972) p. 4.
23. It does not necessarily follow that a recommendation on a more technical question will be more readily accepted. It depends on the individual. Macmillan was inclined to react the other way. 'I am not by nature or, I am afraid, by education very favourably inclined to swallow all that the scientists tell me, because, alas, I do not understand it.' *Parliamentary Debates*, Fifth Series, H. of C., Vol. 605, col. 1048.
24. See pp. 20–1 above.
25. W. S. Churchill, *The Second World War*, Vol. IV, (Cassell, 1951) p. 721.

26. See p. 40 above.

27. *The Memoirs of Lord Gladwyn* (Weidenfeld & Nicolson, 1972) p. 120.

28. See p. 55 above.

29. *FRUS, 1944*, Vol. I, p. 658.

30. See pp. 29–30 above.

31. See p. 30 above.

32. Dilks, *op. cit.*, pp. 653–4.

33. See p. 54 above.

34. Dilks, *op. cit.*, pp. 688–9.

35. See n. 15, p. 114 above.

36. *The Memoirs of Cordell Hull* (Hodder & Stoughton, 1948) pp. 1642–6.

37. For a full analysis of Churchill's views see E. J. Hughes, 'Winston Churchill and the Formation of the United Nations Organisation', *Journal of Contemporary History*, Vol. 9, October 1974.

38. See Appendix C.

39. P M M (44) 4, 8 May 1944, covering note para. 16.

40. See p. 35 above. It may be doubted, however, whether Cadogan would have held to such a position had Eden pressed him to go, even with instructions that he thought unsatisfactory.

41. Sir Charles Webster, *The Congress of Vienna* (Thames & Hudson, 1963) p. 32.

42. J. W. Burton, *World Society* (Cambridge, 1972) pp. 153–5.

43. Dilks, *op. cit.*, p. 706.

44. Churchill, *op. cit.*, Vol VI, p. 190.

45. See p. 55 above.

46. E. R. Stettinius, *Roosevelt and the Russians* (Cape, 1950) pp. 160–3.

47. See p. 41 above.

48. See p. 42 above.

49. See p. 47 above.

50. See p. 53 above.

51. Stettinius, *op. cit.*, p. 142.

52. *Ibid.*, p. 140.

53. R. E. Sherwood, *The White House Papers of Harry L. Hopkins*, Vol. 2 (Eyre & Spottiswoode, 1949) p. 901.

54. See p. 67 above.

55. 'Joint Statement on Voting Procedure' in *Documents of the United Nations Conference on International Organization*, Vol. XI, p. 711.

56. See p. 59 above.

57. Gladwyn Jebb to Charles Webster, *Papers* 3, File 42, 31 July 1945.

58. S. T. Bindoff and G. N. Clark, 'Charles Kingsley Webster 1886–1961', *Proceedings of the British Academy*, Vol. XLVIII, p. 445.

APPENDIX A

The United Nations Plan

W.P. (43) 31
16 January 1943

The aim of British foreign policy must be, first, that we should continue to exercise the functions and to bear the responsibilities of a World Power; and, secondly, that we should seek not only to prevent Europe from being dominated by any one Power, but to preserve the freedom of Europe as essential to our own.

2.   We cannot realise these objectives through our own unaided efforts. We can only hope to play our part either as a European Power or as a World Power if we ourselves form part of a wider organisation.

3.   Towards the achievement of these objectives we have already entered into certain major commitments, namely, the Atlantic Charter, the Mutual Aid Agreement with the United States and the Anglo-Soviet Treaty.

4.   It is impossible to say whether the League of Nations can ever be revived in its old form, or even whether we would wish to see it revived as it was. Certainly we should make every effort to preserve those technical and humanitarian services of the League which have been so conspicuously successful in the past and for which there will be scope in the future. It is perhaps needless to add that the I.L.O. would continue in existence, its functions indeed being extended if necessary. In the meantime, we have the conception of the United Nations, a conception at once less ambitious and more practical than the conception of the League. Upon this idea of the United Nations we must build up the machinery of international co-operation.

5.   International co-operation between the United Nations will not provide the necessary cohesion and stability unless the Great Powers are prepared to accept the responsibilities of leadership *within* the United Nations. For this purpose the Great Powers must agree between themselves on a common world policy and be prepared, as leaders of the United Nations, to take joint action to enforce it. Failing this, we shall be confronted by the prospect of a world in precarious balance, with the Great Powers, each with its circle of client States, facing each other in a rivalry which will merge imperceptibly into hostility.

6.   The leadership of the United Nations will have to come from three, at least, of the Great Powers — the British Commonwealth, the United States, and Russia. In view of the attitude of the United States, China, too, must be included as one of the Great Powers; though it is to be expected that for a long time to come she will not be a Great Power in anything but the name. We should, therefore, regard the conception of the Four Powers, working within the framework of the United Nations, as the immediate basis of our present and post-war foreign policy. Later on this conception may be widened to include other States in the category of Great Powers.

7.   The successful application of the United Nations conception will, however, depend on the validity of two assumptions:—

   (i) that the United Kingdom, the Union of Soviet Socialist Republics and the United States of America will all, after the war, recognise their world-wide interests and responsibilities and be willing to enter into world-wide commitments in order to guard against other nations again troubling the peace; and

   (ii) that, politically speaking, the real, if not the declared object of the Concert of the Four Powers will be to restrict the power of Germany and Japan for as long a period as possible, and will not be based on the alternative theory that both these Powers should be readmitted to the ranks of Great Powers. (Italy has never been a Great Power except by courtesy, and it would probably not be necessary to treat her and the smaller Axis Allies in the same way as Germany and Japan.)

8.   It follows that the most desirable *political* set-up at the end of the war would be a Council consisting of representatives of the British Commonwealth, the United States, the U.S.S.R., and (*pro forma*) China, to act, as it were, as a provisional Executive Committee of the United Nations.

9.   The future of France is obscure, but from our point of view it would be desirable that, provided she recovers her independence and a measure of her greatness, she should be associated with the other Four Powers in the government of the world, if only because without the assistance of a rejuvenated France the problem of preventing a renewed German effort to dominate the Continent will be much more difficult.

10   For a period after the war and until some more comprehensive international system is established, the Four Powers will thus have to undertake the military responsibility for maintaining order and preventing the building up of aggressive forces in Europe and the Far East. This will entail the maintenance by them of a considerable measure of armaments throughout Europe and in Asia; the complete disarmament of the defeated Powers; and the establishment of an Air Force and Naval policing system towards the financing of which the defeated Powers, relieved of the burden of armaments, should, if practicable, contribute heavily.

11.   The most suitable agency for these purposes would seem to be an Inter-Allied Armistice Commission, which might be charged with the duty of supervising a certain number of Reconstruction activities.

12.   International friction and aggression frequently have their roots in economic and social disharmonies. If standards of living are too unequal, for instance, frictions will be created leading to dangerous crises and even to war itself. Consequently it will be of the highest importance for the Four Powers to concern themselves with world economic and social problems, subject, however, to the considerations advanced in paragraph 15 below.

13.   It will, for instance, be highly desirable, if not essential, to obtain general consent to schemes on the lines of the Clearing Union and the "Commodity Control" schemes, so that an "expansionist spiral" of world trade can be initiated. Unless such an expansion of world trade takes place the economic conditions of many countries, including our own, may become completely intolerable, and desperate solutions may be urged by desperate people.

14.   It will also be desirable to retain some organisation, such as the I.L.O., to smooth out discrepancies in social standards by the encouragement of progressive policies in less advanced countries.

15.   It is at this point that a reconciliation is possible between the power-doctrines underlying our conception of the rôle of the Four Great Powers and the economic interest of smaller States. If the Four Powers accept the responsibilities of effective and over-whelming leadership for reasons of security, they should be very careful to allow economic

affairs, so long as they do not endanger security, to be handled by wider assemblies, whether on a world basis or on regional lines.

16.   The most important and also the most dangerous area which will have to be dealt with is Europe. Here, in Europe, is the cradle, and until recently the home, of the civilisation which has now spread to almost every corner of the globe. Here, too, is to be discovered the source of most of the worst conflicts in modern history.

17.   The major danger in Europe is the strong central position of Germany, with her large population and highly developed industries, which are the bases of her military power. The ultimate safety of Europe will depend on the economic as well as the military disarmament of Germany, and an increase in the relative economic status and power of Germany's neighbours.

18.   In addition, however, the joint occupation of Germany by the three major Allies should be accompanied by a very close control over its economic life. If this control were successful it would represent an important large-scale experiment in European international administration.

19.   The Armistice and Reconstruction Commission (on which the smaller European Allies should be represented) would have wide powers, and might well co-ordinate certain essential European services, such as transport, outside as well as inside Germany.

20.   It is to be hoped that the European neutrals (if any in fact remain at the end of the war) will agree to work in with this Commission, but it should not be the intention of the Allies to force them to do so against their will.

21.   Further, the Allied Forces under the control of the Commission would, in fact, if not in name, constitute an international Police Force, which might at a later stage have a more formal international constitution, and which might also be given a wider field of usefulness in appropriate circumstances.

22.   In some cases, particularly in Eastern Europe, we may hope to amalgamate the smaller Powers into Confederations. Two such Confederations are already under discussion (one centring round Czechoslovakia and Poland, and the other round Greece and Yugoslavia) and others might be formed elsewhere.

23.   Generally speaking, regional groupings should be encouraged, subject always to the principle that there must not be a kind of "limited liability" system, whereby one Power is solely responsible for keeping the peace in any given area. For the conception, if so applied, would give rise to rivalries as between one group and another, and hence sow the seeds of future war. In discussing "regionalism", therefore, we must assume that all the Four Powers (with the exception of China) are in principle equally interested in maintaining the peace everywhere in the world, and that they will speak with one voice and act together whenever and wherever it may be threatened.

24.   Thus the measures taken by the United Nations to pacify Europe and to restore its economic life, will, if they are well conceived and executed, go far towards creating the conditions under which European unity may eventually become a reality. To provide a unifying political framework for the various military and economic measures which are envisaged, it is to be hoped that the Armistice and Reconstruction Commission (see paragraph 19) may at some stage become a "Council of Europe", on which all European States should be represented, including the United Kingdom, the Soviet Union, and, if possible the United States. But the admission of neutrals and *a fortiori* of ex-enemies to full membership of the Council would be a gradual, in some cases a very gradual, process.

25.   The military security and economic welfare of backward areas with the status of colonial dependencies would most appropriately be dealt with by Regional Commissions,

composed of representatives of parent States and of other nations with a major defence or economic interest in the regions concerned. Such regions might be, first, South-East Asia; secondly, Africa; and thirdly, the Western Atlantic. Responsibility for the internal administration of particular territories would rest with the individual parent State concerned.

26.   In various other parts of the world the political and economic affairs of particular areas should be dealt with by regional meetings of all the States concerned. Thus, many of the problems of the American Continent would be handled, as at present, by the Pan-American Union. The British Commonwealth already has its Imperial Conference. The Soviet Union is clearly an entity on a comparable scale. Europe has already been dealt with. A Council of the Far East might conceivably be formed with China as a leading figure. In the Middle East we ourselves might attempt, together with the Soviet Union and the United States, and in co-operation with Turkey, to set up an organisation dealing with Middle Eastern question as a whole. "Backward Areas" have been considered in paragraph 25. But all these Regional Councils would ultimately be subordinate, so far as political issues are concerned, to some Council of the World which, in the early stages after the war at any rate, can for all practical purposes only consist of the representatives of the Four Powers and possibly also of France, who would represent in their turn all the United Nations. (A diagram is attached).

27.   What we want to suggest to the world as a whole, here and now, is that there shall, in the World Council, be some ultimate Court of Appeal, but that in the period after the war it will be necessary for the Great Powers to undertake obligations on behalf of the World Council until the latter can be fully organised.

28.   In any case, unless something like the United Nations Plan can after this war be established on a firm and durable basis, it is only too likely that the course of history will repeat itself and that in the fullness of time Germany will once again resume the struggle for world hegemony, and that she will employ for the purpose the same subtle and gradual methods as were employed so successfully by Hitler between 1933 and 1939. If, therefore, we believe that the United Nations Plan offers the best hope for the future, we should make every possible effort to get it generally agreed without delay.

POLITICAL.

WORLD COUNCIL.

(British Commonwealth, U.S.A., U.S.S.R., China, ?France.)

| British Imperial Conference. | Pan-American Union. | European Council (Armistice and Reconstruction Commission) U.K., U.S.A., U.S.S.R., European Allies: eventually neutrals and ex-enemies. | Far Eastern Council (China, Korea, U.K., U.S.A., U.S.S.R., Canada, ?India, ?Australia: eventually Japan). | S.E. Asia Council (U.K., Australia, Canada, N. Zealand, U.S.A., China, France, Holland, Siam, ?India). | Middle East Council (U.K., ?U.S.A., U.S.S.R., Turkey, Persia, Iraq, Syria, Saudi Arabia, Egypt, ?Palestine). | Africa Council (U.K., ?U.S.A., Union of S.A., France, Portugal, Spain, Abyssinia, Belgium). | Caribbean Commission (U.K., U.S.A., Canada, Holland, France, ?Mexico, Cuba, Puerto Rico, San Domingo, Venezuela). |

ECONOMIC.

WORLD ECONOMIC COUNCIL.

(If Established.)

| Board of Clearing (? and Commercial) Union (4 Powers, plus 8 others). | International Investment Board. | Commodity Control. | I.L.O. (Governing Body). | League of Nations Humanitarian and Economic Services (Directors responsible to Four/Five Powers). | Relief Organisation (Seven-Power Executive Committee). |

N.B.—

1. Political issues arising in the economic councils would be referred either to one of the political regional councils or to the World Council.
2. The "Africa Council" would only apply to Africa south of the Sahara. Alternatively there might be more than one Council for Africa.

United Nations Plan for Organising Peace

W.P. (43) 300
7 July 1943

Memorandum by the Secretary of State for Foreign Affairs

As foreshadowed in the last paragraph of my memorandum on the Post-War Settlement (W.P. (43) 292), I circulate to my colleagues herewith a paper which should be considered as replacing the original "United Nations Plan" contained in W.P. (43) 31 of the 16th January last.

A. – GENERAL CONSIDERATIONS

1. *The Atlantic Charter*

The principles embodied in the Charter will be the basis of any international world order after the war. But they will need to be applied and interpreted so as to provide definitely both for a world security system and for world economic arrangements.

2. *Necessity for an International System and International Machinery*

(i) It is improbable that the League of Nations can be revived in its old form, but it is highly desirable that some international machinery, embodying many of the good features of the League, should be established on the conclusion of hostilities.

(ii) In any case, every effort should be made to preserve those technical and humanitarian services of the League which have been so conspicuously successful in the past, and for which there will be scope in the future.

(iii) The International Labour Office should also continue in existence as such, its functions being expanded as necessary.

(iv) But, quite apart from these existing machines, world opinion will undoubtedly demand with increasing insistence that some system should be devised for ensuring political co-operation, the sphere in which the League was least successful. The foundations upon which such a system must be built already exist in the idea of the United Nations.

3. *Position and Duties of the World Powers*

International co-operation between the United Nations will not provide the necessary cohesion and stability unless the World Powers are prepared to accept the responsibilities of leadership *within* the United Nations. For this purpose these Powers, before the war in Europe comes to an end, should agree between themselves on a common world policy and be prepared, as leaders of the United Nations, to take joint action to enforce it. Failing this, we shall be confronted by the prospect of a world in precarious balance, with the World Powers, each with its circle of client States, facing each other in a rivalry which may merge imperceptibly into hostility.

4. *What States should rank as World Powers*

(i) *The Four Powers*
The leadership of the United Nations will have in some way to be shared between the British Commonwealth (and more especially the United Kingdom), the United States and the Soviet Union, if only for the reason that the refusal of any one of these Powers to enter into a world system would render any world system impracticable. In view of her vast area and population and her potential development it would be desirable for China, too, to be included in the ranks of the World Powers, who between them would thus comprise about two-thirds of the population of the globe. We should therefore regard the conception of these Four Powers, working within the framework of the United Nations, as the basis of any scheme for world organisation.

(ii) *France*
The future of France is obscure, but it would seem essential that, when she has recovered a measure of her greatness, she should be given the same position as the Four Powers, if only because without the willing assistance of a rejuvenated France the problem of recreating a sound and free Europe would be much more difficult.

(iii) *Germany, Japan and Italy not to be re-admitted as World Powers*
It must be assumed that the policy of the United Nations towards the Axis Powers will be to restrict the power for evil of Germany and Japan for as long a period as is necessary, and will not be based on the alternative theory that both these Powers should be readmitted in the foreseeable future to international society on the same footing as the Four (or Five) Powers mentioned above. Italy, on the other hand, has never been a world Power in any real sense, and, in addition, she probably went to war against the real wishes of a considerable proportion of her population. It is therefore possible to contemplate a non-Fascist Italy adhering to the United Nations after the war (although not in any leading capacity) perhaps after some period of probation, and the same applies in varying degrees to the minor Axis allies.

5. *The World Council*

(i) *Composition*
It follows that there should be a World Council, consisting in the first place of the Union of Soviet Socialist Republics, the United States of America, China and the United Kingdom, and possibly also of France. To these might be added the representatives of smaller Powers chosen on a regional basis (see paragraph 24), and with certain defined functions (see sub-paragraph (ii) below). Should it prove difficult to obtain the general agreement of the United Nations to this or any other method of selection, or to these functions, the Four (or Five) Powers should, nevertheless, constitute themselves a Provisional World Council until such time as general agreement can be obtained.

(ii) *Functions*

The functions of any World Council would be two-fold, as follows:

  (a) Since all the World Powers would always be present, its primary and most important task would be to smooth out any frictions existing between them so as to achieve that unity of purpose without which no ordered progress will be possible and the peace of the world is bound to be threatened. Where necessary, discussions on these subjects could be limited to the World Powers themselves.

  (b) But, in addition, it would have to take such dispositions for the restraint of aggression and for ensuring the peaceful settlement of disputes as the needs of a general security system may dictate. It may be hoped that the other nations (whether numbered during this war among the United Nations or among the neutrals) will, as a result of their recent experience, consent to the assumption by the World Powers of leadership for that purpose. Naturally the decisions of the World Powers on all such subjects must be unanimous. The smaller Powers should, however, be given adequate representation on the Council and allowed to influence its decisions. In addition, smaller Powers should always be summoned to sit on the Council when their special interests are under discussion. If the smaller Powers accept this method there is no reason why they should not play an important role in the discussions of the Council. But no opposition on their part should be allowed to prevent the World Powers from taking the necessary action for the restraint of aggression and for ensuring the peaceful settlement of disputes. In other words, the final *decision* on such questions should rest with the World Powers acting unanimously.

6. Judicial and Arbitral Machinery

The experience of the League and other bodies has shown the advantage of establishing arbitral and fact-finding machines for the settlement of the various kinds of disputes that arise between nations. It will be the duty of the Council to see that such machinery is used, and it may be hoped that only rarely will the Council itself be called upon to make the actual decisions.

7. Armaments

An essential part of any future world order will be some agreement between the World Powers as to the forces to be maintained by each of them for internal and external purposes, and also the adoption of some principle regulating the armament of smaller Powers. The armaments which the latter can claim to maintain will in turn depend on (1) how far the policy and undertakings of the World Powers, together with the machinery instituted, guarantee the security of the smaller Powers, and (2) on how far the latter are themselves prepared to play their part, whether active or passive, in a general security system. National independence should no longer be considered as a natural right, but as a privilege entailing for the independent State such corresponding obligations and contributions as may be necessary to ensure the maintenance of international well-being, security and peace. If a satisfactory solution of these points is achieved, the principle to be adopted might be that the armament of each country should be proportionate to the part it would be called upon to play in that system.

8. Immediate Post-War Period

  (i) For a period after the war, during which they will have a virtual monopoly of armed strength, the World Powers will, however, have to undertake by themselves the military responsibility for maintaining order and preventing the building up of aggressive forces in Europe and the Far East. This will entail the maintenance by them of a considerable measure of armaments throughout Europe and in Asia; the complete disarmament of the defeated Powers; and the establishment of a policing system towards the financing of which the defeated Powers, relieved of the burden of armaments, should if practicable, contribute heavily.

(ii) For these immediate purposes the most suitable agencies would seem to be some such bodies as United Nations Commissions, which would have the task, one in Europe, and one in the Far East, of co-ordinating the activities of the various Armistice Commissions and those of other United Nations bodies (see paragraphs 14 and 18). In such Commissions the smaller Allied Powers would co-operate.

B. – ECONOMIC AND SOCIAL CONSIDERATIONS

9. *Economic Aspects of World Order*

International friction and aggression frequently have their roots in economic and social disharmonies. Thus, if standards of living are too unequal, stresses will be created leading to dangerous crises and even to war itself. Consequently, it will be of the highest importance for the United Nations, and in particular for the World Powers, to concern themselves with world economic and social problems.

10. *Relief and Reconstruction*

It will, for instance, be highly desirable, if not essential, to obtain general consent before the end of the war to schemes which will be proof that the combined United Nations can bring and intend to bring early relief to the peoples of disorganised countries. These should include schemes covering monetary control, primary products (especially food-stuffs), etc., so that an "expansionist spiral" of world trade can be initiated. Unless such an expansion of world trade takes place, the economic conditions of many countries may become completely intolerable, and desperate solutions may be urged by desperate people.

11. *Development of Backward Countries*

It will also be necessary to inaugurate steps to smooth out discrepancies in social standards by the encouragement of progressive policies in the less advanced countries. This will require internationally concerted measures to assist the development of the more backward countries. It will also be necessary to utilise the International Labour Office to bring about progressive improvement in labour conditions in the industries of the less advanced countries.

12. *Rôle of Smaller States in World Economic Organisations*

It is at this point that a reconciliation is possible between the military and political realities underlying the conception of the rôle of the World Powers as defined above and the economic interest of smaller States. If the World Powers accept the responsibilities of leadership as the only practicable means of maintaining the peace, they should be careful to see that schemes which deal with economic issues, so long as they do not endanger security, are handled by wider assemblies, whether on a world basis or on regional lines. In other words, the construction of any world authority should be guided by considerations of function. Politically the World Powers, as alone possessing any considerable force, should not hesitate to take the lead. Economically, on the other hand, many Powers other than the World Powers would have much to contribute, and, in so far as they can contribute, they should have a real voice in the direction of affairs.

C. – APPLICATION OF THE PLAN TO EUROPE

13. Action in regard to Germany

(i) It is likely that any United Nations plan will have to be applied in the first instance to Europe. Moreover, the European situation is potentially more dangerous than the Far Eastern as a cause of future wars. The major danger in Europe is the strong central position of Germany, with her large population, natural resources, and highly developed industries, which are the bases of her military power. The maintenance of peace in Europe will consequently depend on the economic as well as the military disarmament of Germany, and on an increase in the relative economic status and power of Germany's neighbours.

(ii) In order to secure this result, the joint occupation of Germany by the three major Allies should be accompanied in the early stages by a very close control over the German economic machine. If this control were successful it would represent an important large-scale experiment in European international administration.

(iii) To prevent the re-emergence of anything like an aggressive German "Unitary State" it would probably in addition be desirable –
    (a) to encourage "particularist" or federal tendencies in any local governments which may set themselves up in Germany when the collapse takes place, subject always to not allowing such Governments to escape the consequences of the war, and
    (b) so to organise the occupation of Germany as to foster any particularist, and even eventually separatist tendencies that may reveal themselves.

(iv) If these political and economic precautions were taken, and Germany was occupied for a considerable number of years, it might not be desirable at once and radically to alter the 1937 (*i.e.*, pre-*Anschluss*) boundaries of the Reich, with the exception of the transfer of East Prussia, Danzig, and certain districts of Eastern Germany to Poland. If such transfers took place, however, they should in principle be accompanied by transfers of population. Finally, the Kiel Canal should be internationalized and an international régime applied to the principal German waterways.

14. The United Nations Commission for Europe

(i) But the best safeguard of all against renewed German attempts to dominate the Continent would lie in the creation of a United Nations Commission for Europe (see paragraph 8 (ii)), consisting of representatives of the United Kingdom, the Soviet Union and the United States, with whom a French representative should, if practicable, be associated on an equal footing. Also associated with them, as might be required, would be representatives of the smaller European Allies, and also of Canada and South Africa, if these Dominions so desired and were prepared to make a military contribution to the European policing system. The Commission might be established at some central point in Europe (*e.g.* Copenhagen or Vienna), and would have wide powers. It might well, for instance, in addition to the functions described in paragraph 8 (ii) above, co-ordinate certain essential services – such as transport – outside as well as inside the Axis territories. Apart from that it would be the organ for exercising all the powers of the United Nations necessary to cope with civil disturbances and any minor hostilities that may flare up after major hostilities have been abandoned.

(ii) It is to be hoped that the European *neutrals* (if any, in fact, remain at the end of the war) would agree to work in with this Commission. If they did not do so agree [sic], however, the United Nations should not shrink from exercising pressure on them.

(iii) Further, the Allied Forces which would be under the higher control of the Commission would, in fact, if not in name, constitute an *International Police Power*, which might at a later stage have a more formal international constitution.

15. European Confederations

(i) In some cases, particularly in Eastern Europe, we may hope to see the amalgamation of the smaller Powers into Confederations. The base for two such Confederations already exist and others might be formed elsewhere. But it is evident that any durable grouping in Eastern Europe can only come about as a result of complete co-operation between the Soviet Government and other leading members of the United Nations.

(ii) It is also assumed that it will not be the intention of the World Powers to attempt to force European nations into unions against their will. Subject to this, it might be possible for the United Nations Commission for Europe, for instance, to encourage "regional" tendencies by centralizing certain services in certain specified areas.

16. The Future of Europe

The measures taken by the United Nations to pacify the peoples of Europe and to restore their means of livelihood and of production will, if they are well conceived and executed, go far towards creating the conditions under which European co-operation may eventually become a reality. To provide a political framework for the various military and economic measures contemplated, it is to be hoped that the United Nations Commission for Europe (see paragraph 14) may at some stage become a "Council of Europe", on which all European States should be represented, including the United Kingdom and the Soviet Union, with the addition, it is to be hoped, of the United States. Neutrals (and Austria) should be admitted to the Council as soon as practicable, and at a fairly early stage Italy and the lesser enemy States; but the admission of Germany must be delayed until at any rate after the occupation has ended and could only then take place as a result of some unanimous decision of the World Council. A Council of Europe in which the United Kingdom, the United States of America, and the Union of Soviet Socialist Republics did not play an active part might become, in course of time, an instrument through which Germany could recover peacefully that hegemony over Europe which she has momentarily established by force of arms during the present war.

D. – APPLICATION TO THE FAR EAST

17. Security Measures in respect of Japan

(i) *Disarmament.* The Far Eastern situation will differ from the European in several important respects. It will be necessary to disarm Japan and for that purpose an Armistice Commission on the lines of that proposed for Germany should be set up. In order to achieve its purpose it must insist on the abolition of fortified zones in Japan and other internal arrangements designed to preserve secrecy as to her intentions. But once these measures have been carried out a prolonged military occupation of Japan may be neither necessary nor desirable, for, in contradistinction to Germany, it should be possible to control Japan's armaments by economic means provided adequate naval and air forces are available in the background.

(ii) *Control of Japan's armaments by indirect means.* It is assumed that Japan will be deprived of her Empire, including Korea and Formosa. This would mean in effect the confinement of the Japanese people to the islands of Japan proper. In such circumstances they will scarcely be able to feed themselves, let alone carry on their industries, without a considerable international trade. Moreover, Japan has only one primary product with an export surplus, silk, and after the war this will lose much of its economic importance owing to the development of Nylon. Unless, therefore, it is proposed to allow a large number of Japanese to starve, it will be necessary to permit the Japanese to develop their imports and exports. But this can be done in such a manner as to allow them to exist but at the same time prevent them from becoming a danger to other countries. The Japanese, it is true, are a united and highly disciplined people who are likely to seek to evade the controls imposed on them. But in order to build up aggressive armaments Japan would have to import the necessary raw materials. If these materials are rationed by an international authority commanding wide control she will be helpless. Such machinery must, therefore, be set up in the first place under the Armistice Commission, but perhaps later developing into a more permanent economic body.

(iii) *Permanent Defence System for the Far East.*   It will also be necessary to construct a permanent defence system, as a further precaution against Japanese aggression and to make possible the economic control of Japan suggested in sub-paragraph (ii) above. For this purpose all suitable bases in the Western Pacific and in Eastern Asia might be put at the disposal of a United Nations Pacific Council of Defence, composed of the United States of America, United Kingdom, Union of Soviet Socialist Republics, China, Canada, (possibly France), Australia, New Zealand, (possibly Portugal) and the Netherlands, which would command the necessary air and naval forces.

18. *Economic and Political Measures*

There will have to be a Relief and Rehabilitation Commission to assist China and other countries, including Japan. Both this body and the Armistice Commission might be co-ordinated by a *United Nations Far Eastern Commission*, and this might some day develop into a "Council of the Far East", which could deal in the first instance with the economic and political problems of that area. Representation of the smaller Far Eastern countries on the World Council (China being in any case a member *ex officio*) might also be arranged by means of this body.

19. *India*

The immediate future of India is too uncertain for her place in the world system to be very exactly defined. It is to be hoped that she will find it as a Dominion. She might immediately be associated in some way with the Permanent Defence System of the Far East (see paragraph 17 (iii)) and/or the South-Eastern Asiatic regional system (see paragraph 24). Communal difficulties might possibly stand in the way of her association with the Middle East regional system (paragraph 22) in spite of her interest in the defence of that area.

E. – EVENTUAL WORLD ORGANISATION

20. *Principles governing "Regionalism"*

Generally speaking, tendencies towards regional groupings should be encouraged, subject always to the principle that no one World Power by itself should be given the task of maintaining order in any particular region. For the contrary principle, if admitted, would give rise to rivalries as between one group and another and hence sow the seeds of future war. In discussing "regionalism", therefore, we must assume that all the World Powers are in principle equally interested in maintaining the peace, and that they will speak with one voice and act together whenever and wherever it may be threatened.

21. *Regional Institutions*

To enable the Great Powers to exercise effective control and to associate the smaller Powers to the greatest possible extent in a world system it may be found convenient to set up regional institutions. Such institutions would have several different objects. They might be used for security, for political and economic collaboration, or for the development and control of dependencies. It has already been mentioned (paragraphs 16 and 18) that a "Council of Europe" and a "Council of the Far East" may eventually result from the immediate measures which must be taken in these two areas. But such developments will take time, and meanwhile regions of smaller extent may be used to obtain the objects mentioned above.

22. Regional Defence Systems (Atlantic and Pacific)

Thus there might come into existence two regional systems whose main object was to maintain security against Germany and Japan. (i) There might be an Atlantic System which associated the United Kingdom, the Union of Soviet Socialist Republics and the United States with the countries of the Western sea-board of Europe (including Denmark) and Canada for purposes of common defence, including the provision of air and sea bases in, *e.g.*, Bergen or the Atlantic Islands. It might well be necessary to sub-divide this system into a Northern and Southern Atlantic system. The latter, if formed, would of course include certain South American States, and notably Brazil and the Argentine. (ii) A similar system could, as contemplated in paragraph 17 (iii), be set up in the Pacific. Here again it might be found desirable to associate with this system some South American State with a Pacific sea-board, such as Mexico, Chile, or Peru.

23. Mixed System (Eastern Europe and Middle East)

A Confederation or Confederations in Eastern Europe might form the nucleus, with the assistance of the World Powers (other than China) of a regional system not only for military, but also for political and economic defence against Germany. The Middle East is in a special position, since it contains neither enemy States nor (except to a very limited extent) colonial areas; but here also there might be a system which should enable the World Powers concerned to some extent to share the responsibility for its defence and provide the leadership necessary to overcome obstacles in the way of political and economic collaboration. Such arrangements, however, should not conflict with the treaty position of Great Britain, under which the independent sovereignty of many of the nations comprised in the area at present rests.

24. Colonial Systems

Three regional systems might be set up for colonial dependencies consisting in the first instance of the "Parent States" concerned, together with other States having a major economic or strategic interest in the area. Thus, dependencies in South Eastern Asia might be associated together not only for economic collaboration but also in order to establish the responsibility of the Powers administering them and to encourage the gradual development of self-government. The Tropical dependencies in Africa might also be combined in one or more regional groups for similar purposes, while the Caribbean Colonies (and the Guineas) might fall into another group.

25. Regional Representation in the World Council

In addition to the functions mentioned above, regions might be used as the means of selecting representatives to sit on the World Council with those of the World Powers. The Pan-American System would naturally be one region and might elect two representatives. Europe might also choose two representatives, possibly one from Western and one from Eastern Europe if the systems suggested in paras. 22 and 23 came into existence. The Far Eastern region, the Middle East and the British Commonwealth of Nations (other than the United Kingdom) might each select one representative.

26. Functions of the Council and Assembly

Such a Council of 11 or 12 members, meeting at regular intervals, would not be too large for effective business under the leadership of the World Powers, while it would link all parts of the world together and serve as a final Court of Appeal for all political or economic issues capable of threatening the peace. But an Assembly of all the United Nations might in addition be summoned at fairly long intervals (say every two years) to receive and discuss reports from the Council and the economic bodies described in para. 10.

27. Alternative Methods of Representation

On the other hand (as already stated in para. 5 (i)), it must be recognised that it may be difficult or impossible to establish such a system of regional representation. If this should prove to be the case it might be possible to fall back on election of seven representatives by an annual Assembly. Failing this, the only alternative would be the Four (Five)-Power Council referred to in para. 5 (i).

28. Where should all this International Machinery be?

How far the Council (and consequently the Assembly) should have a regular meeting place is primarily a matter for consideration by the World Powers. But the Council, like the League Council in its earlier stages, could, if desired, meet at different places according to convenience. The international economic and social bodies would, however, certainly need a permanent centre, which it is suggested might be in the Western Hemisphere, as well as a permanent secretariat in which the existing staffs of the League and the I.L.O. should be incorporated. It might well be that the Council would often in practice find it convenient to meet at that centre.

29. Secretariat

It might be better not to form any elaborate international political secretariat until it is seen how the Council and Assembly are going to work and where the headquarters of the new organisation is likely to be. But it would obviously be necessary to have some "Secretary-General" or "Moderator" with a small staff to produce the agenda, conduct correspondence with the economic and regional organisations and generally make arrangements for the meetings of the Council and Assembly.

APPENDIX C

Future World Organisation

W.P. (44) 370   P.M.M. (44) 4
3 July 1944   8 May 1944

COVERING NOTE TO MEMORANDUM PREPARED FOR DISCUSSION WITH THE
DOMINION PRIME MINISTERS. (P.M.M. (44) 4, 8 MAY 1944)*

IN Article 4 of the Moscow Declaration of November 1943 the Four Powers state —
"that they recognise the necessity of establishing at the earliest practicable date a general
international organisation, based on the principle of the sovereign equality of all
peace-loving States, and open to membership by all such States, large and small, for the
maintenance of international peace and security."

2.   When the Declaration was discussed at the Moscow Conference Mr. Hull suggested that
it might be signed at a later date by the other United Nations. M. Molotov subsequently
proposed that a Commission of the Three Powers should be formed to study Article 4 of the
Declaration. At a later session Mr. Hull suggested "an informal understanding to acquire
material for constituting the Commission" and in reply to M. Molotov agreed to an
"unofficial Commission". He added, "that they could gradually select persons to work
together and decide on the peace: sometimes in Moscow, sometimes London, sometimes in
Washington." Mr. Hull emphasised the secrecy which should surround such discussions.
Agreement was incorporated in the Secret Protocol of the Moscow Conference, para. 2 (b),
as follows:—
"It was recognised as desirable that representatives of the United States of America, the
United Kingdom and the Soviet Union should conduct in a preliminary fashion an
exchange of views on questions connected with the establishment of an international
organisation for the maintenance of international peace and security, the intention being
that this work should be carried out in the first instance in Washington, and also in
London and Moscow."

3.   On the 19th November, 1943, a note was received from the United States Chargé
d'Affaires in London suggesting, on instructions from the State Department, that the Four
Powers should announce that they would welcome the adherence of all peace-loving States
to Article 4 of the Declaration. A corresponding communication was made to the Union of
Soviet Socialist Republics and China. In reply His Majesty's Government in the United

* As explained in the text, this covering note was omitted when the memoranda were
presented to the Cabinet on 7 July. The version of memoranda A and B which follows is the
revised version as contained in W.P. (44) 370; passages underlined show alterations from
P.M.M. (44) 4. The alterations were made to accommodate Churchill's views while retaining
the essential principles approved by the Dominion Prime Ministers in May. Memoranda C—E
were unchanged and are reproduced from P.M.M. (44) 4.

Kingdom suggested that this step was premature in view of the agreement at Moscow to have preliminary Three-Power discussions. The Dominions were informed of the proposal, and the Canadian Government in particular thought that a longer document should be prepared before the signature of the other United Nations was invited. The United States Government accepted the British suggestion and the Soviet Government also, though the latter had agreed to the original United States proposal. The United Kingdom and United States Governments exchanged agenda for the Washington discussions which were communicated to the Soviet Government, and the United States Government suggested a preliminary exchange of papers. Subsequently the United Kingdom Government proposed that memoranda should be written on the five main topics enumerated below. The United States Government agreed that our papers should be written on these topics, though their own might have somewhat different titles. The Soviet Government also agreed generally to the suggested procedure, reserving the question of priority of topics. The five topics are as follows:—

A. Scope and nature of an international organisation.
B. Guarantees and the pacific settlement of disputes.
C. Security.
D. Co-ordination of economic and political international machinery.
E. Method and procedure for establishing a world organisation.

4. These, therefore, are the subject headings of the accompanying Memoranda, which are designed, subject to any observations on the part of the Dominion Prime Ministers, to be handed to the Americans and Russians. An attempt has been made to sketch the outline of a workable World Organisation in the light of experience of international institutions. The proposals do not provide a complete solution of all the problems discussed because many of the premises on which such conclusions could be based do not yet exist. It is suggested, however, that our first aim should be to bring the World Organisation into existence. When it has been established, it should be able to find out by its own experience the methods by which international problems may be solved.

5. The Organisation suggested has much in common with the Covenant of the League of Nations and, in accordance with the expressed intention of the Prime Minister, it tries to retain all the best features of its predecessor. But it is meant to be more flexible, less bound by rigid definitions which hamper or prevent necessary action, and above all endowed with the machinery to make action effective. In short, our plan is based on the acceptance of certain essential principles and we leave the means by which these principles shall be carried out to be adapted to the varying circumstances of human intercourse which cannot be foreseen.

6. It is thus that the institutions of Britain and the Commonwealth have grown, and it is this method that their peoples will best understand. Our method of approach may possibly make less appeal to the more legally minded people of the United States, who attach so much importance to the details of a written constitution, or to the Russians, whose way of thinking is very different from our own, or to the peoples of the Continent of Europe, who have a different system of law and have always desired explicit undertakings no matter how often they have been broken. But, though changes may have to be made to meet these points of view, we believe that something like what we suggest represents the maximum of effective international co-operation that can be secured at the present time.

7. The most essential point is to obtain an organisation embracing the United Kingdom and the other Members of the British Commonwealth, the United States and the U.S.S.R., and, it might perhaps be added, France. This, therefore, should be our primary object and no minor consideration should be allowed to stand in its way.

8. The establishment of a centre where the policies of the principal States of the world can be harmonised is in the great tradition of British policy, and we believe that the present proposals carry on a development which was supported by Castlereagh, Palmerston, Salisbury and Grey before the last war and by Lord Balfour, Sir Austen Chamberlain and Mr. Arthur Henderson in the period between the wars.

9. We attach great importance to the establishment of some permanent machinery by which rapid and effective action may be taken against any threat to world peace. The world has seen so many promises broken that faith in the new institution can only be obtained if the means of action are visible, and will, perhaps, only be confirmed after such action has taken place.

10. It is essential to the interests of the British Commonwealth that the Organisation should be world-wide. We have, therefore, subordinated the creation of regional organisations to this end. But we believe that in due course regional organisations (which will probably develop naturally) may play an important part in the world and that if they are suitably guided within the World Organisation their advantages will outweigh their disadvantages.

11. In *Memorandum A* we have assumed that the World Council will consist of the Four Powers and a number of other States. We have left open the method by which these States are chosen because we think that it would be premature to put forward a cut-and-dried scheme at this stage. We have not even laid down the principle that one of the members of the Commonwealth other than the United Kingdom should always have a place on the World Council. Such a demand may very likely provoke a counter demand from the Soviet Government that one of the constituent republics of the U.S.S.R. should always have a seat on the World Council. Whether it can be ensured that another British Commonwealth country in addition to the United Kingdom shall always have a place on the Council must obviously depend on the number of Council members. But we recognise that it should be our object to obtain this result.

12. We have also left open the questions of the Secretariat and the seat of the Organisation, problems closely interrelated. They raise issues on which it is likely to be difficult to come to an agreement and we think that it would be better to postpone them to a later stage of the discussions.

13. Under our proposals, great power would rest in the hands of the World Council. It would, for instance, take the initiative in action to maintain peace, and other members would be bound to follow its decisions. We have, however, left open the question of placing permanently a special responsibility on the Great Powers for the maintenance of international peace and security. By doing so the association of the United States in the burden would be more explicitly obtained, but it may well be possible to secure that advantage without such definition as might seem to imply too great a recognition of the position of the Great Powers in the Organisation.

14. We have not mentioned the Colonial question and prefer to leave it to the United States Government to raise the question if they so desire.

15. In *Memorandum B* the machinery for the pacific settlement of disputes and the maintenance of peace and security has been made as flexible as possible. The members of the British Commonwealth have always been opposed to such guarantees of territorial integrity and political independence as those contained in Article X of the Covenant. Our proposals contain three main propositions:—

(i) That the members of the Organisation shall promise to settle all disputes in such a manner as not to endanger the maintenance of international peace and security without, however, guaranteeing the territorial integrity and political independence of member States. (We have attempted in this manner, so far as can be done at the present stage of international relations, to throw the balance rather more in the direction of change.)

(ii) That the World Council shall be given the initiative to take action for the maintenance of peace and security. (It is only in this way that machinery can be set up to make the promises of the members effective.)

(iii) That action by the Organisation shall be based on principles rather than on elaborate definition (which we believe defeats its own purpose.)

16.   In *Memorandum C* we have merely edited in a form suitable for communication to the Americans and Russians the two papers already blessed by the Chiefs of Staff as suitable to be used as a basis for discussions. The way is thus left open to utilise existing machinery for co-operation in military matters if it is found possible to do so at the end of the war. We have suggested that the members should be prepared to place military forces at the disposal of the World Council, by which means we hope the burden on the Members of the British Commonwealth may be reduced.

17.   We have only made a passing reference to the regulation of armaments, which the United States Government have placed on their list of topics. But our own proposals would enable this country eventually to deal with this question constructively as part of the process for sharing the burden of the armaments necessary to maintain international peace and security, rather than by the negative means of limitation of armaments by scales and numbers.

18.   In *Memorandum D* we have endeavoured to find a method of giving the necessary co-ordination to the new and untried economic and technical organisations without depriving them of the necessary control over their own actions. Here again the questions of organisation must be worked out in the light of experience, but it is essential that these institutions should be co-ordinated in order that the problems of full employment and the proper use of resources may be solved.

19.   The United States Government will naturally decide for itself the best methods by which an international organisation can secure the assent of Congress. But we have put forward the proposals contained in *Memorandum E* as an assistance to their thinking on this subject, and we attach considerable importance to choosing the right method of associating other States with the work of the Four Powers.

20.   Before *Memoranda A to E* are given to the United States and Soviet Governments, we should like to feel sure that other British Commonwealth Governments agree that these papers are on the right lines as a basis for the preliminary and informal discussions, which it is hoped will take place at Washington at the end of May or early in June. It is suggested in *Memorandum E* that the aim of the Washington talks should be to reach a measure of agreement which could find expression in a Draft Declaration to be referred to Governments and subsequently published. It is contemplated that the progress made in the Washington talks would be the subject of further consultation between British Commonwealth Governments before any such declaration were published.

MEMORANDUM A

Scope and Nature of the Permanent Organisation

I. – THE PRINCIPLES AND OBJECTS OF THE ORGANISATION.

1.   The World Organisation will consist of independent States freely associated and working together for the better realisation of the common good of mankind.

2.   The principles and objects of the Organisation should be stated in the preamble of the document which brings it into existence. The Organisation should be as simple and flexible as possible. Thus the statement of its principles and objects becomes specially important, since they lay down the conditions in which action is taken by the members of the Organisation.

3.   Article 4 of the Moscow Declaration lays down that the Organisation shall be based on the "sovereign equality" of States. Two principles follow from these words. In the first place members must agree to respect each other's political independence, and secondly all members enjoy equality of status, though not necessarily equality of function.

4.   Members should not be entitled to receive the benefits of the Organisation unless they are prepared to accept the obligations that go with them. Moreover, it is the assumption of such obligations by all members that ensures to all the benefits of the Organisation. This should be recognised, therefore, as one of the principles of the Organisation.

5.   The object of the Organisation is stated in Article 4 to be the "maintenance of international peace and security", and this must be regarded as its primary purpose.

6.   But if recourse to violence is ruled out, means must be provided by which members of the Organisation can settle their disputes by other than violent methods; and the establishment of machinery for achieving this must be one of the objects of the Organisation.

7.   Moreover, in order that international peace and security shall be maintained there must be in the world some means by which States meet together to review and harmonise their political action. One of the objects of the Organisation, therefore, must be to create a meeting place where statesmen can come together for that purpose.

8.   But international peace and security must be made positively, and not only kept by the negative means of suppressing violence. They will be confirmed and strengthened by guarding the right of man to seek his freedom, and by increase in the well-being of human society. Statesmen of the United Nations have declared this to be both the purpose and the condition of development in international order.

9.   It will be necessary, therefore, for the Organisation to create institutions to promote the betterment of world-wide economic conditions and the removal of social wrongs, and to support and extend institutions which now exist for these purposes.

10.   Thus the principles and objects of the Organisation, and consequently the conditions in which its members receive its benefits and accept its obligations and on which actions taken under its authority are based, may be described as follows:—

11.   *Principles.*

   (i) That all members of the Organisation undertake to respect each other's political independence.

   (ii) That all members are equal in status though not necessarily in function.

   (iii) That all members undertake to fulfil towards each other the obligations which are the conditions of receiving the benefits of the Organisation.

12.   *Objects.*

   (i) To ensure that peace and security shall be maintained so that men shall not live in fear of war.

   (ii) To provide means by which all disputes arising between States may be so dealt with that peace and security are not endangered.

   (iii) To provide a centre in which the political action of States can be reviewed and harmonised, and directed towards a common end.

(iv) To promote the betterment of world-wide economic conditions and the well-being of all men by international agreement so that the fear of want may be removed from the world.

(v) To guard and enlarge the freedom of man by institutions for the removal of social wrongs.

II. – THE NATURE OF THE ORGANISATION.

13.   In Article 4 of the Moscow Declaration it is laid down that the organisation is to be founded on the sovereign equality of its members. Its members will, therefore, retain control of their own actions except so far as they are limited by the obligations into which they freely enter and by international law.

14.   Nothing has been more clearly proved during the present war than the interconnexion of peace and security in all parts of the world. The future organisation must recognise this fact and be a world organisation in which all peaceful States in every part of the world can co-operate together for their mutual benefit.

15.   Though the status of all members is equal and all will enjoy the same rights and undertake the corresponding obligations, their differences in power make necessary some recognition of differences in function. The initiative for the formation of the organisation has come from the Four Powers, the United States, the U.S.S.R., the United Kingdom and China, and it is generally recognised that its success will depend more upon their continued co-operation than on any other single factor. The machinery of the organisation should make it possible for them to carry out the responsibilities which they will have agreed to undertake. They must be given, therefore, a special position in the organisation in order effectively to maintain peace and security. In general, as regards all States, the more power and responsibility can be made to correspond, the more likely is it that the machinery will be able to fulfil its functions.

16.   We look forward to the liberation of France and her restoration to the ranks of the Great Powers.

17.   It is presumed that there will come into existence a number of specialised technical organisations through which States will combine together for various purposes. There are already such organisations in existence as part of the system of the League of Nations. The relations of these bodies to one another and to the main organisation are considered in Memorandum D. Here it need only be said that such bodies are unlikely to survive as effective instruments in a world from which reasonable security is absent.

18.   Just as there are special functional organisations, so there may be regional associations for various purposes when there is obvious advantage to be obtained by limitation of the sphere of action. In particular there should be some regional organisation for the Continent of Europe if only to prevent a repetition of the circumstances which have caused two World Wars to originate in that area. The condition of Europe at the close of this war will demand the special care and assistance of the three Great Powers and means must be found to prevent its becoming the centre of a third world tragedy. It is possible that out of some "United Nations Commission for Europe", as proposed in paragraphs 9 and 10 of Mr. Eden's memorandum of the 1st July, 1943 (annexed), there might grow a European organisation which, under the guidance of the three major allies, might foster peaceful tendencies, heal the wounds of Europe, and at the same time prevent Germany from again dominating the Continent. Such regional associations might also come into existence for economic co-operation, for the promotion of welfare in colonial territories, &c. It is, however, essential that they should not conflict with the world-wide organisation but rather assist it to carry out its purposes.

III. – CONSTITUTION OF THE ORGANISATION.

19.   It is generally recognised that it will be necessary to set up two main bodies, one as a centre of discussion on which all States are represented and the other, a smaller body, as a centre of action. It is suggested that these bodies be termed the World Assembly and the World Council respectively.

20.   *Membership.* – It is assumed that at the outset all the United Nations will be invited to be members of the Organisation. What States now neutral shall be admitted and at what period is a matter for consideration. The enemy States cannot be admitted until they have shown by their conduct that they accept the objects of the organisation and intend to pursue them.

21.   All the members of the organisation should share in some manner in the admission of new members. It will have to be considered how far it is necessary to lay down conditions under which a State shall cease to be a member of the Organisation.

22.   *World Assembly.* – The sovereign equality of all members should be recognised by their representatives meeting together on a footing of equality in a World Assembly at least once a year. The right of information and criticism should belong to all members of the organisation.

23.   It is not suggested that this body should have all the powers that were possessed by the Assembly of the League. The specialised and technical bodies should undertake some of the duties which that body performed and the initiative in preventing breaches of the peace should lie with the World Council.

24.   It is a matter for consideration whether the World Assembly should have the control over finance and the admission of new members which the Assembly of the League possessed; but it is suggested that the States cannot be expected to contribute to the finances of an organisation without some share in their determination, nor to belong to a society to which other States may be admitted without consultation with them.

25.   *World Council.* – This body should be sufficiently small and compact to ensure action and of such a character as to possess the confidence of all members of the organisation.

26.   The constitution of this body raises many difficult problems. The relation between the Great Powers and other States has been a matter of dispute for over a century. It is clearly necessary that the Four Powers, which between them are directly responsible for the peace and security of nearly two-thirds of the world's inhabitants, should always be represented on it. The principle has been generally accepted that where the interests of any State are specially affected it should have the right to lay its case before the Council.*

27.   It is desirable that the World Council should be strictly limited in size, and it has been suggested in some quarters that its membership should be restricted to the three or four Powers upon whom the responsibility for maintaining peace principally depends. It is, however, open to question whether the other States would agree to the establishment of a Council so limited in number. In any case the number and method of their representation is a matter for grave consideration and the manner in which the decisions of the Council shall be made may depend on the method adopted. The object would be to ensure that the other States on the World Council command general confidence. Some form of election is probably essential and the World Assembly might† be used for this purpose.

28.   In such a Council some means must be found to ensure that the various regions of the World are adequately represented. The size and area of States vary so greatly and are so

---

* *In the May version the order of the last two sentences was reversed.*
† *'can obviously' in the May version.*

unevenly distributed over the Continents that some agreement on this subject is essential. Thus, the Caribbean area has more independent States than all the rest of Latin America, which includes Brazil, Argentina and Chile. Both Europe and South America have many more States than North America or Asia. Hitherto States as different in power and status as Canada and Panamá have had equal rights of representation. The principles [*sic*] of rotation has deprived the Council of experienced statesmen, while the creation of "semi-permanent" seats was much resented by some of the States that did not enjoy the privilege.

29. If the principle which governs the election of the Governing Body of the I.L.O. could be accepted, a more satisfactory result might be obtained, but it is difficult to find the principle to apply to a political body.

30. Should Regional Associations of sufficient importance be formed (e.g., a regional organisation for Europe) they might furnish a basis for representation on the Council. But for the most part States do not recognise other States as "representing" them on institutions in which they have a major interest.

31. It is clear that this subject will need careful examination — not only amongst the Four Powers themselves but with the other States whose wishes must be taken into account.

32. The main *function* of the World Council will be to ensure such intercourse between the statesmen of the countries represented on it as to enable them to secure solutions of international problems by discussion and co-operative action. For this purpose regular meetings with an appropriate procedure and secretariat are indispensable. No other single factor is likely to be so influential in producing harmony between the policies of States. The experience of the last thirty years shows that there is no adequate substitute for it.

33. The functions suggested for the World Council as the body responsible for the peace of the world are described in Memorandum B.

34. It will also be necessary for the World Council to give some common direction to the functional bodies. This question is considered in Memorandum D.

35. In general it is hoped that the Council may become a centre where Governments reconcile their attitudes towards major international problems so as to be able to act decisively towards a common end.

36. *Permanent Court of International Justice.* — It is assumed that there will be general agreement that a Permanent Court of International Justice will be set up. The proposals of the Informal Inter-Allied Committee which recently reported on this question seem to indicate the general lines that should be followed.

37. *Secretariat.* — A permanent secretariat will be indispensable. The experience of the League of Nations and the I.L.O. should be utilised. It is assumed, however, that a number of new specialised technical bodies will come into existence. Further consideration of this question might, therefore, await more definite information concerning them.

38. The suggestion that the head of the Secretariat should be given the right of bringing before the World Council any matter which in his opinion threatens the peace of the world might well be incorporated in the rules of the Organisation.

39. *Specialised and Technical Organisations.* — This question is considered in Memorandum D. The position of the International Labour Organisation will need special consideration.

40. *Seat of the Organisation.* — This problem should be left open until further information is available on the number and character of the functional organisations.

41. *Name of the Organisation.* – The term "United Nations" is now in general use and there does not seem to be any strong reason to substitute any other for it.

ANNEX

Extract from Mr. Eden's memorandum of 1 July 1943 'Suggested Principles which would govern the conclusion of hostilities with the European members of the Axis'

'...

(9)   There should be established a supervisory body entitled "United Nations Commission for Europe", composed of high-ranking *political* representatives of the United Kingdom, the United States and the U.S.S.R., of France and the minor European Allies, and, if so desired, of any Dominion prepared to contribute to the policing of Europe. The Commission should be situated at some convenient point on the Continent.

The Commission would act as the supreme United Nations authority in Europe to direct and co-ordinate the activities of the several Armistice Commissions, the Allied Commanders-in-Chief and any United Nations civilian authorities that may be established; and to deal with current problems, military, political and economic, connected with the maintenance of order.

A "Steering Committee", consisting of the representatives of the United Kingdom, the United States and the U.S.S.R. and of France, if she recovers her greatness, should be established as the directing body of the Commission. In the "Steering Committee" the unanimity rule should apply.

(10)   It is likely that a number of civilian authorities will be set up by agreement between the United Nations, some on a world and others on a European basis. Apart from the United Nations Relief and Rehabilitation Administration and the Inter-Governmental Committee which may emerge from the Bermuda Conference, the establishment of a United Nations Shipping Authority and a United Nations Inland Transport Authority for Europe have been suggested. Analogous bodies may well be required to control telecommunications and propaganda and to handle reparation and restitution and other economic problems. These authorities might, in respect of their European activities, establish their headquarters in the same city as the United Nations Commission for Europe, to whom they would be responsible and provide the necessary technical advice.'

MEMORANDUM B

The Pacific Settlement of Disputes, the Question of Guarantees and the Conditions in which Action should be taken for the Maintenance of Peace and Security

I. – INTRODUCTION.

IF war is to be prevented there must be in existence a means to make those decisions which in the past have been made by violence. If an organisation is set up to achieve this end there must be some guarantee that its members will be protected should States, inside or outside it, threaten to subject them to violence. For the purpose of providing protection, action may have to be taken against an offending State, and this necessitates some statement of how and when such action shall be taken.

2.   The maintenance of peace and security is not merely an end in itself but a means by which an ordered and progressive community of States may come into existence. The principles and objects of such a society have been indicated in Part I of Memorandum A, and it is on them that all action by the Organisation should be based. A state of peace should be regarded as not simply the acceptance of the *status quo* but active co-operation between States for the objects and principles of the Organisation.

3.   Such ends cannot be obtained by any system of procedure however skilfully designed. Everything depends on the unity of purpose of those States which possess the greatest means of carrying out their purposes. It is impossible to ensure that these States will always be in agreement, and no set of rules will do so. But an agreement to act under certain specific principles in a World Organisation will make their co-operation easier and will enable other States to be associated with them for their common purpose.

4.   If all the Great Powers are members of the Organisation and show their intention of acting in accordance with it, all States will be more ready to accept the responsibilities commensurate with their power. The absence of the United States and, for a long period, of the Union of Soviet Socialist Republics from the League of Nations caused the United Kingdom to review its responsibilities. For the same reason smaller States were often reluctant to accept full responsibility.

5.   For the same reason also there was great anxiety on the part of many States to define very closely the occasion for action by the organs and members of the League of Nations. As is explained below, this attempt failed in its purpose. Moreover, public opinion did not understand the elaborate safeguards against arbitrary action that existed. It is suggested that the methods embodied in the constitution of the Organisation should be simple and flexible. They should be extended and elaborated only as the result of experience.

6.   It is believed also that, whatever procedure be adopted, it is only by setting up some definite security system such as is suggested in Memorandum C that reality will be given to the promises made and that the States of the world will come to believe that by accepting the rights and responsibilities given to them by the Organisation they will be spared such sufferings as they are now enduring.

II. – THE PACIFIC SETTLEMENT OF DISPUTES.

7.   Disputes between States are divided into two main categories, those, often termed "justiciable", that can be settled by a legal tribunal, and those in which other considerations are predominant.

8.   It is the second class which produces the most intractable and dangerous disputes, including those in which the legal position is entirely clear. In the past, States have promised not to attempt settlement of their disputes by violent means, but they have not promised to settle their disputes. It is suggested that it might be well if they now promised to "settle" their disputes in the sense that they will not allow them to endanger peace and security.

9.   *Justiciable Disputes.* – It would seem that there is likely to be general agreement that justiciable disputes should be generally settled by a Permanent Court of International Justice. The Informal Inter-Allied Committee suggested in its recent report that the Court be open to all States, whether they accept compulsory jurisdiction or not. It would be possible for the International Organisation to make the acceptance of such an obligation a condition of membership, but in such a case it would be necessary to allow States to make certain reservations.

10.   The difference between accepting compulsory jurisdiction with reservations and retaining full freedom of action is likely to have more psychological than practical effect, especially if the World Council can obtain Advisory Opinions from the Court on some point in a dispute, which has been submitted to it.

11.   *Other Disputes.* – Reference to the World Council is the obvious method of dealing with other disputes. Though other elaborate methods of conciliation have been set up they have hardly ever been used and they have the disadvantage of placing the case in the hands of persons who are not responsible for the consequences of failure to preserve peace. It is only in the World Council itself that a body of rules and a technique of procedure can be gradually established as the result of accumulated experience.

12.   It should be for the World Council to decide what method should be used for dealing with the dispute. Any decision of this nature should be regarded as a decision of procedure and consequently be adopted by a majority vote.

13.   Even on questions of principle (as opposed to questions of procedure) decisions might be taken by (say) a two-thirds majority of the Council rather than by unanimity. In all such cases all the Four Powers should of course be included in the majority.* In any event, the votes of the parties to the dispute should not be taken into account.

14.   States are not likely to bind themselves to accept the decisions of the Council in all cases. Nor would it be likely that they would undertake the obligation to enforce it on other States in all cases. But it would still be the function of the World Council, and particularly of the Great Powers on it, to see that disputes did not threaten peace and security and for the other States to co-operate with it to the utmost of their power for that purpose, so that there would still be large opportunities for action to deal with even the most difficult disputes.

15.   For, as has been indicated, if peace and security are to be maintained, some method must be devised for the settlement of all disputes between States. "Settlement" in this sense may, as is often the case in domestic disputes, show that no remedy exists for a legitimate grievance. But if States promise to "settle" their disputes in the sense defined in paragraph 8 above, the balance is thrown more in the direction of change. The *status quo* is sufficiently safeguarded by the mere existence of a universal system for the maintenance of peace and security. Should the dispute be such as to threaten peace and security, it will be for the World Council (and in such cases action will depend largely on the Great Powers) to decide what action should be taken to deal with it.

16.   If the dispute involves the Great Powers themselves the machinery for decision may prove inadequate; but there is hope that the habit of co-operative leadership in the settlement of other disputes and the restraints imposed by their own promises to one another and to other States may suffice to achieve a settlement, even where the machinery seems to be inadequate to do so. Much will depend on whether a sufficient number of States, great and small, come to attach so much importance to the preservation of the system that they are prepared to run risks and make sacrifices to support and preserve it.

17.   There was considerable agreement in the period between the two wars that the vague words of Article XIX of the Covenant of the League of Nations were hardly a sufficient recognition of the fact that there must be a change in the world. When, in the thirties, it was perceived that there was no great desire in some countries to go to war to defend some of the frontiers erected by the Peace Treaties, there was much discussion of a process which became known as "Peaceful Change". Examination of this concept shows that it cannot be obtained by a clause in a Covenant, but can only be a continual process achieved through

---

* *In the May version this sentence read 'We leave this important question open, but it seems desirable that in all such cases all the Four Powers should be included in the majority.'*

discussion and compromise between the Great Powers and, in their due place, the smaller States concerned. But it is essential that such a process be guided by principle and subject to an ordered procedure, and it is necessary, therefore, that it should take place within an international organisation.

18.   It may be hoped that the international functional organisations which are being brought into existence will contribute to furthering the process of peaceful change in an orderly manner.

III. – THE QUESTION OF GUARANTEES.

19.   In considering this question the history of the guarantees given in the Covenant of the League of Nations must be taken into account, since it throws great light on the nature of the problem. For by Article X the Members of the League "undertook to respect and preserve as against external aggression the territorial integrity and existing political independence of all Members." The formula had first been devised by President Wilson for the Western Hemisphere and it was at his instance that it was applied universally. No method was laid down as to how the obligation should be carried out except that the Council should "advise" upon that question.

20.   *Territorial Integrity.* – There was much opposition to the proposed Article, attention being concentrated on the question of "territorial integrity". Lord Cecil suggested that the guarantee should be withdrawn if the State concerned refused to accept a modification of frontier desired by a large majority of the members of the League of Nations. The vague phraseology of Article XIX of the Covenant was all that resulted from this proposal. Mr. Lansing and Dr. Miller were also opposed to inserting Article X, though the latter came to believe that it made little difference. Sir Robert Borden tried to abolish it before the Covenant was signed, and the Canadian Delegation renewed the attempt at the First Assembly. In 1923 an interpretative resolution was adopted by the Assembly (though as Persia dissented it had no legal force) which laid down that it was for each State to decide how it should carry out its obligations under this head, while the Council was to take into account, in any advice that it might give, the geographical situation and special conditions of each State.

21.   In fact, Article X was hardly ever used in the disputes which came before the League of Nations. But it was constantly referred to when some State wished to remind others that its existing frontiers were guaranteed by them. It was also constantly used by critics of the League of Nations to show that its members had guaranteed for all time frontiers which they possessed no legal means of changing without the consent of the State concerned.

22.   Much smaller attention has been paid to this subject in recent discussions, though there may, of course, be a shift of interest when the treaties that register any changes of frontier which may be made come into existence. There is, however, reason to think that many States will be more interested in the establishment of some concrete security system ready for immediate action than in guarantees of frontiers which in themselves do little to prevent the invasion and occupation of territory by the armed forces of another State.

23.   Many other States would be likely to refuse to accept an Organisation which committed them to a guarantee of the territorial integrity of all States.

24.   It is suggested, therefore, that no such guarantee be included in the obligations undertaken by members of the Organisation.

25.   *Political Independence.* – The question of "political independence" raises issues of a rather different character. The Moscow Declaration has already based the Organisation on the "sovereign equality" of all States, which implies that the Members of the Organisation

will retain legal control over their own actions except in so far as they agree by treaty to limit it. All States naturally attach the highest value to their political independence, and the principal statesmen have made repeated declarations that they intend to respect the independence of other States.

26. But an undertaking to respect the political independence of other States does not necessarily involve a commitment to guarantee it. It is, moreover, not easy to define exactly what political independence is. One State may control the actions of another State by indirect means. It is impossible to distinguish the line which divides such actions from what is generally regarded as the legitimate influence which one State may exercise on the actions of another. The objection to any guarantee of "political independence", therefore, is that it could only extend to external and legal forms. It could not take into account more indirect methods.

27. For this reason the inclusion of a guarantee of political independence in the obligations of the Organisation seems undesirable. But it should be recognised that mutual respect for the political independence of its members is one of the essential principles of the Organisation as already pointed out in Part I of Memorandum A.

28. *The Maintenance of International Peace and Security.* – By the Covenant of the League, States undertook to inflict sanctions on another State which broke its promises to submit a dispute to pacific settlement *and* resorted to war. It was for each State to determine its own actions after the Council (or Assembly) had declared that the occasion for action had arisen. Doubt was constantly expressed as to the sufficiency of this promise, though, so far as words can guarantee action, a definite promise was made. But the duty of enforcing action to be taken was laid on the members.

29. Also by Article XI of the Covenant the duty of safeguarding the "peace of nations" was laid on the League, but no specific obligations as regards the action to be taken were laid on the Members.

30. The Four Powers have already, by Article 4 of the Moscow Declaration, laid down that the main purpose of the international organisation is the "maintenance of international peace and security", and have asserted by Article 5 that "they will consult with one another and, as occasion requires, with other members of the United Nations, with a view to joint action on behalf of the community of nations" for this purpose until a system of general security is inaugurated. It would seem that it is along these lines that any guarantee should be given.

31. The duty of co-operating to the utmost of their power in the maintenance of international peace and security should be undertaken by all members of the Organisation. The degree of such co-operation must obviously depend on the geographical situation of States, the amount of their resources, their own internal situation and possibly other factors which cannot be accurately weighed in advance. But the duty of co-operating to the utmost of their power in an Organisation which is essential to the peace and security of all should be laid upon all members.

32. The duty of maintaining international peace and security should be laid in the first instance on the World Council acting on behalf of the other members of the Organisation. It will be for the World Council to take the initiative to give effect to the undertaking to maintain international peace and security. The head of the Secretariat should, however, as suggested in paragraph 38 of Memorandum A, be given the right to bring before the Council any matter which in his opinion threatened international peace and security.

33. It is for consideration whether any special obligations for the maintenance of international peace and security should be explicitly assumed within the permanent Organisation by the Four Powers who have undertaken such a responsibility pending the establishment of a general system.

34.   If regional organisations are set up for security purposes, part of the responsibility in the first instance might fall on them, but, as is suggested in Memorandum A, paragraph 18, not in such a manner as to conflict with the final responsibility of the World Council for the maintenance of peace and security.

IV. — THE CONDITIONS IN WHICH ACTION SHOULD BE TAKEN FOR THE MAINTENANCE OF PEACE AND SECURITY.

35.   It is generally recognised that there must be some statement in the constitution of the Organisation as to the conditions in which action is taken to maintain international peace and security. In the Covenant of the League of Nations and in the attempts to elaborate the Covenant great attention was given to this question.

36.   In the Covenant the sanctions of Article XVI came into force only if there was resort to war after a Member had broken the promises made in Articles XII—XIV. Even then each State necessarily determined for itself whether the *casus foederis* had arisen.

37.   In Article X the guarantees were against "external aggression" only. It was by this article that the unfortunate word "aggression" was introduced into the Covenant and became the subject of so many debates at Geneva. But the more the word was discussed the more difficult it became to define exactly what it meant. The definition of aggression was considered important because it was thought that it might affect the right of the Council to advise that sanctions be employed. The most notable contribution to the debate was the suggestion that aggression should be determined by the acceptance or refusal of arbitration or some other peaceful method of settling disputes. But this did not cover the preparations for aggression, nor did it take the time element sufficiently into account. Moreover, the discussion and analysis of aggression enabled States to use a procedure calculated to defeat the objects of the Covenant. Illustration of this fact was given by the Japanese attack on China in Manchuria.

38.   In Article XI sanctions were not mentioned, and the obligations of the Council were stated in the most general terms. These obligations could be interpreted as giving the right to take drastic action, but in the light of other articles it was difficult to find in them any right to use force against a State. In actual practice a number of dangerous situations that arose between small States were dealt with successfully under Article XI, and a technique which involved such matters as the setting up of commissions of enquiry and the establishment of neutral zones was gradually developed.

39.   In the Protocol of 1924 an attempt was made to make the sanctions "automatic" by setting up an elaborate set of rules. But the discussions showed that such a course was impossible. Sanctions depend upon the will of Governments and peoples and cannot be automatically brought into existence.

40.   As has been noted above, one test of aggression is the acceptance or refusal of some method of settling the dispute. But the acceptance may be merely a method of delay while preparations for aggression are being made (as in the case of Italy's attack on Abyssinia) or actual force is used (as in Japan's attack on China). It can be argued that in both these cases the lack of effective action was due not to any defect in the Articles of the Covenant but to the lack of will on the part of the other States, and notably of the Great Powers involved, to go to war with the recalcitrant State. But it was also true that Japan was able to use her right of veto under Article XI to place obstacles in the way of the necessary enquiry, and that preventive action against Italy, before she attacked, was difficult to take legally under the Covenant. Under the Locarno Treaties the signatory States could act without League authority in the case of "flagrant aggression", but not preventively. If the question of Germany's rearmament had been brought before the Council it is not easy to see what sanctions could have been taken against her under the Covenant.

41.   In actual fact there was never any doubt, in the cases in which the League of Nations was concerned, as to the identity of the aggressor, though sometimes as to the character of the provocation to aggression. States, it is true, adapted their actions and procedure to the language and resolutions adopted at Geneva and later to the Pact of Paris. But in no case were the real intentions and motives of the aggressive States concealed from the Governments of the other members of the League or from public opinion. The discussions at the Council and the Assembly made them sufficiently clear.

42.   This experience suggests that too rigid a definition of the occasion for action is as likely to hinder as to facilitate the maintenance of peace and security. If the World Council is given power to act for this purpose it will be able to work out for itself the necessary procedure in the light of experience. It will be easier also in such circumstances to refer matters to regional associations if any such come into existence which can be used for that purpose.

43.   At the same time the principles and objects governing the actions of Members will have been laid down in the Preamble to the document bringing the Organisation into existence. These, as suggested in Part I of Memorandum A, should include not only the maintenance of peace and security but also respect for the "sovereign equality" and "political independence" of its Members. If, therefore, it is laid down that the World Council shall only take action in accordance with these principles and objects, action for other purposes will be excluded. It is suggested that States will be protected from arbitrary action by the World Council as much by this safeguard as by elaborate definition, while the World Council will be more free to act to protect States from violence.

V. – CONCLUSIONS.

44.   *As to the Pacific Settlement of Disputes –*

(i)   That all States should promise to settle their disputes by peaceful means in such a manner that international peace and security are not endangered.

(ii)   That justiciable disputes should generally be decided by a Permanent Court of International Justice.

(iii)   That other disputes should be subjected to a process of discussion and conciliation in the World Council, which should have power to determine the procedure to be followed without the consent of the parties to the dispute.

45.   *As to Guarantees –*

(i)   That all Members should undertake to co-operate to the utmost of their power in the maintenance of international peace and security, and that the World Council should be required to take the initiative for this purpose.

(ii)   That no guarantee should be given of the territorial integrity of Members.

(iii)   That no guarantee should be given of the political independence of Members, but that respect for it should be recognised as one of the principles of the organisation.

46.   *As to the conditions in which action should be taken for the maintenance of peace and security –*
That there should be no attempt to lay down in advance any rigid definition of the occasions on which such action should be taken, but that the Members of the Organisation and the World Council should only be empowered to take action in accordance with the principles and objects of the Organisation.

MEMORANDUM C

Security
The Military Aspect of any Post-War Security Organisation

I. – INTRODUCTION.

THE Moscow Declaration on General Security contemplates the creation, at the earliest possible date, of an international organisation charged with the maintenance of world peace and security. This organisation is to be founded on the principle of the sovereign equality of all peace-loving States, and all such States are to be eligible for membership.

2.   An attempt is made in the present paper to sketch out the general lines on which the organisation of International Security might be attempted after the conclusion of the present war. The proposals deal, however, with the form which the Permanent Security Organisation might eventually take and do not relate to the intervening period. During this last period it is evident that some temporary arrangements will have to be made, but these will be obviously affected if there is some previous general agreement as to the form which the permanent organisation might assume.

II. – GENERAL CONSIDERATIONS.

Nature of the Organisation.

3.   The proposed world organisation, whatever its form, is bound to fail unless:–
   (a) The United Kingdom, United States, U.S.S.R. and China continue to co-operate whole-heartedly in its support.
   (b) The Governments and peoples of those Powers at least retain the will to enforce peace.
   (c) The organisation is simple, its objects are clear-cut, and the machinery is of a kind to which member States are already accustomed.

The Objects.

4.   The objects should be:–
   (a) To disarm Germany and Japan;
   (b) To keep them disarmed; and
   (c) To prevent them or any other aggressor from again upsetting the peace of the world.

The Means.

5.   The proposed organisation will have to rely, in the main, on the combined military forces of the United Nations and, in particular, of the Four Powers, working together to a common end. Most of the States concerned are already accustomed to such a system.

6.   Economic measures, also, may operate to deter potential aggressors, but unless backed by force or the effective threat of it are unlikely to prove an adequate check on a State which is, itself, ready to resort to force.

The Idea of an "International Police Force".

7.   In some quarters it is contended that the co-ordination of military forces could best be expressed in a completely international "Police Force". Whatever its theoretical merits, this postulates a greater advance in international co-operation than States are yet prepared to make, as it implies the existence of a world State. Practical questions of size, composition, maintenance, location and command would give rise to controversies on which international agreement would almost certainly be unobtainable.

8.   We conclude that the time has not yet come for the creation of such an international force.

III. – PROPOSALS.

Higher Military Organisation.

9.   The proposed world organisation implies the existence of some sort of World Council. This Council will need military advice, and this advice will have to be given by States, not individually, but in concert. Apart from the "strategic" side of the work, *e.g.*, the preparation of plans to resist potential aggression, there are a number of general questions such as the regulation of armaments on which combined military advice will be required.

10.   If the Higher Military Organisation is to advise the World Council and provide machinery whereby plans can be made in advance and the efforts of the forces of member States co-ordinated, it follows that it must form part of, and receive directions from, the World Council.

11.   It thus becomes clear that there will have to be a Military Staff Committee serving the World Council.

Composition of the Military Staff Committee.

12.   Since for many years to come the Four Powers will have to play the predominant part in safeguarding world peace, the permanent members of this Committee should be the military representatives of those Powers. The co-operation of States other than the Four Powers will, however, be essential in providing forces and making available bases, shipping and other facilities, and these States will expect to be given a voice corresponding to their obligations. These States should therefore be associated in some form or other with the work of the Military Staff Committee. The form which this association should take raises difficult problems, and must depend to a considerable extent on the form which the World Council itself takes. As a beginning, the Committee might be strengthened, when dealing with particular security problems, by the addition of military representatives of States having special concern with the question under discussion.

13.   It is important that the members of the World Council should not receive military advice from more than one source. It is therefore essential that the members of the Military Staff Committee should be the supreme military authorities in their own countries or their representatives.

Functions of the Military Staff Committee.

14.   The primary duty of the Committee would be to prepare and keep up to date plans for the prevention of any renewed aggression by Germany or Japan, or by any other State which might at any time give signs of becoming an aggressor. The Committee would also be responsible for any necessary co-ordination of the national forces of the member States.

Force at the Disposal of the World Council.

15.   For the purpose of dealing with major aggression, it is contemplated that, when necessary, the full resources of all member States would be made available. To deal with minor emergencies, part of the obligation to be assumed by member States would be the earmarking of a quota of their national forces or other resources to be at the disposal of the Council. It would be for the World Council to decide, on the advice of the Military Staff Committee: —

(i)   What the size and composition of the quotas of individual States should be.

(ii)   In the event of an emergency arising, what particular forces should be called upon to deal with it.

16.   The mere existence of national forces and their availability in emergency would not, however, by itself, suffice to ensure the maintenance of security, even if plans for their employment were made in advance by the Military Staff Committee. It would be essential that these forces should have worked together in time of peace if their co-operation were to be smooth and efficient in time of emergency. In this connection it is difficult to exaggerate the psychological effect of constant co-operation.

Co-operation between Forces of Different States.

17.   In time of peace co-ordination could best be fostered —
(a)   By the joint garrisoning or occupation of certain areas; and
(b)   By means of joint cruises and flights and other joint exercises.
The method by which these objects should be achieved would require detailed study, and the necessary rights and facilities for joint garrisoning or occupation, joint exercise and joint access to ports and airfields, would have to be secured by agreement between member States and, where necessary, by expressed provisions in the peace treaties with ex-enemy States.

IV. — REGIONS.

18.   There is considerable support for the suggestion that, for purposes of an international security system, the world should be divided into fixed regions, each containing forces which, under the supreme control of a World Council, would be responsible for preventing aggression in that region. It has been argued that such an arrangement would limit the military commitments of the smaller States and increase efficiency and rapidity of action.

19.   From a military point of view, there are certain objections to a world organisation constructed on a basis of separate regions. These objections may be stated as follows: —
(a)   It is impossible to draw a boundary of a region so as to confine within it all military operations which the member States in that region might have to undertake.
(b)   If an attempt were made to fix the operational boundary of a region, States on the perimeter would necessarily form part of the neighbouring geographical region. Thus neighbouring regions would overlap extensively.
(c)   The defence arrangements of some Powers are based primarily on sea and air power, which do not lend themselves to regionalisation.
The advantages of regional organisation may be summarised as follows: —
(a)   The main attraction of a regional political organisation is that it would give the smaller nations a more direct concern in security problems, and so encourage their co-operation in security measures, thus reducing the burden on the Four Powers.
(b)   Regional organisation might increase the efficiency and rapidity of both political and military action by member States of the region.
(c)   A regional organisation, through its attached military staff, would facilitate military co-operation between the States concerned.

20.   An argument in favour of the proposals contained in this paper is that the suggested military organisation is not dependent on the existence of regional political councils, yet could be adapted to a regional system if the latter proved desirable on political grounds. In such a case the Military Staff Committee would serve to co-ordinate the activities of the military staffs attached to the regional organisations.

V. – CONCLUSIONS.

21.   Our conclusions, therefore, are as follows:—
   (a) Any complete international "Police Force" is impracticable in present circumstances.
   (b) The success of any world security organisation depends on the whole-hearted co-operation of the principal member States and on their resolution to use force to prevent aggression.
   (c) The object, in the first instance, of any world security organisation should be the prevention of renewed aggression by Germany and Japan.
   (d) Forces to support the World Council would have to be placed by Member States at its disposal in the manner contemplated in paragraph 15.
   (e) Military advice and direction would be afforded to such World Council as may be set up by a military staff composed of the supreme military authorities of appropriate member States or their representatives.
   (f) National forces associated for the above purpose should train and work together in peace to the greatest possible extent.
   (g) There would be some military difficulty in the division of the world for security purposes into fixed geographical regions, but, if Regional *Political* Councils were set up as part of some world organisation, it would follow that they should have Military Advisory Staffs, and this might facilitate local co-operation.

NOTE. – It will be noticed that the system proposed above differs from the system which existed prior to the war in the following three main points:—
   (a) The establishment of an effective Military Staff Committee of the World Council with power to formulate plans and to co-ordinate the action of national forces prior to any emergency which may necessitate their action.
   (b) The joint garrisoning of certain areas by combined detachments of national forces.
   (c) The training and exercising together of national forces in peace-time, making use of certain specified seaports and airfields.

MEMORANDUM D

Co-ordination of Political and Economic International Machinery

THERE will inevitably be set up, as part of the permanent international system, a number of specialised international bodies dealing with economic and social questions. Some of these bodies have already been considered in considerable detail, e.g., the Permanent Organisation for Food and Agriculture. Others are in earlier stages of development. There are already in existence the technical organisations attached to the League of Nations, such as those which deal with Health, the abolition of the Drug Traffic, Transport, &c.

2.   It will be necessary to make provision –
   (a) To co-ordinate the activities of these bodies on their technical side.
   (b) To bring them into relation with the World Organisation.

3.   The obvious methods by which these objects can be achieved are by means of discussions both between the specialised organisations themselves and in the world organisation, and by means of an economic and social secretariat attached to the World Council.

4.   No doubt some form of consultation will be arranged between the specialised bodies themselves so that their activities may be directed towards a common end. This co-ordination will be assisted by the existence of an economic and social secretariat attached to the World Council. The specialised international bodies should also have the obligation of sending reports to the World Organisation as well as to their constituent members. These reports can be considered and discussed in the World Organisation, so far as it is desirable to do so, in order to facilitate co-operation between the specialised bodies and the maintenance of international peace and security.

5.   These discussions will be assisted by the existence of an economic and social secretariat attached to the World Council, and these may thus come into being for economic and social questions as equivalent to the machinery which (see Memorandum A, paragraph 38), will, it is hoped, be in existence for political questions.

MEMORANDUM E

Method and Procedure for Establishing a World Organisation

IT may be hoped that the exchange of memoranda and preliminary discussions between the three Powers will result in a considerable measure of agreement. The question thus arises how such agreement shall be recorded, in what form it shall be submitted to the three Governments for their approval, and how and when the views of the other United Nations shall be obtained.

2.   In Article 4 of the Moscow Declaration the Four Powers recognised the necessity of establishing an international organisation "at the earliest practicable date", and an obligation lies on them to make every effort to fulfil this promise.

3.   Moreover, if agreement can be obtained between the United Nations on a definite scheme to maintain international peace and security a new hope will arise in the world which may do much to render less difficult the painful process of reconstruction. The reception of the Moscow Declaration by public opinion shows how anxious the world is to receive some assurance that such a scheme is ready for adoption.

4.   There appear to be considerable advantages in obtaining at the earliest possible moment agreement on the essentials of the permanent International Organisation, leaving the more detailed working out of its several parts to a later stage.

5.   If it is decided to set up any regional associations in any part of the world it will be much easier to fashion them in accordance with a general plan after the outline of the World Organisation has been determined.

6.   Moreover, the existence of such an agreement will facilitate negotiation for the establishment of specialised and technical bodies. It will also make possible the adaptation of such parts of the temporary machinery set up immediately after the war as it is desired to incorporate in the permanent Organisation.

7.   In the Moscow Declaration the Four Powers have assumed a responsibility for the maintenance of peace and security pending the establishment of a general system of security. This duty is likely to be less onerous if the other United Nations, and possibly States now neutral, are associated with the Four Powers for that purpose at the earliest possible date. In this way the new permanent Organisation will more quickly become a reality and take its proper position in the new world community.

8.   Moreover, the Treaties of Peace will be more easily made if the form and character of the new permanent organisation are already known. Solutions of difficult problems will be more easily found and there is less likelihood of decisions being made which are incompatible with the terms of the permanent organisation.

9.   It is suggested, therefore, that the aim of the preliminary talks at Washington should be to reach such agreement as can be referred to the three Governments in the form of a Draft Declaration similar to that signed at Moscow but containing in its several clauses a more extended survey of the objects and principles of the permanent International Organisation and an outline of the machinery which it is proposed to set up to obtain them.

10.   It may be necessary to omit from the draft Declaration many important particulars, *e.g.*, the exact methods by which the members of the World Council are chosen and their number. Some of these points may perhaps be left to the new organisation itself to determine. But it may be hoped that agreement may be obtained on what political bodies shall be set up, *e.g.*, a World Assembly, a World Council and a World Court; on the principles on which action will be taken for the pacific settlement of disputes and the maintenance of international peace and security; on the necessity for agreeing some permanent method by which the military forces necessary to maintain international peace and security can be co-ordinated; and on the principles which shall govern the relations of the specialised organisations with one another and with the World Council and World Assembly.

11.   It will then be for the Governments of the three Powers to determine how far they can approve the draft Declaration and it may be necessary to have a more formal exchange of views between them for this purpose.

12.   If agreement is thus obtained it will be necessary to communicate it to the other United Nations for consideration, and immediately thereafter to publish it. After a suitable interval the United Nations would be invited to attend a Conference at which the Declaration, with such amendments as had been found desirable, would be definitely adopted.

13.   It should then be possible to set up a body to work out a more detailed instrument in the form of a Convention or Treaty on the lines of the Declaration. It would be the coming into force of this instrument, after the ordinary procedure required for ratification, which would bring the Permanent Organisation into existence. The exact date on which it was put into force might well be left to be determined by the Four Powers who are specially responsible for the maintenance of international peace and security in the interim period.

14.   This method would have the advantage that, while the Permanent Organisation can, of course, only be brought into existence with the full consent of the Governments concerned after they have consulted the peoples which they represent, its form and character will have been to a large extent decided in consequence of the adoption of the Declaration. Many of the Governments of the United Nations might find it impossible to sign a treaty at that stage. Some of them may not survive the transition from war to peace. But many of them could record their agreement to a Declaration of the kind described and so prepare the way for themselves or their successors to take part in the preparation and signature of the final instrument.

Proposals for the Establishment of a General International Organization

There should be established an international organization under the title of The United Nations, the Charter of which should contain provisions necessary to give effect to the proposals which follow.

CHAPTER I. – PURPOSES

The purposes of the Organization should be:

1. To maintain international peace and security; and to that end to take effective collective measures for the prevention and removal of threats to the peace and the suppression of acts of aggression or other breaches of the peace, and to bring about by peaceful means adjustment or settlement of international disputes which may lead to a breach of the peace;

2. To develop friendly relations among nations and to take other appropriate measures to strengthen universal peace;

3. To achieve international cooperation in the solution of international economic, social and other humanitarian problems; and

4. To afford a center for harmonizing the actions of nations in the achievement of these common ends.

CHAPTER II. – PRINCIPLES

In pursuit of the purposes mentioned in Chapter I the Organization and its members should act in accordance with the following principles:

1. The Organization is based on the principle of the sovereign equality of all peace-loving states.

2. All members of the Organization undertake, in order to ensure to all of them the rights and benefits resulting from membership in the Organization, to fulfill the obligations assumed by them in accordance with the Charter.

3. All members of the Organization shall settle their disputes by peaceful means in such a manner that international peace and security are not endangered.

4. All members of the Organization shall refrain in their international relations from the threat or use of force in any manner inconsistent with the purposes of the Organization.

5.   All members of the Organization shall give every assistance to the Organization in any action undertaken by it in accordance with the provisions of the Charter.

6.   All members of the Organization shall refrain from giving assistance to any state against which preventive or enforcement action is being undertaken by the Organization.

The Organization should ensure that states not members of the Organization act in accordance with these principles so far as may be necessary for the maintenance of international peace and security.

CHAPTER III. – MEMBERSHIP

1.   Membership of the Organization should be open to all peace-loving states.

CHAPTER IV. – PRINCIPAL ORGANS

1.   The Organization should have as its principal organs:
     (a) A General Assembly;
     (b) A Security Council;
     (c) An international court of justice; and
     (d) A Secretariat.

2.   The Organization should have such subsidiary agencies as may be found necessary.

CHAPTER V. – THE GENERAL ASSEMBLY

Section A

Composition

All members of the Organization should be members of the General Assembly and should have a number of representatives to be specified in the Charter.

Section B

Functions and Powers

1.   The General Assembly should have the right to consider the general principles of cooperation in the maintenance of international peace and security, including the principles governing disarmament and the regulation of armaments; to discuss any questions relating to the maintenance of international peace and security brought before it by any member or members of the Organization or by the Security Council; and to make recommendations with regard to any such principles or questions. Any such questions on which action is necessary should be referred to the Security Council by the General Assembly either before or after discussion. The General Assembly should not on its own initiative make recommendations on any matter relating to the maintenance of international peace and security which is being dealt with by the Security Council.

2.   The General Assembly should be empowered to admit new members to the Organization upon recommendation of the Security Council.

3.   The General Assembly should, upon recommendation of the Security Council, be empowered to suspend from the exercise of any rights or privileges of membership any member of the Organization against which preventive or enforcement action shall have been taken by the Security Council. The exercise of the rights and privileges thus suspended may be restored by decision of the Security Council. The General Assembly should be empowered, upon recommendation of the Security Council, to expel from the Organization any member of the Organization which persistently violates the principles contained in the Charter.

4.   The General Assembly should elect the non-permanent members of the Security Council and the members of the Economic and Social Council provided for in Chapter IX. It should be empowered to elect, upon recommendation of the Security Council, the Secretary-General of the Organization. It should perform such functions in relation to the election of the judges of the international court of justice as may be conferred upon it by the statute of the court.

5.   The General Assembly should apportion the expenses among the members of the Organization and should be empowered to approve the budgets of the Organization.

6.   The General Assembly should initiate studies and make recommendations for the purpose of promoting international cooperation in political, economic and social fields and of adjusting situations likely to impair the general welfare.

7.   The General Assembly should make recommendations for the coordination of the policies of international economic, social, and other specialized agencies brought into relation with the Organization in accordance with agreements between such agencies and the Organization.

8.   The General Assembly should receive and consider annual and special reports from the Security Council and reports from other bodies of the Organization.

Section C

Voting

1.   Each member of the Organization should have one vote in the General Assembly.

2.   Important decisions of the General Assembly, including recommendations with respect to the maintenance of international peace and security; election of members of the Security Council; election of members of the Economic and Social Council; admission of members, suspension of the exercise of the rights and privileges of members, and expulsion of members; and budgetary questions, should be made by a two-thirds majority of those present and voting. On other questions, including the determination of additional categories of questions to be decided by a two-thirds majority, the decisions of the General Assembly should be made by a simple majority vote.

Section D

Procedure

1.   The General Assembly should meet in regular annual sessions and in such special sessions as occasion may require.

2.   The General Assembly should adopt its own rules of procedure and elect its President for each session.

3.   The General Assembly should be empowered to set up such bodies and agencies as it may deem necessary for the performance of its functions.

CHAPTER VI. – THE SECURITY COUNCIL

Section A

Composition

The Security Council should consist of one representative of each of eleven members of the Organization. Representatives of the United States of America, the United Kingdom of Great Britain and Northern Ireland, the Union of Soviet Socialist Republics, the Republic of China, and, in due course, France, should have permanent seats. The General Assembly should elect six states to fill the non-permanent seats. These six states should be elected for a term of two years, three retiring each year. They should not be immediately eligible for re-election. In the first election of the non-permanent members three should be chosen by the General Assembly for one-year terms and three for two-year terms.

Section B

Principal Functions and Powers

1.   In order to ensure prompt and effective action by the Organization, members of the Organization should by the Charter confer on the Security Council primary responsibility for the maintenance of international peace and security and should agree that in carrying out these duties under this responsibility it should act on their behalf.

2.   In discharging these duties the Security Council should act in accordance with the purposes and principles of the Organization.

3.   The specific powers conferred on the Security Council in order to carry out these duties are laid down in Chapter VIII.

4.   All members of the Organization should obligate themselves to accept the decisions of the Security Council and to carry them out in accordance with the provisions of the Charter.

5.   In order to promote the establishment and maintenance of international peace and security with the least diversion of the world's human and economic resources for armaments, the Security Council, with the assistance of the Military Staff Committee referred to in Chapter VIII, Section B, paragraph 9, should have the responsibility for formulating plans for the establishment of a system of regulation of armaments for submission to the members of the Organization.

Section C

Voting

(NOTE – The question of voting procedure in the Security Council is still under consideration.)

Section D

Procedure

1.   The Security Council should be so organized as to be able to function continuously and each state member of the Security Council should be permanently represented at the headquarters of the Organization. It may hold meetings at such other places as in its judgment may best facilitate its work. There should be periodic meetings at which each state member of the Security Council could if it so desired be represented by a member of the government or some other special representative.

2.   The Security Council should be empowered to set up such bodies or agencies as it may deem necessary for the performance of its functions including regional subcommittees of the Military Staff Committee.

3.   The Security Council should adopt its own rules of procedure, including the method of selecting its President.

4.   Any member of the Organization should participate in the discussion of any question brought before the Security Council whenever the Security Council considers that the interests of that member of the Organization are specially affected.

5.   Any member of the Organization not having a seat on the Security Council and any state not a member of the Organization, if it is a party to a dispute under consideration by the Security Council, should be invited to participate in the discussion relating to the dispute.

CHAPTER VII. – AN INTERNATIONAL COURT OF JUSTICE

1.   There should be an international court of justice which should constitute the principal judicial organ of the Organization.

2.   The Court should be constituted and should function in accordance with a statute which should be annexed to and be a part of the Charter of the Organization.

3.   The statute of the court of international justice should be either (a) the Statute of the Permanent Court of International Justice, continued in force with such modifications as may be desirable or (b) a new statute in the preparation of which the Statute of the Permanent Court of International Justice should be used as a basis.

4.   All members of the Organization should *ipso facto* be parties to the statute of the international court of justice.

5.   Conditions under which states not members of the Organization may become parties to the statute of the international court of justice should be determined in each case by the General Assembly upon recommendation of the Security Council.

CHAPTER VIII. – ARRANGEMENTS FOR THE MAINTENANCE OF INTERNATIONAL PEACE AND SECURITY INCLUDING PREVENTION AND SUPPRESSION OF AGGRESSION

Section A

Pacific Settlement of Disputes

1.   The Security Council should be empowered to investigate any dispute, or any situation

which may lead to international friction or give rise to a dispute, in order to determine whether its continuance is likely to endanger the maintenance of international peace and security.

2.   Any state, whether member of the Organization or not, may bring any such dispute or situation to the attention of the General Assembly or of the Security Council.

3.   The parties to any dispute the continuance of which is likely to endanger the maintenance of international peace and security should obligate themselves, first of all, to seek a solution by negotiation, mediation, conciliation, arbitration or judicial settlement, or other peaceful means of their own choice. The Security Council should call upon the parties to settle their dispute by such means.

4.   If, nevertheless, parties to a dispute of the nature referred to in paragraph 3 above fail to settle it by the means indicated in that paragraph, they should obligate themselves to refer it to the Security Council. The Security Council should in each case decide whether or not the continuance of the particular dispute is in fact likely to endanger the maintenance of international peace and security, and, accordingly, whether the Security Council should deal with the dispute, and, if so, whether it should take action under paragraph 5.

5.   The Security Council should be empowered, at any stage of a dispute of the nature referred to in paragraph 3 above, to recommend appropriate procedures or methods of adjustment.

6.   Justiciable disputes should normally be referred to the international court of justice. The Security Council should be empowered to refer to the court, for advice, legal questions connected with other disputes.

7.   The provisions of paragraphs 1 to 6 of Section A should not apply to situations or disputes arising out of matters which by international law are solely within the domestic jurisdiction of the state concerned.

Section B

Determination of Threats to the Peace or Acts of Aggression and Action With Respect Thereto

1.   Should the Security Council deem that a failure to settle a dispute in accordance with procedures indicated in paragraph 3 of Section A, or in accordance with its recommendations made under paragraph 5 of Section A, constitutes a threat to the maintenance of international peace and security, it should take any measures necessary for the maintenance of international peace and security in accordance with the purposes and principles of the Organization.

2.   In general the Security Council should determine the existence of any threat to the peace, breach of the peace or act of aggression and should make recommendations or decide upon the measures to be taken to maintain or restore peace and security.

3.   The Security Council should be empowered to determine what diplomatic, economic, or other measures not involving the use of armed force should be employed to give effect to its decisions, and to call upon members of the Organization to apply such measures. Such measures may include complete or partial interruption of rail, sea, air, postal, telegraphic, radio and other means of communication and the severance of diplomatic and economic relations.

4.   Should the Security Council consider such measures to be inadequate, it should be empowered to take such action by air, naval or land forces as may be necessary to maintain

or restore international peace and security. Such action may include demonstrations, blockade and other operations by air, sea or land forces of members of the Organization.

5.   In order that all members of the Organization should contribute to the maintenance of international peace and security, they should undertake to make available to the Security Council, on its call and in accordance with a special agreement or agreements concluded among themselves, armed forces, facilities and assistance necessary for the purpose of maintaining international peace and security. Such agreement or agreements should govern the numbers and types of forces and the nature of the facilities and assistance to be provided. The special agreement or agreements should be negotiated as soon as possible and should in each case be subject to approval by the Security Council and to ratification by the signatory states in accordance with their constitutional processes.

6.   In order to enable urgent military measures to be taken by the Organization there should be held immediately available by the members of the Organization national air force contingents for combined international enforcement action. The strength and degree of readiness of these contingents and plans for their combined action should be determined by the Security Council with the assistance of the Military Staff Committee within the limits laid down in the special agreement or agreements referred to in paragraph 5 above.

7.   The action required to carry out the decisions of the Security Council for the maintenance of international peace and security should be taken by all the members of the Organization in cooperation or by some of them as the Security Council may determine. This undertaking should be carried out by the members of the Organization by their own action and through action of the appropriate specialized organizations and agencies of which they are members.

8.   Plans for the application of armed force should be made by the Security Council with the assistance of the Military Staff Committee referred to in paragraph 9 below.

9.   There should be established a Military Staff Committee the functions of which should be to advise and assist the Security Council on all questions relating to the Security Council's military requirements for the maintenance of international peace and security, to the employment and command of forces placed at its disposal, to the regulation of armaments, and to possible disarmament. It should be responsible under the Security Council for the strategic direction of any armed forces placed at the disposal of the Security Council. The Committee should be composed of the Chiefs of Staff of the permanent members of the Security Council or their representatives. Any member of the Organization not permanently represented on the Committee should be invited by the Committee to be associated with it when the efficient discharge of the Committee's responsibilities requires that such a state should participate in its work. Questions of command of forces should be worked out subsequently.

10.   The members of the Organization should join in affording mutual assistance in carrying out the measures decided upon by the Security Council.

11.   Any state, whether a member of the Organization or not, which finds itself confronted with special economic problems arising from the carrying out of measures which have been decided upon by the Security Council should have the right to consult the Security Council in regard to a solution of those problems.

Section C

Regional Arrangements

1.   Nothing in the Charter should preclude the existence of regional arrangements or agencies for dealing with such matters relating to the maintenance of international peace

and security as are appropriate for regional action, provided such arrangements or agencies and their activities are consistent with the purposes and principles of the Organization. The Security Council should encourage settlement of local disputes through such regional arrangements or by such regional agencies, either on the initiative of the states concerned or by reference from the Security Council.

2.   The Security Council should, where appropriate, utilize such arrangements or agencies for enforcement action under its authority but no enforcement action should be taken under regional arrangements or by regional agencies without the authorization of the Security Council.

3.   The Security Council should at all times be kept fully informed of activities undertaken or in contemplation under regional arrangements or by regional agencies for the maintenance of international peace and security.

CHAPTER IX. – ARRANGEMENTS FOR INTERNATIONAL ECONOMIC AND SOCIAL COOPERATION

Section A

Purpose and Relationships

1.   With a view to the creation of conditions of stability and well-being which are necessary for peaceful and friendly relations among nations, the Organization should facilitate solutions of international economic, social and other humanitarian problems and promote respect for human rights and fundamental freedoms. Responsibility for the discharge of this function should be vested in the General Assembly and, under the authority of the General Assembly, in an Economic and Social Council.

2.   The various specialized economic, social and other organizations and agencies would have responsibilities in their respective fields as defined in their statutes. Each such organization or agency should be brought into relationship with the Organization on terms to be determined by agreement between the Economic and Social Council and the appropriate authorities of the specialized organization or agency, subject to approval by the General Assembly.

Section B

Composition and Voting

The Economic and Social Council should consist of representatives of eighteen members of the Organization. The states to be represented for this purpose should be elected by the General Assembly for terms of three years. Each such state should have one representative, who should have one vote. Decisions of the Economic and Social Council should be taken by simple majority vote of those present and voting.

Section C

Functions and Powers of the Economic and Social Council

1.   The Economic and Social Council should be empowered:–
   (a) to carry out, within the scope of its functions, recommendations of the General Assembly;

(b) to make recommendations, on its own initiative, with respect to international economic, social and other humanitarian matters;

(c) to receive and consider reports from the economic, social and other organizations or agencies brought into relationship with the Organization, and to coordinate their activities through consultations with, and recommendations to, such organizations or agencies;

(d) to examine the administrative budgets of such specialized organizations or agencies with a view to making recommendations to the organizations or agencies concerned;

(e) to enable the Secretary-General to provide information to the Security Council;

(f) to assist the Security Council upon its request; and

(g) to perform such other functions within the general scope of its competence as may be assigned to it by the General Assembly.

Section D

Organization and Procedure

1. The Economic and Social Council should set up an economic commission, a social commission, and such other commissions as may be required. These commissions should consist of experts. There should be a permanent staff which should constitute a part of the Secretariat of the Organization.

2. The Economic and Social Council should make suitable arrangements for representatives of the specialized organizations or agencies to participate without vote in its deliberations and in those of the commissions established by it.

3. The Economic and Social Council should adopt its own rules of procedure and the method of selecting its President.

CHAPTER X. – THE SECRETARIAT

1. There should be a Secretariat comprising a Secretary-General and such staff as may be required. The Secretary-General should be the chief administrative officer of the Organization. He should be elected by the General Assembly, on recommendation of the Security Council, for such term and under such conditions as are specified in the Charter.

2. The Secretary-General should act in that capacity in all meetings of the General Assembly, of the Security Council, and of the Economic and Social Council and should make an annual report to the General Assembly on the work of the Organization.

3. The Secretary-General should have the right to bring to the attention of the Security Council any matter which in his opinion may threaten international peace and security.

CHAPTER XI. – AMENDMENTS

Amendments should come into force for all members of the Organization, when they have been adopted by a vote of two-thirds of the members of the General Assembly and ratified in accordance with their respective constitutional processes by the members of the Organization having permanent membership on the Security Council and by a majority of the other members of the Organization.

CHAPTER XII. – TRANSITIONAL ARRANGEMENTS

1.   Pending the coming into force of the special agreement or agreements referred to in Chapter VIII, Section B, paragraph 5, and in accordance with the provisions of paragraph 5 of the Four-Nation Declaration, signed at Moscow, October 30, 1943, the states parties to that Declaration should consult with one another and as occasion arises with other members of the Organization with a view to such joint action on behalf of the Organization as may be necessary for the purpose of maintaining international peace and security.

2.   No provision of the Charter should preclude action taken or authorized in relation to enemy states as a result of the present war by the Governments having responsibility for such action.

NOTE – In addition to the question of voting procedure in the Security Council referred to in Chapter VI, several other questions are still under consideration.

APPENDIX E

Webster and Smuts Draft Preambles to the Charter

1. *Webster's Original Draft* (cf. Diary entry 21 December 1944 and n. 41 pp. 54 and 115)

[The square brackets reflect comments made by P. S. Falla in a minute of 2 January 1945, but it is not possible to tell when Webster added (in his own handwriting in the original) the words after "peoples" in the last paragraph.]

THE HIGH CONTRACTING PARTIES
In order to achieve international co-operation for the maintenance of international peace and security
    By the acceptance of principles and the institution of methods to ensure that armed force is only used [used only] in the interests of the community of nations, [and not for national ends,]
    By the provision of means by which all disputes that threaten the maintenance of international peace and security shall [can] be settled,
    By the establishment of conditions under which justice and respect for the obligations of international law [and treaties] can be maintained,
    By the employment of international machinery for the [promotion of the] economic and social advancement of all peoples, and ensuring respect for human rights and fundamental freedoms
Agree to this Charter of the United Nations.

2. *Original South African draft*

Preamble
We the United Nations, assembled in Conference to seek a new way of life for the nations, and to prevent a recurrence of the fratricidal strife which has now twice in our generation brought untold sorrows and losses on mankind, and to establish an international organisation to that end:
Do hereby declare in this Charter of the United Nations, our common faith and objects, and the principles on which we seek to found an organisation for the peace progress and welfare of mankind.

Chapter I — The Common Faith
1. We declare our faith in basic human rights, in the sacredness, essential worth, and integrity of the human personality, and affirm our resolve to establish and maintain social and legal sanctions for safeguarding the same:

2. We believe in the practice of tolerance, in the equal rights of individuals and of individual nations large and small, as well as in their inherent right to govern themselves without outside interference, in accordance with their own customs and way of life:

166

3.   We believe in the enlargement of freedom and the promotion of social progress, and in raising the standards of life, so that there may be freedom of thought and expression and religion, as well as freedom from want and fear for all:

4.   We believe in nations living in peace and peaceful intercourse with each other as good neighbours, and in renouncing war as an instrument of national policy.

Chapter II — Purposes

. . . .
. . . .

Chapter III — Principles

. . . .
. . . .

3.   Webster's conflation which, apart from the two points noted, became the final version

[Webster's own handwritten note reads] 'My conflation of Smuts draft and my draft of Preamble made by me on the night of Wed. 11 April 1945, typed by Nora in the early morning of Thur. 12 April 1945, agreed by Genl Smuts at the Hyde Park Hotel between 9 and 9.30 that morning, duplicated by the secretariat and laid on the table for the British Commonwealth meeting. Smuts made one or two small corrections. See Minutes of Commonwealth Conference 12 April 1945.'

PREAMBLE TO THE CHARTER OF THE UNITED NATIONS

THE HIGH CONTRACTING PARTIES:
DETERMINED
> To prevent a recurrence of the fratricidal strife which has twice in our generation brought untold sorrows and losses on mankind,
> and
> to re-establish the faith of men and women in fundamental human rights, in the sacredness. essential worth and integrity of the human personality, in the equal rights of individuals and of individual nations large and small [and] * in the enlargement of freedom and [the promotion of] † to promote social progress and the possibility of raising the standards of life everywhere in the world.
> and for these ends
> To practice tolerance and to live together in peace and peaceful intercourse with each other as good neighbours,
> In order to make possible co-operation between nations for the maintenance of international peace and security necessary for these purposes,
> By the acceptance of principles and the institution of methods to ensure that armed force is only used in the interests of the community of nations, and not for national ends,
> By the provision of means by which all disputes that threaten the maintenance of international peace and security shall be settled,
> By the establishment of conditions under which justice and respect for the obligations of international law and treaties, and fundamental human rights and freedoms can be maintained,
> By the employment of international machinery for the promotion of the economic and social advancement of all peoples,
Agree to this Charter of the United Nations.

* *Deleted in the final version.*
† *Replacing 'to promote' in the final version.*

Charter of the United Nations

WE THE PEOPLES OF THE UNITED NATIONS DETERMINED
to save succeeding generations from the scourge of war, which twice in our lifetime has brought untold sorrow to mankind, and
to reaffirm faith in fundamental human rights, in the dignity and worth of the human person, in the equal rights of men and women and of nations large and small, and
to establish conditions under which justice and respect for the obligations arising from treaties and other sources of international law can be maintained, and
to promote social progress and better standards of life in larger freedom,
AND FOR THESE ENDS
to practise tolerance and live together in peace with one another as good neighbours, and
to unite our strength to maintain international peace and security, and
to ensure, by the acceptance of principles and the institution of methods, that armed force shall not be used, save in the common interest, and
to employ international machinery for the promotion of the economic and social advancement of all peoples,
HAVE RESOLVED TO COMBINE OUR EFFORTS TO ACCOMPLISH THESE AIMS.
Accordingly, our respective Governments, through representatives assembled in the city of San Francisco, who have exhibited their full powers found to be in good and due form, have agreed to the present Charter of the United Nations and do hereby establish an international organization to be known as the United Nations.

CHAPTER I
PURPOSES AND PRINCIPLES

Article 1

The Purposes of the United Nations are:

1.   To maintain international peace and security, and to that end: to take effective collective measures for the prevention and removal of threats to the peace, and for the suppression of acts of aggression or other breaches of the peace, and to bring about by peaceful means, and in conformity with the principles of justice and international law, adjustment or settlement of international disputes or situations which might lead to a breach of the peace;

2.   To develop friendly relations among nations based on respect for the principle of equal rights and self-determination of peoples, and to take other appropriate measures to strengthen universal peace;

3.   To achieve international co-operation in solving international problems of an economic, social, cultural, or humanitarian character, and in promoting and encouraging respect for human rights and for fundamental freedoms for all without distinction as to race, sex, language, or religion; and

4.   To be a centre for harmonizing the actions of nations in the attainment of these common ends.

Article 2

The Organization and its Members, in pursuit of the Purposes stated in Article 1, shall act in accordance with the following Principles.

1.   The Organization is based on the principle of the sovereign equality of all its Members.

2.   All Members, in order to ensure to all of them the rights and benefits resulting from membership, shall fulfil in good faith the obligations assumed by them in accordance with the present Charter.

3.   All Members shall settle their international disputes by peaceful means in such a manner that international peace and security, and justice, are not endangered.

4.   All Members shall refrain in their international relations from the threat or use of force against the territorial integrity or political independence of any state, or in any other manner inconsistent with the Purposes of the United Nations.

5.   All Members shall give the United Nations every assistance in any action it takes in accordance with the present Charter, and shall refrain from giving assistance to any state against which the United Nations is taking preventive or enforcement action.

6.   The Organization shall ensure that states which are not Members of the United Nations act in accordance with these Principles so far as may be necessary for the maintenance of international peace and security.

7.   Nothing contained in the present Charter shall authorize the United Nations to intervene in matters which are essentially within the domestic jurisdiction of any state or shall require the Members to submit such matters to settlement under the present Charter; but this principle shall not prejudice the application of enforcement measures under Chapter VII.

CHAPTER II
MEMBERSHIP

Article 3

The original Members of the United Nations shall be the states which, having participated in the United Nations Conference on International Organization at San Francisco, or having previously signed the Declaration by United Nations of January 1, 1942, sign the present Charter and ratify it in accordance with Article 110.

Article 4

1.   Membership in the United Nations is open to all other peace-loving states which accept the obligations contained in the present Charter and, in the judgment of the Organization, are able and willing to carry out these obligations.

2.   The admission of any such state to membership in the United Nations will be effected by a decision of the General Assembly upon the recommendation of the Security Council.

Article 5

A Member of the United Nations against which preventive or enforcement action has been taken by the Security Council may be suspended from the exercise of the rights and privileges of membership by the General Assembly upon the recommendation of the Security Council. The exercise of these rights and privileges may be restored by the Security Council.

Article 6

A Member of the United Nations which has persistently violated the Principles contained in the present Charter may be expelled from the Organization by the General Assembly upon the recommendation of the Security Council.

CHAPTER III
ORGANS

Article 7

1. There are established as the principal organs of the United Nations: a General Assembly, a Security Council, an Economic and Social Council, a Trusteeship Council, an International Court of Justice, and a Secretariat.

2. Such subsidiary organs as may be found necessary may be established in accordance with the present Charter.

Article 8

The United Nations shall place no restrictions on the eligibility of men and women to participate in any capacity and under conditions of equality in its principal and subsidiary organs.

CHAPTER IV
THE GENERAL ASSEMBLY

Composition

Article 9

1. The General Assembly shall consist of all the Members of the United Nations.

2. Each Member shall have not more than five representatives in the General Assembly.

Functions and Powers

Article 10

The General Assembly may discuss any questions or any matters within the scope of the present Charter or relating to the powers and functions of any organs provided for in the present Charter, and, except as provided in Article 12, may make recommendations to the Members of the United Nations or to the Security Council or to both on any such questions or matters.

Article 11

1. The General Assembly may consider the general principles of co-operation in the maintenance of international peace and security, including the principles governing disarmament and the regulation of armaments, and may make recommendations with regard to such principles to the Members or to the Security Council or to both.

2. The General Assembly may discuss any questions relating to the maintenance of international peace and security brought before it by any Member of the United Nations, or by the Security Council, or by a state which is not a Member of the United Nations in accordance with Article 35, paragraph 2, and, except as provided in Article 12, may make recommendations with regard to any such question to the state or states concerned or to the Security Council or to both. Any such question on which action is necessary shall be referred to the Security Council by the General Assembly either before or after discussion.

3. The General Assembly may call the attention of the Security Council to situations which are likely to endanger international peace and security.

4. The powers of the General Assembly set forth in this Article shall not limit the general scope of Article 10.

Article 12
1. While the Security Council is exercising in respect of any dispute or situation the functions assigned to it in the present Charter, the General Assembly shall not make any recommendations with regard to that dispute or situation unless the Security Council so requests.

2. The Secretary-General, with the consent of the Security Council, shall notify the General Assembly at each session of any matters relative to the maintenance of international peace and security which are being dealt with by the Security Council and shall similarly notify the General Assembly, or the Members of the United Nations if the General Assembly is not in session, immediately the Security Council ceases to deal with such matters.

Article 13
1. The General Assembly shall initiate studies and make recommendations for the purpose of:
   (a) promoting international co-operation in the political field and encouraging the progressive development of international law and its codification;
   (b) promoting international co-operation in the economic, social, cultural, educational, and health fields, and assisting in the realization of human rights and fundamental freedoms for all without distinction as to race, sex, language, or religion.

2. The further responsibilities, functions, and powers of the General Assembly with respect to matters mentioned in paragraph 1 (b) above are set forth in Chapters IX and X.

Article 14
Subject to the provisions of Article 12, the General Assembly may recommend measures for the peaceful adjustment of any situation, regardless of origin, which it deems likely to impair the general welfare or friendly relations among nations, including situations resulting from a violation of the provisions of the present Charter setting forth the Purposes and Principles of the United Nations.

Article 15
1. The General Assembly shall receive and consider annual and special reports from the Security Council; these reports shall include an account of the measures that the Security Council has decided upon or taken to maintain international peace and security.

2. The General Assembly shall receive and consider reports from the other organs of the United Nations.

Article 16
The General Assembly shall perform such functions with respect to the international trusteeship system as are assigned to it under Chapters XII and XIII, including the approval of the trusteeship agreements for areas not designated as strategic.

Article 17
1. The General Assembly shall consider and approve the budget of the Organization.

2. The expenses of the Organization shall be borne by the Members as apportioned by the General Assembly.

3. The General Assembly shall consider and approve any financial and budgetary arrangements with specialized agencies referred to in Article 57 and shall examine the administrative budgets of such specialized agencies with a view to making recommendations to the agencies concerned.

Voting

Article 18

1. Each member of the General Assembly shall have one vote.

2. Decisions of the General Assembly on important questions shall be made by a two-thirds majority of the members present and voting. These questions shall include: recommendations with respect to the maintenance of international peace and security, the election of the non-permanent members of the Security Council, the election of the members of the Economic and Social Council, the election of members of the Trusteeship Council in accordance with paragraph 1 (c) of Article 86, the admission of new Members to the United Nations, the suspension of the rights and privileges of membership, the expulsion of Members, questions relating to the operation of the trusteeship system, and budgetary questions.

3. Decisions on other questions, including the determination of additional categories of questions to be decided by a two-thirds majority, shall be made by a majority of the members present and voting.

Article 19

A Member of the United Nations which is in arrears in the payment of its financial contributions to the Organization shall have no vote in the General Assembly if the amount of its arrears equals or exceeds the amount of the contributions due from it for the preceding two full years. The General Assembly may, nevertheless, permit such a Member to vote if it is satisfied that the failure to pay is due to conditions beyond the control of the Member.

Procedure

Article 20

The General Assembly shall meet in regular annual sessions and in such special sessions as occasion may require. Special sessions shall be convoked by the Secretary-General at the request of the Security Council or of a majority of the Members of the United Nations.

Article 21

The General Assembly shall adopt its own rules of procedure. It shall elect its President for each session.

Article 22

The General Assembly may establish such subsidiary organs as it deems necessary for the performance of its functions.

CHAPTER V
THE SECURITY COUNCIL

Composition

Article 23

1. The Security Council shall consist of eleven Members of the United Nations. The Republic of China, France, the Union of Soviet Socialist Republics, the United Kingdom of Great Britain and Northern Ireland, and the United States of America shall be permanent members of the Security Council. The General Assembly shall elect six other Members of the United Nations to be non-permanent members of the Security Council, due regard being specially paid, in the first instance to the contribution of Members of the United Nations to the maintenance of international peace and security and to the other purposes of the Organization, and also to equitable geographical distribution.

2. The non-permanent members of the Security Council shall be elected for a term of two years. In the first election of the non-permanent members, however, three shall be chosen for a term of one year. A retiring member shall not be eligible for immediate re-election.

3. Each member of the Security Council shall have one representative.

Functions and Powers

Article 24

1. In order to ensure prompt and effective action by the United Nations, its Members confer on the Security Council primary responsibility for the maintenance of international peace and security, and agree that in carrying out its duties under this responsibility the Security Council acts on their behalf.

2. In discharging these duties the Security Council shall act in accordance with the Purposes and Principles of the United Nations. The specific powers granted to the Security Council for the discharge of these duties are laid down in Chapters VI, VII, VIII, and XII.

3. The Security Council shall submit annual and, when necessary, special reports to the General Assembly for its consideration.

Article 25

The Members of the United Nations agree to accept and carry out the decisions of the Security Council in accordance with the present Charter.

Article 26

In order to promote the establishment and maintenance of international peace and security with the least diversion for armaments of the world's human and economic resources, the Security Council shall be responsible for formulating, with the assistance of the Military Staff Committee referred to in Article 47, plans to be submitted to the Members of the United Nations for the establishment of a system for the regulation of armaments.

Voting

Article 27

1. Each member of the Security Council shall have one vote.

2. Decisions of the Security Council on procedural matters shall be made by an affirmative vote of seven members.

3. Decisions of the Security Council on all other matters shall be made by an affirmative vote of seven members including the concurring votes of the permanent members; provided that, in decisions under Chapter VI, and under paragraph 3 of Article 52, a party to a dispute shall abstain from voting.

Procedure

Article 28

1. The Security Council shall be so organized as to be able to function continuously. Each member of the Security Council shall for this purpose be represented at all times at the seat of the Organization.

2. The Security Council shall hold periodic meetings at which each of its members may, if it so desires, be represented by a member of the government or by some other specially designated representative.

3.   The Security Council may hold meetings at such places other than the seat of the Organization as in its judgment will best facilitate its work.

Article 29

The Security Council may establish such subsidiary organs as it deems necessary for the performance of its functions.

Article 30

The Security Council shall adopt its own rules of procedure, including the method of selecting its President.

Article 31

Any Member of the United Nations which is not a member of the Security Council may participate, without vote, in the discussion of any question brought before the Security Council whenever the latter considers that the interests of that Member are specially affected.

Article 32

Any Member of the United Nations which is not a member of the Security Council or any state which is not a Member of the United Nations, if it is a party to a dispute under consideration by the Security Council, shall be invited to participate, without vote, in the discussion relating to the dispute. The Security Council shall lay down such conditions as it deems just for the participation of a state which is not a Member of the United Nations.

CHAPTER VI
PACIFIC SETTLEMENT OF DISPUTES

Article 33

1.   The parties to any dispute, the continuance of which is likely to endanger the maintenance of international peace and security, shall, first of all, seek a solution by negotiation, enquiry, mediation, conciliation, arbitration, judicial settlement, resort to regional agencies or arrangements, or other peaceful means of their own choice.

2.   The Security Council shall, when it deems necessary, call upon the parties to settle their dispute by such means.

Article 34

The Security Council may investigate any dispute, or any situation which might lead to international friction or give rise to a dispute, in order to determine whether the continuance of the dispute or situation is likely to endanger the maintenance of international peace and security.

Article 35

1.   Any Member of the United Nations may bring any dispute, or any situation of the nature referred to in Article 34, to the attention of the Security Council or of the General Assembly.

2.   A state which is not a Member of the United Nations may bring to the attention of the Security Council or of the General Assembly any dispute to which it is a party if it accepts in advance, for the purposes of the dispute, the obligations of pacific settlement provided in the present Charter.

3.   The proceedings of the General Assembly in respect of matters brought to its attention under this Article will be subject to the provisions of Articles 11 and 12.

Article 36

1.   The Security Council may, at any stage of a dispute of the nature referred to in Article 33 or of a situation of like nature, recommend appropriate procedures or methods of adjustment.

2.   The Security Council should take into consideration any procedures for the settlement of the dispute which have already been adopted by the parties.

3.   In making recommendations under this Article the Security Council should also take into consideration that legal disputes should as a general rule be referred by the parties to the International Court of Justice in accordance with the provisions of the Statute of the Court.

Article 37

1.   Should the parties to a dispute of the nature referred to in Article 33 fail to settle it by the means indicated in that Article, they shall refer it to the Security Council.

2.   If the Security Council deems that the continuance of the dispute is in fact likely to endanger the maintenance of international peace and security, it shall decide whether to take action under Article 36 or to recommend such terms of settlement as it may consider appropriate.

Article 38

Without prejudice to the provisions of Articles 33 to 37, the Security Council may, if all the parties to any dispute so request, make recommendations to the parties with a view to a pacific settlement of the dispute.

CHAPTER VII
ACTION WITH RESPECT TO THREATS TO THE PEACE, BREACHES OF THE PEACE, AND ACTS OF AGGRESSION

Article 39

The Security Council shall determine the existence of any threat to the peace, breach of the peace, or act of aggression and shall make recommendations, or decide what measures shall be taken in accordance with Articles 41 and 42, to maintain or restore international peace and security.

Article 40

In order to prevent an aggravation of the situation, the Security Council may, before making the recommendations or deciding upon the measures provided for in Article 39, call upon the parties concerned to comply with such provisional measures as it deems necessary or desirable. Such provisional measures shall be without prejudice to the rights, claims, or position of the parties concerned. The Security Council shall duly take account of failure to comply with such provisional measures.

Article 41

The Security Council may decide what measures not involving the use of armed force are to be employed to give effect to its decisions, and it may call upon the Members of the United Nations to apply such measures. These may include complete or partial interruption of economic relations and of rail, sea, air, postal, telegraphic, radio, and other means of communication, and the severance of diplomatic relations.

Article 42

Should the Security Council consider that measures provided for in Article 41 would be inadequate or have proved to be inadequate, it may take such action by air, sea, or land forces as may be necessary to maintain or restore international peace and security. Such action may include demonstrations, blockade, and other operations by air, sea, or land forces of Members of the United Nations.

Article 43

1.   All Members of the United Nations, in order to contribute to the maintenance of international peace and security, undertake to make available to the Security Council, on its call and in accordance with a special agreement or agreements, armed forces, assistance, and facilities, including rights of passage, necessary for the purpose of maintaining international peace and security.

2.   Such agreement or agreements shall govern the numbers and types of forces, their degree of readiness and general location, and the nature of the facilities and assistance to be provided.

3.   The agreement or agreements shall be negotiated as soon as possible on the initiative of the Security Council. They shall be concluded between the Security Council and Members or between the Security Council and groups of Members and shall be subject to ratification by the signatory states in accordance with their respective constitutional processes.

Article 44

When the Security Council has decided to use force it shall, before calling upon a Member not represented on it to provide armed forces in fulfilment of the obligations assumed under Article 43, invite that Member, if the Member so desires, to participate in the decisions of the Security Council concerning the employment of contingents of that Member's armed forces.

Article 45

In order to enable the United Nations to take urgent military measures, Members shall hold immediately available national air-force contingents for combined international enforcement action. The strength and degree of readiness of these contingents and plans for their combined action shall be determined, within the limits laid down in the special agreement or agreements referred to in Article 43, by the Security Council with the assistance of the Military Staff Committee.

Article 46

Plans for the application of armed force shall be made by the Security Council with the assistance of the Military Staff Committee.

Article 47

1.   There shall be established a Military Staff Committee to advise and assist the Security Council on all questions relating to the Security Council's military requirements for the maintenance of international peace and security, the employment and command of forces placed at its disposal, the regulation of armaments, and possible disarmament.

2.   The Military Staff Committee shall consist of the Chiefs of Staff of the permanent members of the Security Council or their representatives. Any Member of the United Nations not permanently represented on the Committee shall be invited by the Committee to be associated with it when the efficient discharge of the Committee's responsibilities requires the participation of that Member in its work.

3.   The Military Staff Committee shall be responsible under the Security Council for the strategic direction of any armed forces placed at the disposal of the Security Council. Questions relating to the command of such forces shall be worked out subsequently.

4.   The Military Staff Committee, with the authorization of the Security Council and after consultation with appropriate regional agencies, may establish regional subcommittees.

Article 48

1.   The action required to carry out the decisions of the Security Council for the maintenance of international peace and security shall be taken by all the Members of the United Nations or by some of them, as the Security Council may determine.

2.   Such decisions shall be carried out by the Members of the United Nations directly and through their action in the appropriate international agencies of which they are members.

Article 49

The Members of the United Nations shall join in affording mutual assistance in carrying out the measures decided upon by the Security Council.

Article 50

If preventive or enforcement measures against any state are taken by the Security Council, any other state, whether a Member of the United Nations or not, which finds itself confronted with special economic problems arising from the carrying out of those measures shall have the right to consult the Security Council with regard to a solution of those problems.

Article 51

Nothing in the present Charter shall impair the inherent right of individual or collective self-defence if an armed attack occurs against a Member of the United Nations, until the Security Council has taken measures necessary to maintain international peace and security. Measures taken by Members in the exercise of this right of self-defence shall be immediately reported to the Security Council and shall not in any way affect the authority and responsibility of the Security Council under the present Charter to take at any time such action as it deems necessary in order to maintain or restore international peace and security.

CHAPTER VIII
REGIONAL ARRANGEMENTS

Article 52

1.   Nothing in the present Charter precludes the existence of regional arrangements or agencies for dealing with such matters relating to the maintenance of international peace and security as are appropriate for regional action, provided that such arrangements or agencies and their activities are consistent with the Purposes and Principles of the United Nations.

2.   The Members of the United Nations entering into such arrangements or constituting such agencies shall make every effort to achieve pacific settlement of local disputes through such regional arrangements or by such regional agencies before referring them to the Security Council.

3.   The Security Council shall encourage the development of pacific settlement of local disputes through such regional arrangements or by such regional agencies either on the initiative of the states concerned or by reference from the Security Council.

4.   This Article in no way impairs the application of Articles 34 and 35.

Article 53

1.   The Security Council shall, where appropriate, utilize such regional arrangements or agencies for enforcement action under its authority. But no enforcement action shall be taken under regional arrangements or by regional agencies without the authorization of the Security Council, with the exception of measures against any enemy state, as defined in paragraph 2 of this Article, provided for pursuant to Article 107 or in regional arrangements directed against renewal of aggressive policy on the part of any such state, until such time as

the Organization may, on request of the Governments concerned, be charged with the responsibility for preventing further aggression by such a state.

2.   The term enemy state as used in paragraph 1 of this Article applies to any state which during the Second World War has been an enemy of any signatory of the present Charter.

Article 54
The Security Council shall at all times be kept fully informed of activities undertaken or in contemplation under regional arrangements or by regional agencies for the maintenance of international peace and security.

CHAPTER IX
INTERNATIONAL ECONOMIC AND SOCIAL CO-OPERATION

Article 55
With a view to the creation of conditions of stability and well-being which are necessary for peaceful and friendly relations among nations based on respect for the principle of equal rights and self-determination of peoples, the United Nations shall promote:
  (a) higher standards of living, full employment, and conditions of economic and social progress and development;
  (b) solutions of international economic, social, health, and related problems; and international cultural and educational co-operation; and
  (c) universal respect for, and observance of, human rights and fundamental freedoms for all without distinction as to race, sex, language, or religion.

Article 56
All Members pledge themselves to take joint and separate action in co-operation with the Organization for the achievement of the purposes set forth in Article 55.

Article 57
1.   The various specialized agencies, established by inter-governmental agreement and having wide international responsibilities, as defined in their basic instruments, in economic, social, cultural, educational, health, and related fields, shall be brought into relationship with the United Nations in accordance with the provisions of Article 63.

2.   Such agencies thus brought into relationship with the United Nations are hereinafter referred to as specialized agencies.

Article 58
The Organization shall make recommendations for the co-ordination of the policies and activities of the specialized agencies.

Article 59
The Organization shall, where appropriate, initiate negotiations among the states concerned for the creation of any new specialized agencies required for the accomplishment of the purposes set forth in Article 55.

Article 60
Responsibility for the discharge of the functions of the Organization set forth in this Chapter shall be vested in the General Assembly and, under the authority of the General Assembly, in the Economic and Social Council, which shall have for this purpose the powers set forth in Chapter X.

CHAPTER X
THE ECONOMIC AND SOCIAL COUNCIL

Composition

Article 61

1.   The Economic and Social Council shall consist of eighteen Members of the United Nations elected by the General Assembly.

2.   Subject to the provisions of paragraph 3, six members of the Economic and Social Council shall be elected each year for a term of three years. A retiring member shall be eligible for immediate re-election.

3.   At the first election, eighteen members of the Economic and Social Council shall be chosen. The term of office of six members so chosen shall expire at the end of one year, and of six other members at the end of two years, in accordance with arrangements made by the General Assembly.

4.   Each member of the Economic and Social Council shall have one representative.

Functions and Powers

Article 62

1.   The Economic and Social Council may make or initiate studies and reports with respect to international economic, social, cultural, educational, health, and related matters and may make recommendations with respect to any such matters to the General Assembly, to the Members of the United Nations, and to the specialized agencies concerned.

2.   It may make recommendations for the purpose of promoting respect for, and observance of, human rights and fundamental freedoms for all.

3.   It may prepare draft conventions for submission to the General Assembly, with respect to matters falling within its competence.

4.   It may call, in accordance with the rules prescribed by the United Nations, international conferences on matters falling within its competence.

Article 63

1.   The Economic and Social Council may enter into agreements with any of the agencies referred to in Article 57, defining the terms on which the agency concerned shall be brought into relationship with the United Nations. Such agreements shall be subject to approval by the General Assembly.

2.   It may co-ordinate the activities of the specialized agencies through consultation with and recommendations to such agencies and through recommendations to the General Assembly and to the Members of the United Nations.

Article 64

1.   The Economic and Social Council may take appropriate steps to obtain regular reports from the specialized agencies. It may make arrangements with the Members of the United Nations and with the specialized agencies to obtain reports on the steps taken to give effect to its own recommendations and to recommendations on matters falling within its competence made by the General Assembly.

2.   It may communicate its observations on these reports to the General Assembly.

Article 65
The Economic and Social Council may furnish information to the Security Council and shall assist the Security Council upon its request.

Article 66
1. The Economic and Social Council shall perform such functions as fall within its competence in connexion with the carrying out of the recommendations of the General Assembly.

2. It may, with the approval of the General Assembly, perform services at the request of Members of the United Nations and at the request of specialized agencies.

3. It shall perform such other functions as are specified elsewhere in the present Charter or as may be assigned to it by the General Assembly.

Voting

Article 67
1. Each member of the Economic and Social Council shall have one vote.

2. Decisions of the Economic and Social Council shall be made by a majority of the members present and voting.

Procedure

Article 68
The Economic and Social Council shall set up commissions in economic and social fields and for the promotion of human rights, and such other commissions as may be required for the performance of its functions.

Article 69
The Economic and Social Council shall invite any Member of the United Nations to participate, without vote, in its deliberations on any matter of particular concern to that Member.

Article 70
The Economic and Social Council may make arrangements for representatives of the specialized agencies to participate, without vote, in its deliberations and in those of the commissions established by it, and for its representatives to participate in the deliberations of the specialized agencies.

Article 71
The Economic and Social Council may make suitable arrangements for consultation with non-governmental organizations which are concerned with matters within its competence. Such arrangements may be made with international organizations and, where appropriate, with national organizations after consultation with the Member of the United Nations concerned.

Article 72
1. The Economic and Social Council shall adopt its own rules of procedure, including the method of selecting its President.

2. The Economic and Social Council shall meet as required in accordance with its rules, which shall include provision for the convening of meetings on the request of a majority of its members.

CHAPTER XI
DECLARATION REGARDING NON-SELF-GOVERNING TERRITORIES

Article 73

Members of the United Nations which have or assume responsibilities for the administration of territories whose peoples have not yet attained a full measure of self-government recognize the principle that the interests of the inhabitants of these territories are paramount, and accept as a sacred trust the obligation to promote to the utmost, within the system of international peace and security established by the present Charter, the well-being of the inhabitants of these territories, and, to this end:

(a) to ensure, with due respect for the culture of the peoples concerned, their political, economic, social, and educational advancement, their just treatment, and their protection against abuses;

(b) to develop self-government, to take due account of the political aspirations of the peoples, and to assist them in the progressive development of their free political institutions, according to the particular circumstances of each territory and its peoples and their varying stages of advancement;

(c) to further international peace and security;

(d) to promote constructive measures of development, to encourage research, and to co-operate with one another and, when and where appropriate, with specialized international bodies with a view to the practical achievement of the social, economic, and scientific purposes set forth in this Article; and

(e) to transmit regularly to the Secretary-General for information purposes, subject to such limitation as security and constitutional considerations may require, statistical and other information of a technical nature relating to economic, social, and educational conditions in the territories for which they are respectively responsible other than those territories to which Chapters XII and XIII apply.

Article 74

Members of the United Nations also agree that their policy in respect of the territories to which this Chapter applies, no less than in respect of their metropolitan areas, must be based on the general principle of good-neighbourliness, due account being taken of the interests and well-being of the rest of the world, in social, economic, and commercial matters.

CHAPTER XII
INTERNATIONAL TRUSTEESHIP SYSTEM

Article 75

The United Nations shall establish under its authority an international trusteeship system for the administration and supervision of such territories as may be placed thereunder by subsequent individual agreements. These territories are hereinafter referred to as trust territories.

Article 76

The basic objectives of the trusteeship system, in accordance with the Purposes of the United Nations laid down in Article 1 of the present Charter, shall be:

(a) to further international peace and security;

(b) to promote the political, economic, social, and educational advancement of the inhabitants of the trust territories, and their progressive development towards self-government or independence as may be appropriate to the particular circumstances of each territory and its peoples and the freely expressed wishes of the peoples concerned, and as may be provided by the terms of each trusteeship agreement;

(c) to encourage respect for human rights and for fundamental freedoms for all without distinction as to race, sex, language, or religion, and to encourage recognition of the interdependence of the peoples of the world; and

(d) to ensure equal treatment in social, economic, and commercial matters for all Members of the United Nations and their nationals, and also equal treatment for the latter in the administration of justice, without prejudice to the attainment of the foregoing objectives and subject to the provisions of Article 80.

Article 77

1. The trusteeship system shall apply to such territories in the following categories as may be placed thereunder by means of trusteeship agreements:

(a) territories now held under mandate;

(b) territories which may be detached from enemy states as a result of the Second World War; and

(c) territories voluntarily placed under the system by states responsible for their administration.

2. It will be a matter for subsequent agreement as to which territories in the foregoing categories will be brought under the trusteeship system and upon what terms.

Article 78

The trusteeship system shall not apply to territories which have become Members of the United Nations, relationship among which shall be based on respect for the principle of sovereign equality.

Article 79

The terms of trusteeship for each territory to be placed under the trusteeship system, including any alteration or amendment, shall be agreed upon by the states directly concerned, including the mandatory power in the case of territories held under mandate by a Member of the United Nations, and shall be approved as provided for in Articles 83 and 85.

Article 80

1. Except as may be agreed upon in individual trusteeship agreements, made under Articles 77, 79, and 81, placing each territory under the trusteeship system, and until such agreements have been concluded, nothing in this Chapter shall be construed in or of itself to alter in any manner the rights whatsoever of any states or any peoples or the terms of existing international instruments to which Members of the United Nations may respectively be parties.

2. Paragraph 1 of this Article shall not be interpreted as giving grounds for delay or postponement of the negotiation and conclusion of agreements for placing mandated and other territories under the trusteeship system as provided for in Article 77.

Article 81

The trusteeship agreement shall in each case include the terms under which the trust territory will be administered and designate the authority which will exercise the administration of the trust territory. Such authority, hereinafter called the administering authority, may be one or more states or the Organization itself.

Article 82

There may be designated, in any trusteeship agreement, a strategic area or areas which may include part or all of the trust territory to which the agreement applies, without prejudice to any special agreement or agreements made under Article 43.

Article 83

1. All functions of the United Nations relating to strategic areas, including the approval of the terms of the trusteeship agreements and of their alteration or amendment, shall be exercised by the Security Council.

2.   The basic objectives set forth in Article 76 shall be applicable to the people of each strategic area.

3.   The Security Council shall, subject to the provisions of the trusteeship agreements and without prejudice to security considerations, avail itself of the assistance of the Trusteeship Council to perform those functions of the United Nations under the trusteeship system relating to political, economic, social, and educational matters in the strategic areas.

Article 84
It shall be the duty of the administering authority to ensure that the trust territory shall play its part in the maintenance of international peace and security. To this end the administering authority may make use of volunteer forces, facilities, and assistance from the trust territory in carrying out the obligations towards the Security Council undertaken in this regard by the administering authority, as well as for local defence and the maintenance of law and order within the trust territory.

Article 85
1.   The functions of the United Nations with regard to trusteeship agreements for all areas not designated as strategic, including the approval of the terms of the trusteeship agreements and of their alteration or amendment, shall be exercised by the General Assembly.

2.   The Trusteeship Council, operating under the authority of the General Assembly, shall assist the General Assembly in carrying out these functions.

CHAPTER XIII
THE TRUSTEESHIP COUNCIL

Composition

Article 86
1.   The Trusteeship Council shall consist of the following Members of the United Nations:
   (a) those Members administering trust territories;
   (b) such of those Members mentioned by name in Article 23 as are not administering trust territories; and
   (c) as many other Members elected for three-year terms by the General Assembly as may be necessary to ensure that the total number of members of the Trusteeship Council is equally divided between those Members of the United Nations which administer trust territories and those which do not.

2.   Each member of the Trusteeship Council shall designate one specially qualified person to represent it therein.

Functions and Powers

Article 87
The General Assembly and, under its authority, the Trusteeship Council, in carrying out their functions, may:
   (a) consider reports submitted by the administering authority;
   (b) accept petitions and examine them in consultation with the administering authority;
   (c) provide for periodic visits to the respective trust territories at times agreed upon with the administering authority; and
   (d) take these and other actions in conformity with the terms of the trusteeship agreements.

Article 88

The Trusteeship Council shall formulate a questionnaire on the political, economic, social, and educational advancement of the inhabitants of each trust territory, and the administering authority for each trust territory within the competence of the General Assembly shall make an annual report to the General Assembly upon the basis of such questionnaire.

Voting

Article 89

1. Each member of the Trusteeship Council shall have one vote.

2. Decisions of the Trusteeship Council shall be made by a majority of the members present and voting.

Procedure

Article 90

1. The Trusteeship Council shall adopt its own rules of procedure, including the method of selecting its President.

2. The Trusteeship Council shall meet as required in accordance with its rules, which shall include provision for the convening of meetings on the request of a majority of its members.

Article 91

The Trusteeship Council shall, when appropriate, avail itself of the assistance of the Economic and Social Council and of the specialized agencies in regard to matters with which they are respectively concerned.

CHAPTER XIV
THE INTERNATIONAL COURT OF JUSTICE

Article 92

The International Court of Justice shall be the principal judicial organ of the United Nations. It shall function in accordance with the annexed Statute, which is based upon the Statute of the Permanent Court of International Justice and forms an integral part of the present Charter.

Article 93

1. All Members of the United Nations are *ipso facto* parties to the Statute of the International Court of Justice.

2. A state which is not a Member of the United Nations may become a party to the Statute of the International Court of Justice on conditions to be determined in each case by the General Assembly upon the recommendation of the Security Council.

Article 94

1. Each Member of the United Nations undertakes to comply with the decision of the International Court of Justice in any case to which it is a party.

2. If any party to a case fails to perform the obligations incumbent upon it under a judgment rendered by the Court, the other party may have recourse to the Security Council,

which may, if it deems necessary, make recommendations or decide upon measures to be taken to give effect to the judgment.

Article 95

Nothing in the present Charter shall prevent Members of the United Nations from entrusting the solution of their differences to other tribunals by virtue of agreements already in existence or which may be concluded in the future.

Article 96

1.   The General Assembly or the Security Council may request the International Court of Justice to give an advisory opinion on any legal question.

2.   Other organs of the United Nations and specialized agencies, which may at any time be so authorized by the General Assembly, may also request advisory opinions of the Court on legal questions arising within the scope of their activities.

CHAPTER XV
THE SECRETARIAT

Article 97

The Secretariat shall comprise a Secretary-General and such staff as the Organization may require. The Secretary-General shall be appointed by the General Assembly upon the recommendation of the Security Council. He shall be the chief administrative officer of the Organization.

Article 98

The Secretary-General shall act in that capacity in all meetings of the General Assembly, of the Security Council, of the Economic and Social Council, and of the Trusteeship Council, and shall perform such other functions as are entrusted to him by these organs. The Secretary-General shall make an annual report to the General Assembly on the work of the Organization.

Article 99

The Secretary-General may bring to the attention of the Security Council any matter which in his opinion may threaten the maintenance of international peace and security.

Article 100

1.   In the performance of their duties the Secretary-General and the staff shall not seek or receive instructions from any government or from any other authority external to the Organization. They shall refrain from any action which might reflect on their position as international officials responsible only to the Organization.

2.   Each Member of the United Nations undertakes to respect the exclusively international character of the responsibilities of the Secretary-General and the staff and not to seek to influence them in the discharge of their responsibilities.

Article 101

1.   The staff shall be appointed by the Secretary-General under regulations established by the General Assembly.

2.   Appropriate staffs shall be permanently assigned to the Economic and Social Council, the Trusteeship Council, and, as required, to other organs of the United Nations. These staffs shall form a part of the Secretariat.

3.   The paramount consideration in the employment of the staff and in the determination of the conditions of service shall be the necessity of securing the highest standards of efficiency, competence, and integrity. Due regard shall be paid to the importance of recruiting the staff on as wide a geographical basis as possible.

CHAPTER XVI
MISCELLANEOUS PROVISIONS

Article 102

1.   Every treaty and every international agreement entered into by any Member of the United Nations after the present Charter comes into force shall as soon as possible be registered with the Secretariat and published by it.

2.   No party to any such treaty or international agreement which has not been registered in accordance with the provisions of paragraph 1 of this Article may invoke that treaty or agreement before any organ of the United Nations.

Article 103

In the event of a conflict between the obligations of the Members of the United Nations under the present Charter and their obligations under any other international agreement, their obligations under the present Charter shall prevail.

Article 104

The Organization shall enjoy in the territory of each of its Members such legal capacity as may be necessary for the exercise of its functions and the fulfilment of its purposes.

Article 105

1.   The Organization shall enjoy in the territory of each of its Members such privileges and immunities as are necessary for the fulfilment of its purposes.

2.   Representatives of the Members of the United Nations and officials of the Organization shall similarly enjoy such privileges and immunities as are necessary for the independent exercise of their functions in connexion with the Organization.

3.   The General Assembly may make recommendations with a view to determining the details of the application of paragraphs 1 and 2 of this Article or may propose conventions to the Members of the United Nations for this purpose.

CHAPTER XVII
TRANSITIONAL SECURITY ARRANGEMENTS

Article 106

Pending the coming into force of such special agreements referred to in Article 43 as in the opinion of the Security Council enable it to begin the exercise of its responsibilities under Article 42, the parties to the Four-Nation Declaration, signed at Moscow, October 30, 1943, and France, shall, in accordance with the provisions of paragraph 5 of that Declaration, consult with one another and as occasion requires with other Members of the United Nations with a view to such joint action on behalf of the Organization as may be necessary for the purpose of maintaining international peace and security.

Article 107

Nothing in the present Charter shall invalidate or preclude action, in relation to any state which during the Second World War has been an enemy of any signatory to the present Charter, taken or authorized as a result of that war by the Governments having responsibility for such action.

CHAPTER XVIII
AMENDMENTS

Article 108

Amendments to the present Charter shall come into force for all Members of the United Nations when they have been adopted by a vote of two-thirds of the members of the General Assembly and ratified in accordance with their respective constitutional processes by two-thirds of the Members of the United Nations, including all the permanent members of the Security Council.

Article 109

1. A General Conference of the Members of the United Nations for the purpose of reviewing the present Charter may be held at a date and place to be fixed by a two-thirds vote of the members of the General Assembly and by a vote of any seven members of the Security Council. Each Member of the United Nations shall have one vote in the conference.

2. Any alteration of the present Charter recommended by a two-thirds vote of the conference shall take effect when ratified in accordance with their respective constitutional processes by two-thirds of the Members of the United Nations including all the permanent members of the Security Council.

3. If such a conference has not been held before the tenth annual session of the General Assembly following the coming into force of the present Charter, the proposal to call such a conference shall be placed on the agenda of that session of the General Assembly, and the conference shall be held if so decided by a majority vote of the members of the General Assembly and by a vote of any seven members of the Security Council.

CHAPTER XIX
RATIFICATION AND SIGNATURE

Article 110

1. The present Charter shall be ratified by the signatory states in accordance with their respective constitutional processes.

2. The ratifications shall be deposited with the Government of the United States of America, which shall notify all the signatory states of each deposit as well as the Secretary-General of the Organization when he has been appointed.

3. The present Charter shall come into force upon the deposit of ratifications by the Republic of China, France, the Union of Soviet Socialist Republics, the United Kingdom of Great Britain and Northern Ireland, and the United States of America, and by a majority of the other signatory states. A protocol of the ratifications deposited shall thereupon be drawn up by the Government of the United States of America which shall communicate copies thereof to all the signatory states.

4. The states signatory to the present Charter which ratify it after it has come into force will become original Members of the United Nations on the date of the deposit of their respective ratifications.

Article 111

The present Charter, of which the Chinese, French, Russian, English, and Spanish texts are equally authentic, shall remain deposited in the archives of the Government of the United States of America. Duly certified copies thereof shall be transmitted by that Government to the Governments of the other signatory states.

IN FAITH WHEREOF the representatives of the Governments of the United Nations have signed the present Charter.

DONE at the city of San Francisco the twenty-sixth day of June, one thousand nine hundred and forty-five.

List of Persons

Alexander, A. V., First Lord of the Admiralty 1940—5.

Amery, L. S., Secretary of State for India 1940—5.

Anderson, Sir John, Home Secretary and Minister of Home Security 1940; member of the War Cabinet; Lord President of the Council 1941—3; Chancellor of the Exchequer 1943—5.

Armstrong, H. F., Editor of *Foreign Affairs*, and Special Adviser to the U.S. Secretary of State.

Assheton, Ralph, Parliamentary Secretary, Ministry of Labour & National Service 1939—42, Ministry of Supply 1942—3; Financial Secretary to the Treasury 1943—4; later Lord Clitheroe.

Angel, Eduardo Zulueta, Chairman of the Preparatory Commission, Colombian representative.

Attlee, C. R., Lord Privy Seal 1940—February 1942; Deputy Prime Minister February 1942; Secretary of State for Dominion Affairs February 1942—September 1943; Lord President of the Council September 1943—1945; later Prime Minister and Lord Attlee.

Beaverbrook, Lord, Minister of Aircraft Production 1940—1; Member of the War Cabinet; Minister of Supply 1941—2; Minister of Production 1942—3; Lord Privy Seal 1943—5.

Beeson, Edward, Professor at Harvard University.

Berle, Adolf A., Assistant Secretary of State, U.S. State Department.

Bevin, E., Minister of Labour & National Service 1940—5; Secretary of State for Foreign Affairs 1945—50.

Blaisdell, Donald C., Associate Chief, Division of International Security Affairs, U.S. Department of State.

Bowman, Dr. Isaiah, President of Johns Hopkins University; Special Adviser to the U.S. Secretary of State on post-war problems.

Bridges, Sir Edward, Secretary to the Cabinet 1938—46.

Brierly, J. L., Professor of International Law at Oxford.

Bruce, Stanley, Australian High Commissioner in London.

Bucknell, H., Junior Counsel at the United States Embassy in London.

Butler, Nevile, Head of the American Department, Foreign Office, and Secretary-General of the British delegation at San Francisco.

Butler, R. A., Parliamentary Under-Secretary of State for Foreign Affairs 1938—41; President of the Board of Education 1941—5; later Chancellor of the Exchequer, Deputy Prime Minister, Master of Trinity College, Cambridge, and Lord Butler.

Byrnes, James F., United States Secretary of State 1945—7.

Cadogan, Sir Alexander, Permanent Under-Secretary of State for Foreign Affairs 1938—46; leader of British delegation, Dumbarton Oaks.

Cecil, Viscount of Chelwood, Lord Privy Seal 1923—4; Chancellor of the Duchy of Lancaster 1924—7; President of the League of Nations Union 1923—45.

Clark, G. N., a Deputy Director of F.R.P.S.; Chichele Professor of Economic History, University of Oxford; later Provost of Oriel College.

Clark-Kerr, Sir Archibald, British Ambassador in Moscow.

Cohen, Benjamin V., Counsel, U.S. Office of War Mobilization.

Connally, Tom, Senator for Texas; Democratic Chairman of the Senate Foreign Relations Committee.

Cordier, Andrew W., U.S. adviser, San Francisco; later responsible for the Executive Committee of the Preparatory Commission dealing with the General Assembly.

Cooper, Duff, Minister of Information

1940–1; Chancellor of the Duchy of Lancaster 1941–3; British Representative to the French Committee of Liberation in Algiers 1943 and subsequently Ambassador in Paris and Lord Norwich.

Corbett, Percy E., Professor of International Law, McGill University.

Coulson, J. E., Desk Officer, Economic & Reconstruction Department, Foreign Office.

Cranborne, Viscount, Paymaster-General 1940; Secretary of State for Dominion Affairs 1941–February 1942, and September 1943–1945; Lord Privy Seal 1942–3; later Lord Salisbury.

Cripps, Sir Stafford, Ambassador in Moscow 1941–February 1942; Lord Privy Seal and member of War Cabinet February–November 1942; Minister of Aircraft Production November 1942–45; later Chancellor of the Exchequer.

Curtin, John, Prime Minister of Australia.

Davies, Lord, Coal owner and philanthropist. Founder of the Wilson Chair of International Politics at the University College of Wales, Aberystwyth.

Dewey, Thomas E., Governor of New York; Republican Presidential candidate 1944.

Dixon, Pierson, Private Secretary to Anthony Eden.

Dulles, John Foster, Adviser to the United States delegation at San Francisco, and later Secretary of State.

Dunn, Colonel D. Capel, Assistant Secretary (Military), War Cabinet Offices; died with Malkin over the Atlantic, July 1945.

Dunn, J. C., Special Adviser on political relations, U.S. Department of State.

Durbin, E. F. M., Personal Assistant to Attlee, and a junior Minister in Attlee's 1945 administration until his death in a drowning accident.

Eady, Sir Wilfrid, Additional Second Secretary, Treasury and member of Richard Law's interdepartmental committee.

Eden, Anthony, Secretary of State for Foreign Affairs 1940–5 and member of War Cabinet; later Prime Minister and Lord Avon.

Eisenhower, General Dwight D., Supreme Commander Allied Expeditionary Force; President of the United States 1953–60.

Elliott, George F., Military and naval analyst for the *New York Herald Tribune* and military analyst for the Columbia Broadcasting System.

Evatt, Herbert V., Australian Minister for External Affairs; leader of the Australian delegation at San Francisco.

Falla, P. S., Desk Officer, Economic & Reconstruction Department, Foreign Office.

Fleming, J. F., War Cabinet Offices.

Fletcher, Henry P., General Counsel of the Republican National Committee.

Foot, Dingle, Parliamentary Secretary, Ministry of Economic Warfare 1940–5.

Fouques-Duparc, J., Director of the Secretariat of International Conferences, French Ministry of Foreign Affairs; and Secretary-General of the French delegation at San Francisco.

Fraser, P., Prime Minister of New Zealand; leader of the New Zealand delegation at San Francisco.

Freitas-Valle, C. de, Brazilian representative on the Preparatory Commission.

Gerig, Benjamin, Chief, Division of Dependent Area Affairs, U.S. Department of State; Secretary-General of the United States delegation, Dumbarton Oaks.

Gore-Booth, P., First Secretary, British Embassy, Washington; later Permanent Under-Secretary and Lord Gore-Booth.

Gousev, F. T., Soviet Ambassador in London.

Grigg, Sir James, Secretary of State for War 1942–5.

Gromyko, Andrei, Soviet Ambassador in Washington; later Soviet Minister of Foreign Affairs; leader of Soviet delegation at Dumbarton Oaks.

Grove-White, Maj.-Gen., Assistant to Lt. Gen. Macready, Chief of British Army Staff, Washington.

Hackworth, Green H., Legal Adviser, U.S. Department of State. (In his diary Webster frequently wrote 'Hackforth'.)

Hadow, R. H., Counsellor, British Embassy, Washington.

Halifax, Viscount, former Viceroy of India; Secretary of State for Foreign Affairs 1938–40; British Ambassador in Washington 1940–5.

Hall, Donald, Personal Assistant to Richard Law.

Hall, G. H. (p. 53), Parliamentary Under-Secretary of State for the Colonies 1940–2; Financial Secretary to the Admiralty 1942–3; Parliamentary Under-Secretary of State for Foreign Affairs 1943–5.

Harriman, W. Averell, holder of many ministerial appointments in the United States; at the time of Yalta U.S. Ambassador in Moscow.

Harrison, G. W., Desk Officer, Central Department, Foreign Office.

Holt, Captain Vyvyan, Eastern Department, Foreign Office.

Hoo, Chi-tsai Victor, Chinese Vice-Minister of Foreign Affairs.

Hood, Viscount, Desk Officer, Economic & Reconstruction Department, Foreign Office.

Hopkins, Harry L., Special Adviser and Assistant to President Roosevelt.

Hornbeck, Stanley K., Director of the Office of Far Eastern Affairs, U.S. Department of State.

Horsbrugh, Florence, Parliamentary Secretary, Ministry of Health, 1939—45.

Howard, D. F., Head of Southern Department, Foreign Office.

Hull, Cordell, United States Secretary of State 1933—November 1944.

Jacob, Brigadier I., War Cabinet Offices.

Jebb, H. M. Gladwyn, head Economic & Reconstruction Department, Foreign Office; Executive Secretary to the Preparatory Commission; later delegate to the Security Council, Ambassador in Paris and Lord Gladwyn.

Jordan, W. M., former doctoral student of Webster's; later Director of the Political Affairs Division in the Department of Political & Security Council Affairs, United Nations Secretariat.

King, Mackenzie, Prime Minister of Canada.

Koo, V. K. Wellington, Chinese Ambassador in London.

Laithwaite, Sir Gilbert, War Cabinet Offices; joint secretary to the Armistice and Post-War Committee.

Lambert, J., joint secretary to the War Cabinet Committee on Post-War Settlement.

Langer, W. L., Professor at Harvard University.

Law, Richard, Parliamentary Under-Secretary of State for Foreign Affairs 1941—43; Minister of State 1943—5; later Lord Coleraine.

Liang, Yuen-li, Counsellor, Chinese Embassy, London.

Loxley, P., Private Secretary to Cadogan, died in an air crash February 1945.

Mabane, W., Parliamentary Secretary, Ministry of Home Security 1939—42, Ministry of Food 1942—5; Minister of State 1945.

Macartney, C. A., International Department, League of Nations Union 1928—36; F.R.P.S. 1939—46.

MacLeish, Archibald, United States Assistant Secretary of State.

Macmillan, Harold, Minister Resident at Allied Force Headquarters, Mediterranean Command 1942—5; later Prime Minister.

Malkin, Sir William, Legal Adviser to the Foreign Office until his death in an air accident over the Atlantic in July 1945.

Mallory, Walter H., Executive Director of the U.S. Council of Foreign Relations.

Maisky, Ivan M., Assistant People's Commissar for Foreign Affairs, U.S.S.R.

Manuilsky, Dmitri Z., Vice-Chairman of the Preparatory Commission, Ukrainian representative.

Masaryk, Jan, Czechoslovak Minister of Foreign Affairs and chairman of the Czech delegation at San Francisco.

Massigli, René, French Ambassador in London.

Molotov, V. M., Soviet Minister of Foreign Affairs.

Monnet, J., Commissioner for Armament, Supplies and Reconstruction, French National Liberation Committee, Algiers, 1943—4; later Chairman of the Action Committee for the United States of Europe.

Nervo, Luis-Padilla, Mexican representative on the Preparatory Commission.

Noel-Baker, P., Minister of State, Foreign Office, 1945—6.

Notter, Harley A., Chief, Division of International Security and Organization, U.S. Department of State.

Noyes, Charles, Assistant to Stettinius.

Nye, Lt. Gen. Sir Archibald, Vice-Chief of the Imperial General Staff.

Opie, Redvers, Counsellor & Economic Adviser, British Embassy, Washington.

Owen, A. D. K., Private Secretary to Sir Stafford Cripps; joined the Foreign Office in 1945.

Parra-Perez, Caracciolo, Venezuelan Minister of Foreign Affairs and chairman of the Venezuelan delegation at San Francisco.

Pasvolsky, Leo, Special Assistant to the U.S. Secretary of State.

Index